Biometrics
and Kansei Engineering

Khalid Saeed • Tomomasa Nagashima
Editors

Biometrics
and Kansei Engineering

 Springer

Editors
Khalid Saeed
AGH University of Science
    and Technology
Kraków, Poland

Tomomasa Nagashima
Muroran Institute of Technology
Muroran, Hokkaido
Japan

ISBN 978-1-4899-8998-7   ISBN 978-1-4614-5608-7 (eBook)
DOI 10.1007/978-1-4614-5608-7
Springer New York Heidelberg Dordrecht London

Printed on acid-free paper

Springer is part of Springer Science+Business Media (www.springer.com)

Preface

The book I am introducing with Professor Tomomasa Nagashima is on the principles and applications of biometrics (BM) and Kansei engineering (KE) and their techniques. For the first time, biometrics and Kansei engineering are combined together in one book. The idea did not come incidentally. Biometrics in future will imply new technologies that will depend on people's emotions and the prediction of their intention to take an action. For pervasive or ubiquitous networks, we need real-time human–computer interactions. Actually, KE is becoming the complementary part of BM in these as well as other aspects. The authors are indeed indebted to Professor Ryszard Tadeusiewicz for his steady support toward both fields of biometrics and Kansei engineering in Poland and Japan through his lectures, consultation, and worthy advice on many issues.

Biometrics is divided into two categories: physiological (the body features we are born with) and behavioral (or psycho-behavioral as Kansei experts call it). Behavioral BM deals with our behavior – the way we walk, the way we talk, and the way we express our emotions.

Kansei engineering, however, as stated by Professor Tomomasa Nagashima, who I call the godfather of KE, is concerned with the interactions between users and products/services. One of its major activities is focused on the product psychology – engineers need to design the product in accordance with the comfort of the users; hence, they test the reaction of people toward certain products (car interiors, for example). Accordingly, the response of the driver (in the case of cars) can be quicker or more certain toward sudden changes if the dashboard is designed to be user-friendly, well seen with the good relation between car computer and human. The reaction and behavior of individuals certainly differ from person to person based on their personal emotions and character or their exact behavioral biometrics. This is only one real example, which will be studied in detail in the book.

The subject of the book is introduced through two parts: biometrics and Kansei. In the biometrics part, there are eight chapters that cover most of the basic biometrics applications. Principles and new concerns are explained in Chap. 1 and face recognition in unconstrained environment in Chap. 2. Chapter 3 covers a thorough study on iris recognition independently of its rotation angle. Some medical details about the iris anatomy and possible iris diseases are given in this Chap. 3 for a knowledge of the error sources in iris recognition. Consequently, a new mathematical model based on Fourier descriptors was worked out to deal with the iris image under different conditions, particularly with the most difficult problems that result from its deformation and rotation. Human identification by their vascular vessel pattern with the help of the finger vein model is given in Chap. 4. Chapter 5 deals with the operation principles of touch screen dynamics and its user identification studies. These five chapters have been neatly prepared by my team of biometrics in AGH University of Science and Technology in Kraków. The other three chapters of Part I of the book present interesting new aspects in biometrics and have been very well prepared by internationally known biometrics research groups from Japan, USA, and Canada. Chapter 6 shows new methods of biometric identification based on eye movement, the three-dimensional shape of the iris surface, and the contour of the eyelid during blinking. New effective pattern descriptors in eye detection are given in Chap. 7. Chapter 8 introduces a complete discussion on chaotic neural networks and multidimensional data analysis in biometrics.

The Kansei part of the book consists of six chapters (Chaps. 9, 10, 11, 12, 13, and 14) which involve definitions and principles of KE and its essential techniques in some interesting and very important fields and applications in our life. Chapter 9 presents a general description and introduction to the scientific field Kansei Engineering. Chapter 10 discusses the role of KE as a postmodern technology. In Chap. 11, the role of empathy in KE is highlighted among the various concepts in Kansei – an aesthetic thought is introduced. Chapter 12 deals with the methods of measuring Kansei, which involve the techniques for assessing mental and physical states from facial expressions those for assessing closing comfort via physiological responses. Chapters 13 and 14 deal with Kansei from the viewpoint of information technologies. An information-theoretical approach to Kansei is given in Chap. 13 through the relation between Bayesian updating using the notion of binary channel and sequential probability ratio test (SPRT). Chapter 14 also introduces computer agent modeling based on Ontology and a Bayesian network as applied to human care problems.

Thus, through these works, it will be shown how the two parts of BM and KE relate to each other, proving that a closer coordination between them can help study systematically the user's behavior and the feedback to the contiguous computer.

Moreover, some current studies in Kansei allow the association of biometrics features or personal emotion patterns with possible odd states and/or diseases. The KE achievements, for example, are developing such facilities for studying the reason why an infant or a child cries. By analyzing the cry signal, it should be known if it is a call for food or the baby is sick, frightened, or simply feels lonely.

From another viewpoint and for the health and safety of people, according to my own observations and thus my suggestions, cars should have microphones and cameras embedded in the doors and ceiling (in a similar way to air bags or air curtains) that operate immediately after an accident or a similar need. This would allow the car computer to register the current state of the driver and the passengers (their behavior and emotions, if they are shouting or crying, or what they are saying) when they are unable to communicate at all. The car computer then is supposed to send the appropriate information to the nearest hospital, police, or the nearest cars and their drivers and/or computers.

This is, thus, the benefit of using Kansei ideas and basics in biometrics applications and domains for a more comfortable, propitious, and safe life.

A number of scientists and researchers have contributed in reaching the main goals of this book and stand behind its prosperity. The authors hence are indebted to all of them who have contributed to this work and made the book of benefit for other researchers.

Together with Professor Nagashima, I am grateful to all the reviewers of both BM and KE chapters for their constructive comments and critical remarks that made the chapters palpable and readable. In particular, we express our sincere thanks to Professor Toshio Kuwako at Tokyo Institute of Technology, Professor Toshi Kato at Chuo University, Professor Huang Huming at the University of Calgary, Professor Kevin Jia at International Game Technology, and Professor Qinghan Xiao at Defence R&D Canada. They indeed devoted their precious time and carefully put in their efforts to get the result we have.

Finally, I hope the book will add a significant aspect to the scientific literature for the research teams in their current and future fundamental investigation challenges in biometrics and Kansei engineering.

Khalid Saeed
Kraków, Poland

Contents

Part I Biometrics

1 **Biometrics Principles and Important Concerns**   3
Khalid Saeed

2 **Face Recognition in Unconstrained Environment** 21
Przemysław Kocjan and Khalid Saeed

3 **Iris Pattern Recognition with a New Mathematical Model
to Its Rotation Detection** 43
Krzysztof Misztal, Emil Saeed, Jacek Tabor, and Khalid Saeed

4 **Human Identification by Vascular Patterns** 67
Jan Kosmala and Khalid Saeed

5 **A Study on Touch Screen Devices:
User Authentication Problems** 89
Marcin Rogowski and Khalid Saeed

6 **New Proposals for Biometrics Using Eyes** 113
Nobuyuki Nishiuchi and Masayuki Daikoku

7 **Local Texture Descriptors on Biometric Detection: New Local
Quaternary Pattern Descriptors and Case Study on Eye Detection** 129
Jiayu Gu and Chengjun Liu

8 **Chaotic Neural Network and Multidimensional Data Analysis
in Biometric Applications** 153
Kushan Ahmadian and Marina Gavrilova

Part II Kansei Engineering

9 **Introduction to Kansei Engineering** 173
Tomomasa Nagashima

10 Human Being and Kansei Engineering 177
Yoshio Shimizu

11 Concepts of *Kansei* and Aesthetic Thoughts 191
Tomomasa Nagashima, Yoshifumi Okada, and Yuzuko Nagashima

**12 *Kansei* Measurement in Cooperative Development
Techniques** 211
Masayoshi Kamijo and Yoshio Shimizu

**13 Information Theoretic Methodology for Kansei Engineering:
Kansei Channel and SPRT** 233
Tetsuo Hattori and Hiromichi Kawano

14 Kansei Engineering and Service Engineering 259
Takashi Uozumi

Contributors

Kushan Ahmadian University of Calgary, Calgary, Canada

Masayuki Daikoku Faculty of System Design, Tokyo Metropolitan University, Tokyo, Japan

Marina Gavrilova University of Calgary, Calgary, Canada

Jiayu Gu New Jersey Institute of Technology, University Heights, Newark, NJ, USA

Tetsuo Hattori Kagawa University, Kagawa, Japan

Masayoshi Kamijo Interdisciplinary Graduate School of Science and Technology, Shinshu University, Tokida, Ueda, Nagano, Japan

Hiromichi Kawano NTT Advanced Technology, Tokyo, Japan

Przemysław Kocjan AGH, Kraków, Poland

Jan Kosmala ABB, Kraków, Poland

Chengjun Liu New Jersey Institute of Technology, University Heights, Newark, NJ, USA

Krzysztof Misztal AGH University of Science and Technology, Kraków, Poland

Tomomasa Nagashima Graduate School of Engineering, Muroran Institute of Technology, Mizumoto, Muroran, Hokkaido, Japan

Yuzuko Nagashima University of Hawaii at Manoa, Honolulu, USA

Nobuyuki Nishiuchi Faculty of System Design, Tokyo Metropolitan University, Tokyo, Japan

Yoshifumi Okada Muroran Institute of Technology, Muroran, Japan

Marcin Rogowski King Abdullah University of Science and Technology, Thuwal, Saudi Arabia

Emil Saeed Medical University in Bialystok, Bialystok, Poland

Khalid Saeed AGH University of Science and Technology, Faculty of Physics and Applied Computer Science, Kraków, Poland

Yoshio Shimizu Shinshu University, Nagano, Japan

Jacek Tabor Jagiellonian University, Kraków, Poland

Takashi Uozumi Department of Computer Science and Systems Engineering, Muroran Institute of Technology, Hokkaido, Japan

Part I
Biometrics

Chapter 1
Biometrics Principles and Important Concerns

Khalid Saeed

Information can be seen, heard,
touched, smelled and tasted;
it can also be felt,

—by Biometrics

Abstract This chapter will show and discuss some facts, concepts, and approaches concerning the principles of biometrics from research point of view. In particular, the chapter introduces a deep study on the meaning of preprocessing principles as for image analysis and processing in biometrics. The effects and consequences of noisy or unfiltered biometric images are discussed in some detail with examples on fingerprints. Some new biometric features like the human nail lunula are also presented for future eventual consideration. The biometrics error rates with their graphical representation in biometric systems are illustrated in some detail. Also discussed is how the biometric features are not stable and permanent with age. Example of face changes is given for discussion.

1.1 Introduction

Brief introductory information about the history and the reasons of studying biometrics are presented in this chapter.

K. Saeed (✉)
AGH University of Science and Technology, Faculty of Physics and Applied Computer Science,
Al. Mickiewicza 30, Kraków PL-30059, Poland
e-mail: saeed@agh.edu.pl

K. Saeed and T. Nagashima (eds.), *Biometrics and Kansei Engineering*,
DOI 10.1007/978-1-4614-5608-7_1, © Springer Science+Business Media New York 2012

Fig. 1.1 Fingerprints from more than 4,000 years ago (times of Babylon)

1.1.1 What is Biometrics?

The first question that needs to be asked is what biometrics is. Biometrics means *biological measurement*. The name comes from Greek *bios* – life, and *metricos* – measuring [1]. Hence, the term "biometrics" is used to define the science that deals with the computer recognition of individuals based on their biological or behavioral (or both) body characteristics. It is the continuation of the idea of body measurement and the model created by Bertillon in 1882 [2]. Biometric features are the possible characteristics extracted from human body. Face, iris, fingerprints, and voice are all examples of biometric features.

It is worth mentioning here that biometrics is not the plural from "biometric." Biometric is the adjective from biometrics. However, we can see some cited works use the term "biometric" for a "biometrics feature" or a biometrics class. On the other hand "biometry" is the name of another subject. It stands for the mathematical and statistical aspects of biology, and hence it is not the same as biometrics. It is also referred to as "biostatistics" to deal with the use and development of statistical theory and methods to address design, analysis, and interpretation of information in the biological sciences. This and other information about biometry can be found in [3].

Naturally then, a "biometric system" is basically an automatic pattern recognition system that is concerned with biometrics and works on its feature basis. More details about such systems will be given later in this chapter.

In general, there is agreement that fingerprints were the first biometrics ever used. However, there is no clear date at which fingerprinting was first used (whether in Egypt during the pyramid-building era, in China, or in Babylon [4]). However, many references agree the first tracks of biometrics were left in Mesopotamia (Iraq today) after Babylonian people about 4,000 years ago (probably in 1913–1885 B.C.). Human thumbprints were found on ancient Babylonian clay tablets, seals, and pottery. People embodied their fingerprints into the clay tablet on one side of the seal while the business transaction was imprinted on the second side (Fig. 1.1) to legalize a contract and protect it against forgery. By 1880 fingerprint was considered a reliable and important biometrics. As Henry Faulds wrote in Nature [5]:

When bloody finger marks or impressions on clay, glass, etc. exist, they may lead to the scientific identification of criminals. Already I have had experience in two such cases... There can be no doubt as to the advance of having, besides their photographs, a nature-copy of the forever unchangeable finger furrows of important criminals.

1.2 Biometric Feature Classification

Simply, every human body part or sense that carries information about the human being and can be detected and recorded for classification and recognition is a good human representation feature. Human smell, taste, vision, hearing, touching, and feeling are all examples of human information sources. Not all, however, can be measured at the present time because the *information technology* level, particularly when it comes to the information sensors, is not appropriate or fully in accordance with the theoretical results achieved by computer scientists and researchers. Example of this is the human smell detection. Also the emotions or gestures are currently examined for the possibility of people verification. The fundamentals of *Kansei Engineering* are also studied for a link between this science and the principles of *biometrics* (particularly, those of *psychobehavioral* type). This is one of the reasons why this book contains works about the applications of both biometrics and Kansei Engineering. Scientists have always looked for interaction between users and products or service, looking from user's psychological and behavioral point of view. This is actually the *Kansei* concept itself. Readers are encouraged to read Chaps. 10, 11, 12, 13, and 14 of this book for more details about Kansei and its applications.

In general, the biometric features are classified as either of physiological or behavioral type.

1.2.1 Physiological Human Characteristics (Cognitive Biometrics)

Physiological biometrics deals with the human features that we were born with. They usually are dictated by our genetics. The feature data are gathered from our body characteristics. Examples are fingerprints, iris image, face, odor, retina, ear, vascular pattern, lips, hand geometry, DNA, and many other distinct features of the body parts that can be measured through an automatic process.

1.2.2 Behavioral Human Characteristics (Behaviometrics)

This group consists of methods measuring human features indirectly. Behavioral biometrics measures the repeated activities we make in our daily life. Every human

Fig. 1.2 Lunula – the lower
whitish part of the fingernail
(**a**); in some fingers, it is
invisible (**b**)

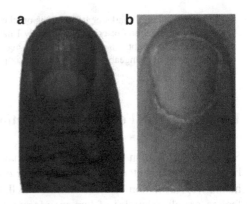

takes actions in his own way, differing from the manner in which others perform
them. Examples are:

> speech (the way we speak, how we use our lips to produce sounds), signature (the way we
> sign or write), keystroke dynamics (the way we type or strike on the keyboard), mouse
> dynamics (how we move and use the computer mouse), gait (the way of walking), and all
> the other movements or gestures a human makes by any part of his body. The author and his
> team have achieved promising results in keystroke dynamics [6] for user authentication, the
> topic that is very important in security and rather practical for internet applications and
> on-line access purposes.

1.2.2.1 Other Interesting New Features

There still are other features which are under studying (teeth layout, ECG signal,
and x-ray [7] are some of the examples). Other interesting new features of
biometrics are the way we move our lips while talking [8] and the manner we
move our hands and fingers [9]. The author has recently been interested in examining the pattern of human nail lunula (Fig. 1.2). In 2011, the author introduced the
idea of using lunula in biometrics [10]. The lower whitish part of the fingernail is
called "lunula" (from Latin) and comes from its lunar shape. Lunula seems to have
a permanent shape, pattern, and color distribution differing from person to another.

It is sometimes invisible in one or more fingers (hidden under the skin at the deep
bed of the fingernail), and some people seem not to have it (Fig. 1.2b). However, we
all have the lunula, and it becomes visible after a simple appropriate lighting from the
other side of the finger and some filtering and denoising [11], as can be seen in Fig. 1.3.

1.3 Why Biometrics?

Why use biometrics for human authentication and identification?

Biometric methods dispense the individual of the necessity to remember PIN
codes or passwords. Unlike the traditional methods of using PIN codes or

Fig. 1.3 The lunula extraction by simple image lighting (**a**) then filtering (**b**) and enhancing (**c**) by simple laboratory methods

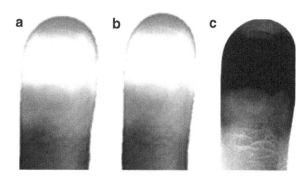

passwords, biometrics offers a unique physiological or behavioral and reliable means for people identification or user authentication. Simply each individual has his own characteristics. Not only are these characteristics unique, but they are also permanent, universal, and collectable. Most of them are comfortable to collect and acceptable by users. Besides, it is possible to forget or lose our classic password; it can also easily be stolen. For more details on biometrics and their advantages in security and privacy, the reader can see, for example, the works in [12, 13].

Biometrics is now almost everywhere. Their systems are and can be used in many aspects of our life, among others they are used in homes, schools (in school library, registration and enrollment, controlling the contact with students, and even food services in some countries), banks, hospitals, markets, streets (vending machines, for example), police, court, and airports. The main reasons are to save money and time.

From the other side, however, a serious question may arise: "Is biometrics or, generally, are the biometric systems reliable?" Does biometrics definitely solve the problems of classic passwords? This is a steadily asked question and a continuously discussed problem in the current time at scientific conferences and researchers' meetings as well as the biometrics business forums all over the world. As the password breaking (such as spoofing) is, unfortunately, developing, there also are anti-spoofing manners/ways/methods that deal with or operate on such an "identity theft." Spoofing and anti-spoofing methods and systems are beyond the topics of this work. However, there is an interesting collection of works on spoofing that the reader can see in [14]. One thing should rather be considered as a fact: "the biometrics exists and will continue to exist and develop with the advance of technology."

Another subject would also be of considerable concern, namely, what would determine which biometric feature is the best to use, and why? This is the most frequently asked question when it comes to the realization of researchers' thoughts or ideas to develop for a commercial use or to simply popularize them. Actually, there are a variety of schools, each supports one or two of the biometric features. However, in many institutions like banks and commercial entrepreneurships, fingerprints, iris, and face are the most commonly used three features. In this book, three physiological features (face, iris, and vein pattern) and one behavioral feature (screen touching) will be discussed to show what is new about them. The touch screen (Chap. 5 of this book) is studied in detail from all possible sides. To the knowledge of the author, this will be the first work on this subject. Screen touching characteristics as a behavioral biometric feature will be introduced predominantly from both software and hardware points of view.

1.4 Biometrics and Pattern Recognition Systems

Since biometrics is a science that deals with human identity on the basis of our body's biological features, their characteristic images, and the patterns they furnish, biometrics should then belong to pattern recognition. Here in this section, a general description of the pattern recognition system is given, but with its input assumed to be acquired from our body characteristics and its basic features, the face image, say.

1.4.1 Accomplishment of BM Systems

Image recognition system, and hence the biometric system, mainly consists of the blocks given in Fig. 1.4.

Let us consider the blocks of Fig. 1.4 individually and start with the explanation of the two important aspects in pattern recognition, namely, the analysis and

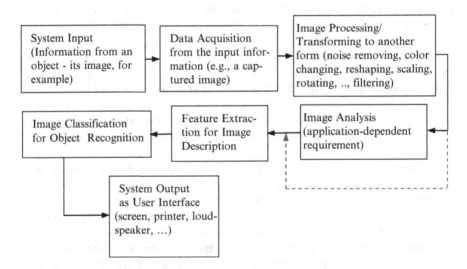

Fig. 1.4 Universal object recognition system

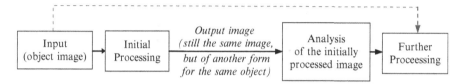

Fig. 1.5 Processing and analysis chart

processing of object images as applied to biometrics. Their meaning will be given here with examples on biometric images. Then, and in order to understand the whole system of biometrics, some basic information will be given about feature extraction as an essential step before image classification for recognition. Readers who are interested in all stages from data acquisition to system output as user interfaces are advised to see the works in [15–17].

1.4.2   Initial Processing and Analysis of Biometric Images

Consider the diagram of Fig. 1.5. The results of image analysis with and without initial processing (preprocessing) are shown through an example. In order to do the image analysis, one should first have it free of noise, clear enough to select the areas of interest. This is achieved during the stage of some initial transformation of the original image, usually called preprocessing. This is only to let the input or the acquired image be receptive and ready for further processing and analysis. *In all initial processing (preprocessing) and hence any processing methods, the output still is an image of another shape of the same object*, as illustrated in Fig. 1.5. Image analysis is not essential in all the cases; the processing procedure may not require such a stage (the dashed line in Fig. 1.5). We should, however, remember that the *image analysis is an irreversible process*. Unlike the processing operation of an image, the thinned form of an image cannot be inversely transformed (back into its original shape) by using the inverse transformation tools like Fourier transform, for example.

However, analysis will always simplify the procedure of feature extraction and hence description for precise classification. The main analysis aspects are *thinning* and *segmentation* [15, 17, 18]. There are varieties of analysis methods on both thinning and segmentation, and it is only a matter of selecting the appropriate one for the assigned application [17, 19, 20]. The thinning is to reduce the image pixels to a minimum while keeping the essential information they carry. The segmentation, however, is to divide the image into parts or regions of similar characteristics – color, brightness, and structure – so that the classification process becomes easier and hence the recognition is faster. For better results of further processing in most algorithms, it has been proved that the image should go under initial processing and analysis. The following example shows exactly this concept.

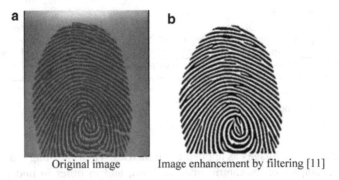

Original image   Image enhancement by filtering [11]

Fig. 1.6 Thinning the fingerprint noisy image to prepare for analysis and further proper processing: (**a**) original image; (**b**) image enhancement by filtering [11]

Fig. 1.7 The thinning results of the image in Fig. 1.6a

1.4.3 Example

This example will first show how the image processing simply means image transformation. Figure 1.6a presents the original image of a fingerprint. Figure 1.6b is its new form after filtering it and removing the noise from it [11].

As can be seen, the output image still clearly belongs to the original object; it carries all the main characteristics and information of the input image. However, the resulting image is easier to deal with in the further steps of classification.

Consider now the original image for direct analysis (without denoising). Figure 1.7 shows the thinning process of the same fingerprint as an image without removing the noise in it.

Let us now consider the thinning process after removing the noise. Figure 1.8 shows the details.

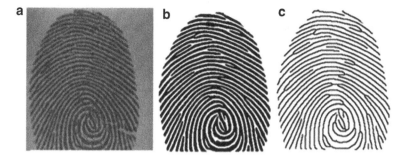

Fig. 1.8 Example of image analysis by thinning its noise-free form: (**a**) original fingerprint image, (**b**) its denoised and enhanced image [11], (**c**) thinning results [18]

Both the denoising and the thinning algorithms used in this comparison were written and implemented by the author's team.

In conclusion, the preprocessing steps are just to have the original object image in a form and shape easier and more receptive to the algorithms applied later for feature extraction and hence better image description for successful classification and recognition.

1.4.4 Feature Extraction and Biometric Image Description

The next block in the process of object recognition system of Fig. 1.4 is the feature extraction of the biometric image for its object (human) description and hence recognition. In order to recognize an object, we must describe it or at least its images first. This implies a reasonable description (and at the lowest possible cost) of the object using only a number of its selected features. These points are usually the object characteristic points. In some algorithms, the relations between the geometrical characteristic points are considered after certain transformation. An example of the last methods is the author's algorithms for image description by the minimal eigenvalues of Toeplitz matrices shown in the chapter [21]. In the mathematical models introduced in it, the author transforms the collection of geometrical points into a sequence of other points that form a clear relation. The sequences are similar for the same object but different from those belonging to other objects. This is an important stage for the final decision of object classification for recognition. The appropriate algorithm should select features in a way that the resulting group of feature points (the feature vector) would substitute the original image's huge number of pixels while keeping the essential information necessary to recognize the described object. Why is this? Good descriptor will always take the place of original image without losing the basic characteristics that describe the original object. The image description by millions of pixels is reduced to only hundreds (or in many cases much less) of feature points and eventually leads to much less computations. Here, we should recall that in all methods or systems of biometrics, the resulting final image is to be recognized as belonging to the object it represents. If the obtained *success rate* (the success rate is a measure of the effectiveness and successful recognition result) is very high with low hardware and software cost, it then means the methods we followed were successful in giving the appropriate form and description of the analyzed image. This of course will always depend on all the stages and steps shown in Fig. 1.4, not only on one or two of them. These steps and those methods will form the fundamentals or essence of every pattern recognition and hence biometrics system.

1.4.5   Biometric System Construction

Biometric systems mainly consist of the following four main components:

1. Scanning hardware or sensors (examples are camera, microphone, text scanner, x-ray, and tomographic equipment). This is to scan the human anatomy being under test for image acquisition, which is an essential tool to read and input data.
2. Analog-to-digital converter – in order to convert the input information to the biometric system into a digital form for the necessary procedure of further digital processing.
3. An appropriate software to manipulate digital data for the DSP or DGP wherever necessary.
4. Database to save the classified image data and compare it with the already enrolled and stored image in the database for classification and hence person recognition.

1.5   Human Measurement and Evaluation on the Basis of Biometric Features

In its simplest meaning, as implicitly discussed above, biometrics serves for human feature measurement. However, the measurement has only one of two purposes (we call them *modes*), either to *identify* people (to answer the question "Who are you?") or to *verify* them (to answer the question "Are you really who you claimed?").

1.5.1   Verification and Identification

To verify people (and hence the term *verification*), we will need to answer with either "Yes" or "No," and therefore it is a matter of binary classification. This kind of evaluation is actually easier than that concerning identification. To identify people, and hence comes the term *identification*, we need to seek in huge contents (database) to evaluate the personality of someone and find out who he is.

When the security aim is to prevent more than one person from using the same identity, then we are concerned with what is called *positive recognition*, where we should follow the *verification mode*. However, when the goal of a biometric system is to prevent one user from making use of more than one identity, then we are dealing with *negative recognition*, and hence *identification mode* is in use.

For more details on verification and identification, the reader can go to [19, 22, 23], where these and other useful terms are discussed thoroughly.

1.5.2 Error Sources in Biometrics

There are some facts that should be known and considered when studying the biometric errors and their sources. Although biometrics has the properties of uniqueness and permanence and has almost steady characteristics, there still exists a possibility that the biometric system may make some errors while verifying human features for their recognition. This happens when we register people features under different conditions of data acquisition (different sensors for data collection) or when they are collected under different conditions like lighting and atmospheric conditions like temperature, image resolution, age, and so on. This leads to the result that for one person we may have two different features, for example, two characteristic face images and two or more fingerprints, which is contrary to the basic assumption that biometric features are unique. Consequently, there is a probability that our features match those of other people, leading to some matching errors. Such situations may appear after bad image-capturing (low resolution camera, for example), and hence we have an error introduced by the device. Or that the methodology we are following has some drawbacks leading to some errors. However, here we are dealing with errors that result from the human when interacting with biometric data acquisition devices: how they give their biometric feature images when conducting the sensors and the way they look at the camera, for example. Errors may also arise when the individual is sick or under treatment, or when they provide their data, for example, their photographs, they supply old ones. This, sometimes, is completely different from their actual look. Such human factors can be summarized and presented in the following examples:

1.5.2.1 Examples of Human Error Sources

As error sources, we can count the variable lighting conditions and different shooting angles, which can significantly affect the recognition results of the tested biometric image. In Chap. 2 of this book (entitled "Face Recognition in

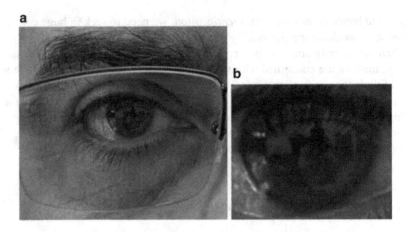

Fig. 1.9 Eye image showing loss of information in the iris (**a**). Such a photo is not accepted for passports. It is covered by the upper eyelid, lash, and glasses. The iris is shown enlarged in (**b**). Many factors would affect the results of recognition with such an image as the input to the authentication system

Unconstrained Environment"), the reader can find a discussion with advanced examples on how the environmental conditions work and how they increase the error rate. In some cases even small changes in illumination and facial expression may change the right extraction of the biometric characteristics.

Another example of biometric error sources is in iris recognition methods. The results are different whenever a part of the iris is covered, for example, by the eyelids, hair, and glasses (Fig. 1.9), causing errors in the classification and hence inaccurate or even incorrect authentication results. Moreover, more serious problems have been proved to exist with the rotated iris images. This is well explained in Chap. 3 of this book. The mathematical model given there actually deals with such problems. The worked out algorithm successfully improves the results by minimizing the role of such changes and hence maximally decreases the error effects.

Other error sources are concerned with aging. Here almost all biometric features can undergo changes with age. Consider the series of photos in Fig. 1.10 taken for one person every 3 years. The difference distinguished by the human eye should be found out and considered by the automatic recognition system; will this be the case for the photographs of Fig. 1.10?

These and other factors that cause differences in the characteristics of the biometric image will always lead to lower accuracy in user authentication. They would also allow for larger fraud tolerance. The fraud value is controlled by some factors, and some tolerance is allowed by the concept of thresholding and its rules. All these tasks will be discussed in the following sections.

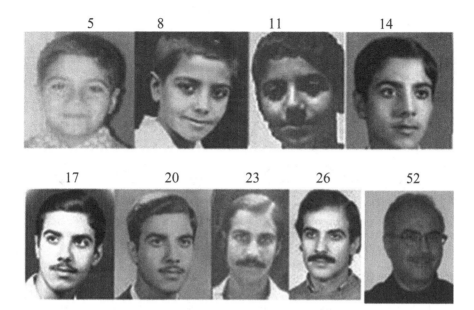

Fig. 1.10 There is an evident difference between face images with time. Nine photos of the same person taken throughout the years. The recognition system should consider such differences while analyzing the photograph

1.5.3 Types of Basic Verification Errors and Their Rates

To study the biometric system accuracy and its tolerance, I will start with defining the possible errors made by the system or its environment in order to evaluate the system performance. Based on the graphical representation of genuine and impostor distribution, a biometric verification system can make two types of errors:

1. Matching the recognition features of person A as belonging to person B, that is, *an acceptance occurs, although the user is an impostor.* This means the two users will be treated as one person, leading to what is called *False Acceptance (FA) or False Matching.* The resulting error is then called *False Acceptance error*, measured as a *ratio* or *rate* and hence the name *False Acceptance Ratio/ Rate – FAR.*
2. Mismatching features of person A and treating them as belonging to another person. That is, *a rejection occurs although the user is genuine.* This in turn leads to what is called *False Rejection (FR)* or *False Nonmatching*, and the error rate is called *False Rejection Ratio – FRR.*

Both False Acceptance and False Rejection rates depend on the input source of information and the percentage of the noise their images contain. Recall the three factors mentioned above for the error sources: sensors, human, and algorithmic approaches.

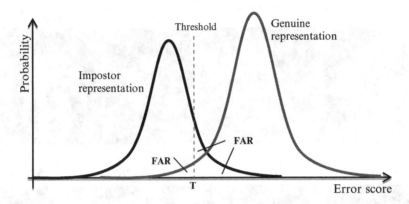

Fig. 1.11 Gaussian distribution for the probability of error to explain *FAR* and *FRR* errors as overlapping areas between the genuine (registered user) and impostor (unregistered user) *curves*

1.5.3.1 Error Graphical Representation

In order to evaluate a biometric system for a degree of success in human recognition on the basis of their biometric features, such errors as those mentioned above should be either eliminated or at least decreased to a minimum. The more we can do to eliminate such errors, the better and more effective will be our system as it would bring lower mismatching probabilities and hence the rate of the recognition success is higher.

Since there is always a possibility of system deviation from the ideal case (normal desired accuracy state), the mismatching (in both meanings, positive and negative) error can be represented by a Gaussian curve (Fig. 1.11). This helps study the probability of system errors. Both genuine distribution (also called true positive) and impostor distribution (true negative) are drawn on one plane. Their overlapping shows some common areas to define the already defined error rates *FAR* and *FRR*. A selected error score value that defines the *system tolerance* or *sensitivity* is called *threshold* (*T* in Fig. 1.11). *T* is fixed according to the application, and a vertical line is drawn at *T* to define these possible basic errors.

Obviously, *FAR* and *FRR* are both *T*-dependent. Thus, if the threshold is selected to be at the cross point of the two curves (T_{cross} in Fig. 1.12), then at this point the probability of the two error rates is equal, $FAR = FRR$, and the error rate is then called Crossover Error Rate, *CER*, or Equal Error Rate, *ERR*.

Another way of illustrating the error rates *FAR* and *FRR* is the direct relation between them, which is shown in Fig. 1.13. Here, the applications of the error studies are presented thoroughly by the detailed illustration in the figure.

Increasing the threshold *T* will result in a higher value of *FRR*, while decreasing *T* would cause an increase in *FAR*. On the other hand, the position of *T*-line, that is, the value of the threshold for a given system, is actually application dependent. We cannot assign, for example, a lower value for *T* to decrease the *FRR* (and hence, to increase *FAR*) and make the system more tolerant to system inputs just to obtain a

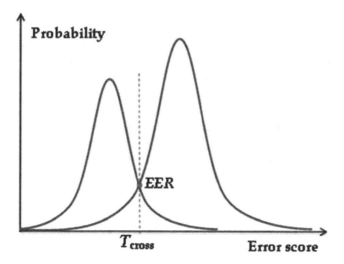

Fig. 1.12 Equal error rate illustration

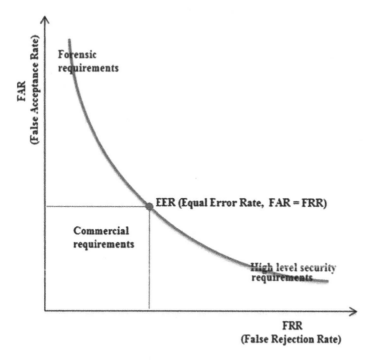

Fig. 1.13 *FAR* is high (forensic and criminal applications) for low *FRR*, while *FRR* should be very high (in high-security requirements), although *FAR* is very low then. *EER* is the most practical tolerance for commercial use (in banking, for example)

system of higher success rate. The reason is simply we would obtain a nonsecure system at the time when the matter requires high-security conditions. Therefore, in security applications, the *FRR* is not as important as the *FAR* [24]. *FAR* should be very low (in some applications may reach 0.00001 %) at a bit higher *FRR* (e.g., 0.01 %) so that only authorized people can be given an access. However, in forensic applications the tolerance should be very low, and hence *FRR* should be at the lowest possible levels (the closest to zero), and obviously, the system should not miss any single person suspected of committing a crime. In commercial applications, banking systems, for example, *T* is selected around what is called *EER* (*Equal Error Ratio*) where *FAR* = *FRR*. Here, the time of recognition proce-dure should also be taken into consideration; it is usually about 1–4 s, depending on the commercial application.

1.5.3.2 Further Study of Errors

We should first recall that in many normal cases, the environmental conditions and the sensor nature and accuracy play a role in creating new errors if not increasing the already mentioned ones. Examples are the scaling, rotation, and translation of the image before or while acquiring the input information to the biometric system. The impact of such errors on the classification results is large and should always be considered. In some biometric features, like the eye iris, the collected information would cause serious errors when the image is, for example, rotated. This problem and its consequences together with the suggested solution, as mentioned above, are given in Chap. 3 of this book. The impact on FRR and FAR is also given there.

Moreover, it is also possible to depict the system performance for all threshold values. This is obtained by the *Relative Operating Characteristic* (*ROC*) *curve*, which plots FAR against (1 − *FRR*) or *FRR* for various values of threshold *T*. *ROC* curves in *ROC* space are discussed thoroughly in [25]. *ROC* curve is also called *Receiver Operating Characteristic* and discussed in detail in [22], where the authors use the *ROC* curve for validating the claimed performance levels. In their paper about security and privacy in biometrics [23], Prabhakar et al. give a very interesting study of *ROC* curve, *FRR*, *FAR*, and other measuring means and error rates like *Failure To Capture* (*FTC*) and *Failure To Enroll* (*FTE*) to summarize the accuracy of biometric systems. They also show through examples how the biomet-ric desired accuracy depends greatly on the application.

1.6 Conclusions and Future Work

A brief history of biometrics was first given to have an itemized study about its principles and how people have been dealing with human body measurement for more than four millennia. Classification of biometrics and its types were presented in this chapter to show both known and completely new body features and characteristics. Emphasis was put on the role of initial processing in biometric image processing for classification and hence people recognition purposes. Some new details about visible and invisible fingernail lunula and its image processing were introduced for future consideration. Biometric errors and their sources that originate from human, device sensors, designed software, or algorithms were presented with examples of the common human biometric errors. The error rates like *FAR* and *FRR* were discussed circumstantially so that the reader can understand the rules of setting remarkable tolerance and accepting different error rate allowance according to the application and purpose of the employed biometric feature. The biometric feature extraction methods were also considered at a glance. The author has proved his team's methods of preprocessing and analysis, particularly those on image denoising [11] and its thinning [18, 26], are operative and practical in treating biometric images.Intensive work is done on removing the possibly existing drawbacks or undesired features in these and other algorithms. This would definitely result in improving the algorithmic level of performance and their operation time for faster, productive action and universal applications.

Acknowledgment   This work was partially supported by AGH University of Science and Technology in Cracow, grant no. 11.11.220.01.

References

1. Schneier B (1999) Inside risks: the uses and abuses of biometrics. Commun ACM 42(8):136
2. Rhodes HTF (1956) Alphonse Bertillon: father of scientific detection. Abelard-Schuman, London
3. Molenberghs G (2006) Biometry and biometrics. Sensor Rev 26(1). Online http://www.emeraldinsight.com/journals.htm. Accessed 28 May 2012
4. Cummins H (1941) Ancient finger prints in clay. Sci Mon 52:389–402, Reprinted in Journal of Criminal Law and Criminology 34(4):468–481. December 1941
5. Faulds H (1880) On the skin-furrows of the hand. Nature 22(574):601–624. doi:10.1038/022605a0
6. Rybnik M, Panasiuk P, Saeed K, Rogowski M (2012) Advances in the Keystroke Dynamics: the Practical Impact of Database Quality. Lecture Notes in Computer Science – LNCS 7564, Springer-Verlag Heidelberg, Germany, 204–215
7. Shamir L, Ling S, Rahimi S, Ferrucci L, Goldberg IG (2009) Biometric identification using knee X-rays. Int J Biometrics 1(3):365–370
8. Abdulla WH, Calverly Yu P (2009) Lips tracking biometric for speaker recognition. Int J Biometrics 1(3):288–306
9. Nishiuchi N, Komatsu S, Yamanaka K (2010) Biometric verification using the motion of fingers: a combination of physical and behavioral biometrics. Int J Biometrics 2(3):222–235
10. Saeed K (2011) A note on problems with biometrics methodologies. In: Proceedings of IEEE-ICBAKE conference, IEEE CS Press – CD, Takamatsu, Japan, 19–21 Sep 2011, pp 20–22
11. Godzwon M, Saeed K (2012) Biometrics image denoising algorithm based on Contourlet transform. Lecture Notes in Computer Science – LNCS 7594, Springer-Verlag Heidelberg, Germany, 735–742
12. Boulgouris NV, Plataniotis KN, Micheli-Tzanakou E (eds) (2009) Biometrics: theory, methods, and applications. Wiley, Hoboken

13. Saeed KJ, Pejaś J, Mosdorf R (eds) (2006) Biometrics, computer security systems and artificial intelligence applications. Springer Science + Business Media, New York
14. Nishiuchi N, Yamaguchi T (2008) Spoofing issues and anti-spoofing. Int J Biometrics 1(2)
15. Russ JC (2011) The image processing handbook. Taylor and Francis Group, Boca Raton, FL
16. Jain AK (1989) Fundamentals of digital image processing. Prentice-Hall, Englewood Cliffs, NJ
17. Saeed K (2004) Image analysis for object recognition. Bialystok University of Technology, Bialystok
18. Saeed K, Tabedzki M, Rybnik M, Adamski M (2010) K3M: a universal algorithm for image skeletonization and a review of thinning techniques. Appl Math Comput Sci 20(2):317–335
19. Bolle RM, Connell JH, Pankanti S, Ratha NK, Senior AW (2010) Guide to biometrics. Springer, New York
20. Gonzalez RC, Woods RE (2008) Digital image processing. Prentice Hall, Upper Saddle River, NJ
21. Saeed K (2012) Carathéodory–Toeplitz based mathematical methods and their algorithmic applications in biometric image processing. Appl Numer Math. doi:10.1016/j.apnum.2012.05.004
22. Dass SC, Zhu Y, Jain AK (2006) Validating a biometric authentication system: sample size requirements. IEEE Trans Pattern Anal Mach Intell 28(12):1302–1319
23. Prabhakar S, Pankanti S, Jain AK (2003) Biometric recognition: security and privacy concerns. IEEE Mag Secur Privacy 1(2):33–42. doi:10.1109/MSECP.2003.1193209
24. Wilson C (2010) Vein pattern recognition: a privacy-enhancing biometric. CRC Press, Boca Raton
25. Kelkboom EJC, Molina GG, Breebaart J, Veldhuis RNJ, Kevenaar TAM, Jonker W (2010) Binary biometrics: an analytic framework to estimate the performance curves under Gaussian assumption. IEEE Trans Syst Man Cybern A: Syst Humans 40(3):555–571
26. Saeed K, Tabedzki M, Rybnik M, Adamski M (2012) Biometrics image thinner. Accepted for patent in South Korea

Chapter 2
Face Recognition in Unconstrained Environment

Przemysław Kocjan and Khalid Saeed

Abstract This chapter addresses the problem of face recognition from images with lighting problems such as shadows or brightness level. Authors describe face recognition processing, including major components such as face detection, tracking, alignment, and feature extraction. Technical challenges of building a face recognition system are pointed out. The chapter emphasizes the importance of subspace analysis and learning, providing not only an understanding of the challenges therein but also the most successful solutions developed to date. In the following sections, authors present brief history of face recognition systems, show problems that affect results of these systems, and present their own approach based on finding fiducial points in face image and their further use for face recognition.

2.1   Introduction

Face recognition is a task that humans perform routinely and effortlessly in their daily lives. Our brains perform this task remarkably easily and accurately, although this apparent simplicity is dangerously misleading. The automatic face recognition is a problem that is still far from being solved. Wide availability of powerful and low-cost desktop and embedded computing systems has created an enormous interest in automatic processing of digital images and videos in a number of applications, including biometric authentication, surveillance, human-computer interaction, and multimedia management. In spite of more than 20 years of

P. Kocjan (✉)
AGH, Kraków, Poland
e-mail: przemyslaw.kocjan@gmail.com

K. Saeed
AGH University of Science and Technology, Faculty of Physics and Applied Computer Science, Al. Mickiewicza 30, Kraków PL-30059, Poland
e-mail: saeed@agh.edu.pl

K. Saeed and T. Nagashima (eds.), *Biometrics and Kansei Engineering*,
DOI 10.1007/978-1-4614-5608-7_2, © Springer Science+Business Media New York 2012

extensive research and large number of papers published in journals and conferences dedicated to this area, we still cannot claim that artificial systems are comparable to human performance.

Automatic face recognition is intricate primarily because of differences in conditions like lighting and viewpoint changes induced by body movement during image acquisition. Aging, facial expressions, occlusions etc., also make the problem more difficult. Researchers from the areas of computer vision, image analysis and processing, pattern recognition, machine learning, and many other are working cooperatively, motivated not only by the fundamental challenges this recognition problem generates but also by numerous practical applications in which human identification is needed. The interest of scientists is also increased by the fact that with the rising public concern for security, the need for identity verification such as face recognition is more apparent. Also, advances in technology, such as in digital cameras and mobile devices, made face recognition more important and easier to approach.

Face recognition has an important advantage over many other biometric technologies – it is a nonintrusive, noninvasive, and easy-to-use method. Because of this, it became one of three identification methods used in e-passports and the biometric of choice for many other security applications. Hietmeyer [1] considered six biometric attributes. From all of them, face scored the highest compatibility in a Machine Readable Travel Documents (MRTD) [2].

A face recognition system is expected to identify faces in images and videos automatically. This system may operate in either or both of two modes: face verification (authentication) and face identification (recognition). Face verification compares a query face image of supposedly known person against this person's template face image stored by the system (one-to-one match). Face identification compares a query face image of unknown identity against all the template images in the database to determine the identity of the query face (one-to-many matches). Another face recognition scenario involves a watch-list check, where a query face is matched to a list of suspects (one-to-few matches).

The performance of face recognition systems has improved significantly since the first automatic face recognition system developed by Kanade [3]. Currently face detection, facial feature extraction, and recognition can be performed in real time for images captured under constrained conditions.

2.2   Early Approaches to the Face Recognition Problem

The need of face recognition rises from the moment when machines become more "intelligent" and powerful and gained the ability to improve, supplement, or substitute human abilities and senses.

The subject of face recognition is as old as computer vision because of not only the practical importance of the topic but also the theoretical interest from cognitive scientists. Clearly, using a face to recognize people is not the only method of differentiation between people. Humans also use different senses (e.g., hearing) in order to recognize each other. Machines may utilize a wider range of recognition techniques using, for example, fingerprint images or iris scans. Despite the fact that other methods of identification can be more accurate, face recognition, because of its noninvasive nature and because it is human's primary method of person identification, remains a major area of research.

Since the beginning of the research in that field of technology, there were two main approaches to face recognition: feature based (geometrical) and appearance based (pictorial).

The geometrical approach uses the spatial configuration of facial features. It means that the main geometrical features of the face such as the positions of eyes, nose, and mouth are first located and then faces are classified on the basis of various geometrical distances and angles between these features. On the other hand, the pictorial approach uses templates of the facial features. That method is using the templates of the major facial features and entire face to perform recognition on the frontal views of the faces. Many of the projects based on those two approaches have some similar common extensions that handle different poses and backgrounds.

Apart from these two techniques, there are other more recent template-based approaches. In one of the methods, templates are formed from the image gradient. The other one is principal component analysis approach, which can be interpreted as a suboptimal template approach. Finally there is the deformable template approach that combines elements of both the pictorial and feature geometry approaches and can be applied to faces at varying poses and expressions.

Perhaps the most famous early example of a face recognition system is the one developed by Kohonen in 1989 [4]. It was demonstrated there that a simple neural network could perform face recognition for aligned and normalized face images. The type of network he employed computed face description by approximating the eigenvectors of the face image autocorrelation matrix. These eigenvectors are now known as eigenfaces.

Kohonen's system was, however, not a practical success, because of the need for precise alignment and normalization. In the following years many researchers tried face recognition schemes based on edges, inter-feature distances, and other neural network approaches. While several methods were successful on small databases of aligned images, none successfully addressed the more realistic problem, where database is large and the location and scale of the face are unknown.

A year later, Kirby and Sirovich [5] introduced an algebraic manipulation technique which made it easy to directly calculate the eigenfaces and showed that less than 100 of them were required to accurately describe carefully aligned and normalized face images. Turk and Pentland [6] demonstrated in 1991 that the residual error when coding using the eigenfaces can be used both to detect faces in cluttered natural imagery and to determine the precise location and scale of faces in an image. They then proved that by coupling this method for detecting and localizing faces with the eigenface recognition method, one could achieve reliable real-time recognition of faces in a minimally constrained environment. This demonstration that simple, real-time pattern recognition techniques could be combined to create a useful system sparked an explosion of interest in the topic of face recognition.

With the rapid evolution of the technology and the commercialization of technological achievements, face recognition became more and more popular not only as research subject but also for the use in security systems.

This fact gave the motive to many researchers and also companies to develop techniques for automatic recognition of faces. These products have many applications, also in security and human-computer interaction. For instance, a face-recognizing machine could allow automated access control for buildings or enable a computer to recognize the person using it at the moment. Most existing face recognition systems, however, can recognize only frontal or nearly frontal images of faces. By recognizing faces under varying pose, one would make the conditions under which face recognition systems operate less rigid.

2.3 Face Recognition in a Changing Environment

The progress in face recognition has been promising over the years. However, the same task for unconstrained environments – where we have to take into account changes of viewpoint, illumination, expression, occlusion, accessories, and so on – is still far from being solved.

2.3.1 Problem

Subspace analysis techniques for face recognition are based on the fact that a class of patterns of interest, such as the face, resides in a subspace of the input image space. If we consider a small grayscale image of size 64×64 which has 4,096 pixels, this picture can express a large number of pattern classes, such as trees, houses, and faces. However, among the 256^{4096}, which is more than 10^{9864} possible configurations of pixels, only a few correspond to faces. Because of this, the original image representation is highly redundant. The dimensionality of this representation could be greatly reduced when only the face patterns are of interest.

With the eigenface or principal component analysis (PCA) [6, 7] approach, a small number of eigenfaces [8] are derived from a set of training face images by using the Karhunen-Loeve transform or PCA. These modeling techniques allowed to efficiently represent face image as a feature vector of low dimensionality. The features in such subspace provide more valuable and richer information for recognition than the raw image.

The manifold or distribution of all faces accounts for variation in face appearance, whereas the nonface manifold accounts for everything else. Closer look into manifolds in the image space shows that they are highly nonlinear and nonconvex [9, 10]. Figure 2.1a illustrates face versus nonface manifolds and (b) illustrates the manifolds of two individuals contained in one face manifold. Distinguishing between the face and nonface manifolds in the image space is the task of face

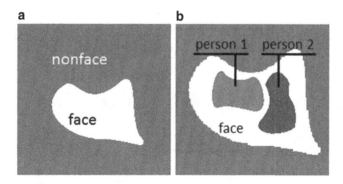

Fig. 2.1 (**a**) Face versus nonface manifolds, (**b**) face of different individuals

Fig. 2.2 Sample intrasubject variations in pose, illumination, expression, occlusion, and brightness [16]

detection. Face recognition, however, is concerned with distinguishing multiple individuals in the single face manifold.

As shown in Fig. 2.1, the classification problem associated with face detection is highly nonlinear and nonconvex, even more so for face matching. Face recognition evaluation reports (e.g., [11, 12]) and other independent studies indicate that the performance of many state-of-the-art face recognition methods deteriorates with changes in lighting, pose, and other factors [13–15].

Whereas shape and reflectance are intrinsic properties of a face object, the appearance (i.e., the texture look) of a face is also subject to several other factors, including the facial pose (or, equivalently, camera viewpoint), illumination, and facial expression. Figure 2.2 shows an example of significant intrasubject variations caused by some of these factors.

To complicate the problem, we could add various imaging parameters, such as aperture, exposure time, lens aberrations, and sensor spectral response which also increases intrasubject variations. Face-based person identification is even more difficult with possible small intersubject variations (Fig. 2.3). All these factors are present in the image data, so "the variations between the images of the same face due to illumination and viewing direction are almost always larger than the image variation due to change in face identity" [17]. This variability makes it

Fig. 2.3 Similarity of frontal faces between son and father (**a**) [81, 82], twins (**b**) [81]

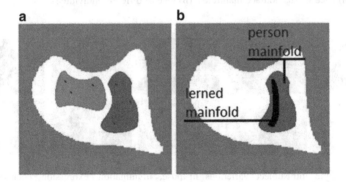

Fig. 2.4 Challenges in face recognition from subspace viewpoints. (**a**) Euclidean distance is unable to differentiate between individuals. (**b**) The learned manifold of classifier is unable to characterize unseen images of the same individual face

difficult to extract the consistent intrinsic information of the face objects from their respective images.

As illustrated above, the entire face manifold is highly nonconvex, and so is the face manifold of any individual under various circumstances. Linear methods such as PCA [6, 18], independent component analysis (ICA) [19], and linear discriminant analysis (LDA) [20] project the data linearly from a high-dimensional space (e.g., the image space) to a low-dimensional subspace. Because of this fact, they are unable to preserve the nonconvex variations of face manifolds necessary to differentiate among individuals. In a linear subspace, Euclidean and Mahalanobis distances are normally used for template matching. Unfortunately they do not perform well for distinction between face and nonface manifolds and between manifolds of individuals (Fig. 2.4a). This crucial fact limits the possibility of linear methods to achieve highly accurate face detection and recognition.

Another problem is the ability to generalize, illustrated by Fig. 2.4b. A canonical face image of 112×92 resides in a 10,304-dimensional feature space. The number of examples per person available for learning the manifold is usually much smaller than the dimensionality of the image space. A system trained on so few examples may not generalize well to unseen instances of the face.

2.3.2 Proposed Solutions

To deal with difficulties mentioned above, it is possible to choose one out of two strategies. First method is to construct a "good" feature space in which the face manifolds become simpler, that is, less nonlinear and nonconvex than those in the other spaces. This method needs two things to be done. First thing is the normalization of face images geometrically and photometrically, such as using morphing and histogram equalization. Second thing is the extraction of features from the normalized images which are stable with respect to such variations as ones based on Gabor wavelets.

The second strategy is to construct classification engines able to solve difficult nonlinear classification and regression problems in the feature space and to generalize better. Since the first option reduces the nonlinearity and nonconvexity, it does not solve the problems completely, and classification engines able to deal with such difficulties are still necessary to achieve high performance. A successful algorithm should combine both strategies.

When thinking about first strategy, it is necessary to mention the geometric feature-based approach used in the early days of face recognition [21–24], where facial features such as eyes, nose, mouth, and chin are detected. Properties of and relations between these features are used as descriptors for face recognition. Advantages of this approach include efficiency when achieving data reduction and insensitivity to variations in illumination and viewpoint. However, facial feature detection and measurement techniques developed to date are not reliable enough, as mentioned before, for the geometric feature-based recognition [25]. Such geometric properties alone are inadequate for face recognition because the rich information contained in the facial texture or appearance is discarded. These are reasons why early techniques are not effective. The statistical learning approach learns from training data, like appearance images or features extracted from appearance, to extract good features and construct classification engines. During the learning, both prior knowledge about faces and variations seen in the training data are taken into consideration.

The appearance-based approach, such as PCA- [6] and LDA [20]-based methods, incorporates more advanced face recognition techniques. Such an approach generally operates directly on an image-based representation. It extracts features in a subspace derived from training images. Using PCA, a face subspace is constructed to represent optimally only the face object. Using LDA, a discriminant subspace is constructed to optimally distinguish faces of different persons. Comparative reports (e.g., [20]) show that LDA-based methods generally yield better results than PCA-based ones.

Although these linear, holistic, appearance-based methods avoid instability of the early geometric feature-based algorithms, they are not accurate enough to describe subtleties of original manifolds in the original image space. This is due to their limitations in handling nonlinearity in face recognition. Fortunately such linear methods can be extended using nonlinear kernel techniques (kernel PCA [26] and kernel LDA [27]) to deal with this nonlinearity [28–31]. In these approaches, a nonlinear projection (dimension reduction) from the image space to a feature space is performed. The manifolds in the resulting feature space become simple, yet with subtleties preserved. The kernel methods may achieve good performance on the training data; however, it may not be so for unseen data because of their much greater flexibility than the linear methods and overfitting thereof.

Another approach to handle the nonlinearity is to construct a local appearance-based feature space using appropriate image filters, so the distributions of faces are less affected by various changes. Local feature analysis (LFA) [32], Gabor wavelet-based features (such as elastic graph bunch matching, EGBM) [33–35], and local binary pattern (LBP) [36] have been used for this purpose.

Some of these algorithms may be considered as combining geometric (or structural) feature detection and local appearance feature extraction to increase stability of recognition performance when viewpoint, illumination, or expression changes. Face recognition algorithms can be divided based on pose dependency into pose dependent and pose invariant. One can distinguish three types of pose-dependent algorithms (viewer-centered images). The first are feature based (analytic) which detect a set of geometrical features on the face such as nose, mouth, chin, and eyes. The second are appearance based (holistic) such as PCA and LCA, and the third are hybrid, such as LFA or EGBM, which are the combination of the two previous. In the pose-invariant algorithms, 3D face models are utilized to reduce the variations in pose and illumination. Gordon and Lewis [37] proposed an identification system based on 3D face recognition. The 3D model used by them is represented by a number of 3D points associated with their corresponding texture features. This method requires an accurate estimate of the face pose. Lengagne et al. [38] proposed a 3D face reconstruction scheme using a pair of stereo images for recognition and modeling. However, they did not implement the recognition module. Atick et al. [39] proposed a reconstruction method of 3D face surfaces based on the Karhonen-Loeve (KL) transform and the shape-from-shading approach. They also discussed the possibility of using eigenhead surface face recognition applications. Yan and Zhang [40] proposed a 3D reconstruction method to improve the performance of face recognition by making reconstruction method, introduced by Atick et al., rotation invariant. Zhao and Chellappa [41] proposed a method to adapt a 3D model from a generic range map to the shape obtained from shading for enhancing face recognition performance in different lighting and viewing conditions.

A large number of local features can be produced with varying parameters in the position, scale, and orientation of the filters. For example, more than 100,000 local appearance features can be produced when an image of 100×100 is filtered with Gabor filters of five scales and eight orientations for all pixel positions, causing increased dimensionality. Some of these features are effective and important for the classification task, whereas the others may not be so. AdaBoost methods have been used successfully to tackle the feature selection and nonlinear classification problems [42–44].

Researchers put much effort in creating recognition system resistant to shadows, low brightness level, or flashes. Some of these problems can be dealt with using mathematical tools. One of the difficulties that researchers still deal with is images with unusual lighting. In the situation when the intensity variability in input images changes, we have to deal with different types of variability in the area of the face and its background. Local shadows change the form of individual parts of the face, that is, nose, mouth, and eyes, and distort the boundaries of the face area. Global shadows significantly reduce efficiency of discrimination of various face areas against general background or completely hide them.

The results of face recognition systems are very sensitive to variability in the face area. The analysis of the recent literature devoted to face recognition from images with lighting problems [45–53] leads to the observation that there exist some methods to solve this problem, such as:

- Processing of images in order to equalize brightness variation (intensity equalization)
- Reduction of intensity gradient (gamma correction, logarithmic transformation), invariant (in respect to intensity) image representation using the LBP (local binary patterns) and LTV (logarithmic total variation)
- Representation of face images with lighting problems using the eigenbase decompositions and corresponding models based on eigenfaces
- Representation of face images with lighting problems with spectral features using the wavelets and cosine transformation with elimination of low-frequency components
- Extension of face recognition system database with new patterns having all distortions related to lighting problem of face images

The eigenbasis approaches are usually obtained using PCA and LDA [45–47] and more recently also using CCA (Canonical Correlation Analysis [50]), at the same time using DCT (Discrete Cosine Transform) as face images with lighting problems preprocessing step.

For example, in [45] it was shown that in order to solve recognition task using the PCA and LDA, face images should be transformed into spectral features using 2DDCT. At the same processing step, the low-frequency spectral components are removed, as corresponding to "shadow" components.

2.3.3   Authors' Approach

Authors of this chapter also tried to solve the aforementioned problem. We tried to overcome the difficulties caused by shadows using Toeplitz matrices [54] where different ways of calculating coefficients in matrices are presented. Attempt to use this approach in face recognition [55] was performed with 25 points marked on each face form database.

Also different types of classifiers were used to determine usefulness of proposed matrices. Although the points could be determined manually, there are many algorithms which could perform this task automatically, that is, ASM or AAM. Authors propose a way of determining some of fiducial face points by performing a

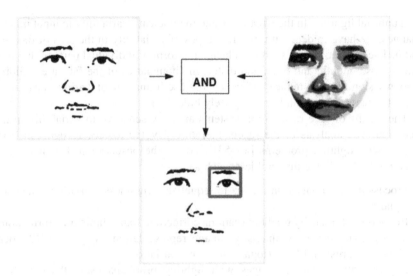

Fig. 2.5 Part of the process of determining the second coordinate of the eye [56]

couple of morphological operations like adaptive threshold and binarization in each of RGB channel (Fig. 2.5). Research shows that Toeplitz matrices perform successfully on small databases, although increasing the size of the database causes the results to deteriorate.

Figure 2.6 represents the scheme of the authors' algorithm. A process of selection and extraction of characteristic points is performed step by step. After successful feature point localization, feature points are used in Toeplitz matrix. The steps of the algorithm are easy to perform and implement.

The algorithm works with color images. After loading image, the first step that has to be done is correct face localization.

To detect faces in images, P. Viola and M. Jones algorithm is used. Characteristic feature of this approach is high efficiency. Speed of the algorithm is 15 fps on Pentium III 700 MHz with resolution 384 × 288 pixels. The algorithm works with grayscale images, so color images have to be transformed. It is estimated that rate of correct face detection is 93.7%.

After conversion to grayscale, an image is searched for faces. When it is localized, it is being cut off from image and rescaled to size of 240 × 240 pixels.

An image is transformed into the HSV color space to perform skin color classification. Acronym HSV stands for hue, saturation, and value. Hue has values from 0° to 360°, saturation from 0 to 1, and value from 0 to 1.

As a result we obtain black and white image with some noise that can be easily removed using median filter. On computer equipped with Intel Pentium Dual CPU T3400, processing time from beginning of the program to obtaining black and white image took less than 200 ms. Medium values from test showed 192 ms. Result can be further reduced with optimization. Final image with detected skin is presented in Fig. 2.7b.

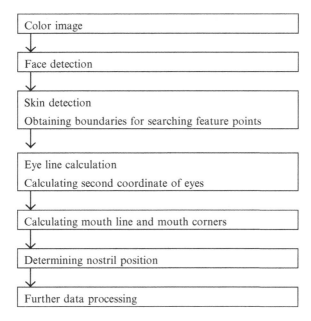

Fig. 2.6 The main stages of the algorithm

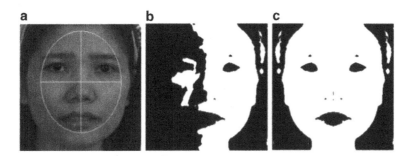

Fig. 2.7 (**a**) Input image with boundaries, (**b**) the result of skin detection, (**c**) mirror image of the detected skin

Skin detection does not always give a correct result. It may be caused by not equally illuminated face or skin color differences caused by makeup or illness. As can be seen in Fig. 2.7b, the skin was not detected on the whole face. Using the symmetry of the face, we can approximate that the detected skin is more or less equally distributed on both sides.

Creating mirror image allows to set boundaries more correctly. Calculating boundaries that are visible in Fig. 2.7a is relatively simple. To obtain them, we are using the idea of image moments. We need to calculate the zero moment (M_{00})

and the first moments for y (M_{10}) and x (M_{01}) from binary mask in Fig. 2.7c. Then using equations below, it is possible to set a center of the object in image:

$$Yc = \frac{M_{10}}{M_{00}}, \tag{2.1}$$

$$Xc = \frac{M_{01}}{M_{00}}, \tag{2.2}$$

Calculation of the second moments (M_{11}, M_{02}, M_{20}) and (2.3), (2.4), allowing for creation of the ellipse

$$L = 1, 5\sqrt{\left[(a+c) + \sqrt{\left(bb + (a+c)^2\right)}\right]/2}, \tag{2.3}$$

$$W = 1, 5\sqrt{\left[(a+c) - \sqrt{\left(bb + (a+c)^2\right)}\right]/2}, \tag{2.4}$$

Parameters a, b, and c are:

$$a = \left(\frac{M_{02}}{M_{00}}\right) - XcXc, \tag{2.5}$$

$$b = \left(\frac{M_{11}}{M_{00}}\right) - XcXc, \tag{2.6}$$

$$c = \left(\frac{M_{20}}{M_{00}}\right) - YcYc, \tag{2.7}$$

When boundaries were successfully set, we are now able to search for the first coordinate of the eye. In order to do so, we are using Sobel filter in two dimensions OX and OY.

The face is divided in two parts, left and right. For each side of the face, we are creating a projection. Obtained function $H(y)$ (see Fig. 2.8a) is multiplied by function $W(y)$ (see Fig. 2.8b) in order to minimize the influence of the mouth and nostrils.

After multiplication of the $H(y)$ by $W(y)$, we obtain the function shown in Fig. 2.8c. Maximum value of this function denotes the eye line and the first coordinate of the eye.

The second coordinate is calculated by performing adaptive binarization. As a result, we obtain a binary image with the eyes, nostrils, and mouth remaining on it. Additionally, the threshold is performed in the color image (RGB) on every channel. Then logical operation AND is executed for every pixel in the image.

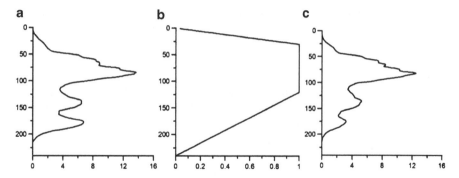

Fig. 2.8 (**a**) Projection *H(y)*, (**b**) function *W(y)*, (**c**) function *F(y)*

When the pixel value is "black" in both images, we obtain a "black" pixel. Otherwise, the pixel is white. The result of this operation is shown in Fig. 2.5.

Vertical projection for eyes is performed in the last step after thresholding and the AND operation. The maximum value denotes the second coordinate of the eye position.

The mouth line is calculated in a similar way to the eye line. The projection is multiplied by the function *W(y)*. This function was modified in a way that minimizes the influence of the eyes.

The position of the mouth corners and width of the jaw and the nostrils are also acquired using projection approach. The maximum value of the projection result denotes the coordinates of features we are looking for.

The obtained feature points will be used for the image description. These points are used to build Toeplitz matrices and calculate their minimal eigenvalues [54].

This simple algorithm is able to work under different lighting conditions (part of the shadows is being removed), and it is robust to elements of environment because feature points are not being searched for outside face area. Skin detection process works also in case of people with dark skin carnation.

2.4   Examples of Face Recognition Algorithms

A number of face recognition algorithms are based on feature-based methods that detect a set of geometrical features on the face such as the positions of the eyes, eyebrows, nose, and mouth [57]. Geometric properties and relations such as areas, distances, and angles between the features are selected as the descriptors of faces. Therefore, the geometric attributes provide benefits in data reduction and make the algorithm less sensitive to variations in illumination, viewpoint, and expressions. Typically, 30–40 feature points per face are generated. The performance of face recognition based on geometrical features depends on the accuracy of the feature location algorithm. However, there are no perfect answers to the problem of how many feature points shall be acquired for the best performance, what the important features are, or how to extract them automatically. Face recognition based on geometrical feature matching is possible for face images at very low resolution. However, precision will suffer, and on large databases this method does not satisfy accuracy demands.

Ivancevic et al. [58] stated that there are about 80 landmark points on a human face and the number of points chosen is application dependent. However, some authors used more than 80 facial points in their algorithms. One example of such work is Cootes et al. [59] where 122 landmark points are used. On the other hand many authors base their algorithms on much smaller number of points – for example, Huang and Huang [60] used 90 facial feature points, Kobayashi and Hara [61] used 30 facial characteristic points, Pantic and Rothkrantz [62] used 19 facial fiducial points, Valstar and Pantic [63] used 20 facial fiducial points, Cohn et al. [64] used 46 fiducial points, and Zhang et al. [65] used 34 fiducial points.

Also a lot of effort was put in the works describing feature point tracking [64, 66], action unit recognition for facial expression analysis [62, 63, 67–69], review papers in facial expression analysis [70–72], and many others.

Appearance-based face recognition algorithms are alternative group of methods which proceed by projecting an image into the subspace and finding the closest point in such subspace [73]. Two well-known linear transformation methods that have been most widely used for dimensionality reduction and feature extraction are the principal component analysis (PCA) [20] and linear discriminant analysis (LDA) [73]. Object classes that are closer together in the output space are often weighted in the input space to reduce potential misclassification. The PCA could be operated either on the raw face image to extract the fisherface or on the eigenface to obtain the discriminant eigenfeatures [20]. Feature representation methods that combine the strengths of different realizations of PCA methods can be found in [74]. Kernel PCA [75] and the generalized discriminant analysis (GDA) using Kernel approach [76] have proved they are successful in pattern regression and classification tasks. Independent component analysis (ICA) provides a set of basis vectors that possess maximum statistical independence [77]. Face recognition techniques based on elastic graph matching [34] and support vector machines (SVMs) [78] also showed successful results. Line edge map approach [57] extracts lines from a face edge map as features, based on a combination of template matching and geometrical feature matching. The nearest feature line classifier [79] attempts to extend the capacity covering variations of pose, illumination, and expression for a face class by finding the candidate person that has the minimum distance between the feature point of query face and the feature lines connecting any two prototype feature points. A modified Hausdorff distance measure was also used to compare face images for recognition [79].

The environment proposed by the authors in [83] (called FaReS-Mod) only gives an option to design system based on two algorithms – PCA and LDA. These algorithms lack robustness to shadows and changing environment. Pictures used in the environment were all nearly frontal images and were captured under more or less constrained environment. The system created by this environment is not very

Fig. 2.9 Seven eigenfaces calculated from input images [6]

robust and cannot be used for images in less rigid environment; however, it does have an educational aspect. It allows to track every stage of face recognition process as it works.

We will briefly describe the basic idea of a face recognition algorithm using eigenface recognition described by Turk and Pentland [6] and face recognition based on elastic bunch graph matching [34] by Wisskot et al.

The main idea of PCA approach is to extract the relevant information from a face image, encode it as efficiently as possible, and compare one encoded face with a database of models encoded similarly. The approach includes extracting the information contained in an image of a face to somehow capture the variation in a collection of face images, independent of any judgment on features, and use this information to encode and compare individual face images. In mathematical terms, one has to find the principal components of the distribution of faces or the eigenvectors of the covariance matrix of the set of face images. These eigenvectors can be thought of as a set of features which together characterize the variation between face images. Each image location contributes to each eigenvector so that we can display the eigenvector as a sort of ghostly face which we call an eigenface. Some of these faces are shown in Fig. 2.9.

Each face image in the training set can be represented exactly in terms of a linear combination of the eigenfaces. The number of possible eigenfaces is equal to the number of face images in the training set. However, the faces can also be approximated using only the "best" eigenfaces – those that have the largest eigenvalues and which therefore account for the most variance within the set of face images. Computational efficiency is the primary reason for using a smaller number of eigenfaces.

If we consider the training set of face images $\Gamma_1, \Gamma_2, \Gamma_3, \ldots, \Gamma_M$, the average face of the set is defined by $\Psi = \frac{1}{M} \sum_{n=1}^{M} \Gamma_n$. Each face differs from the average by the vector $\Phi_i = \Gamma - \Psi$. Set of very large vectors is then subject to principal component analysis which seeks a set of M orthonormal vectors u_n and their associated eigenvalues x_k which best describes the distribution of the data.

Since a complete algorithm can be found in many publications, we did not find it necessary to present it here.

Eigenfaces seem adequate for describing face images under controlled conditions. To perform identification task, new face image (Γ) is transformed into eigenface components by simple operation $\omega_k = u_k^T(\Gamma - \Psi)$ for $k = 1 \ldots M'$. This describes a set of point-by-point image multiplications and summations, operations performed at approximately frame rate on image processing hardware.

Since PCA approach cannot deal with nonlinearity as mentioned earlier, we think that presenting hybrid approach like EBGM in contrast would be more interesting.

Without going into details how individual faces and general knowledge about faces are represented by respectively labeled graphs and the face bunch graph (FBG) [34], we are now going to explain how these graphs are generated. Authors have used a method to generate initial graphs for the system, one graph for each pose, together with pointers to indicate which pairs of nodes in graphs for different poses correspond to each other. Once the system has an FBG (possibly consisting of only one manually defined model), graphs for new images can be generated automatically by elastic bunch graph matching. Initially, when the FBG contains only a few faces, it is necessary to review and correct the resulting matches, but once the FBG is big enough (approximately 70 graphs), one can rely on the matching and generate large collections of model graphs automatically.

Manual definition of graphs is done in three steps. At first the authors mark a set of fiducial points for a given image. Most of these points are positioned at well-defined features which are easy to locate, such as the left and right pupil, the corners of the mouth, the tip of the nose, the top and bottom of the ears, the top of the head, and the tip of the chin. These points were selected to make manual positioning easy and reliable. Additional fiducial points are positioned at the center of gravity of certain easy-to-locate fiducial points. This allows an automatic selection of fiducial points in the regions where well-defined features are missing, for example, at the cheeks or the forehead. Then, edges are drawn between fiducial points, and edge labels are automatically computed as the differences between node positions. Finally, the Gabor wavelet transform provides the jets for the nodes. In general, the set of fiducial points should cover the face evenly.

A key role in elastic bunch graph matching is played by the function evaluating the graph similarity between an image graph and the FBG of identical pose. It depends on the jet similarities and the distortion of the image grid relative to

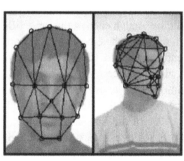
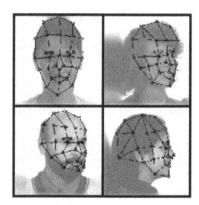

grids for face finding

grids for face recognition

Fig. 2.10 Object-adapted grids for different poses. The nodes are positioned automatically by elastic graph matching against the corresponding face bunch graphs [34]

the FBG grid. Since the FBG provides several jets for each fiducial point, the best one is selected and used for comparison. These best fitting jets serve as local experts for the image face.

The goal of elastic bunch graph matching on a query image is to find the fiducial points and thus to extract the graph which maximizes the similarity with the FBG from the image. In practice, one has to apply a heuristic algorithm to find near-optimum results within a reasonable time. Authors use a coarse-to-fine approach in which they introduce the degrees of freedom of the FBG progressively: translation, scale, aspect ratio, and finally local distortions. Authors introduce phase information and increase the focus of displacement estimation in the similar way: no phase, phase with focus 1, and then phase with focus 1 up to 5. The matching schedule described here assumes faces of known pose and approximately standard size so that only one FBG is required.

The resulting graph is called the image graph and is stored as a representation of the individual face of the image (Fig. 2.10).

To minimize computing effort and to optimize reliability, authors extract a face representation in two stages. The first stage called the normalization stage is described in greater detail in [80]. Its purpose is to estimate the position and size of the face in the original image so that the image can be scaled and cut to standard size. The second stage takes this standardized image as an input and extracts a precise image graph appropriate for face recognition purposes. In the experiments on the face database, original images had a format of 256×384 pixels, and the faces varied in size by a factor of 3. The poses were known and did not need to be determined. The normalization stage used three FBGs of appropriate pose which differed in face size. Authors arbitrarily picked approximately 30 images to form each FBG. More careful selection of images to cover a wider range of variations can only improve system performance. The grids used in the construction of the FBGs put little emphasis, that is, few nodes, on the interior of the face and have fewer nodes than those used for the second stage (see Fig. 2.10 for two examples). The smaller number of nodes speeds up the process of face finding. Using a matching scheme similar to the one described earlier, authors match each of the three FBGs to the input image. Authors select the graph that matches best, cut a frame of appropriate size around it from the image, and resize it to 128×128 pixels. The poses could be determined analogously [80], although here they are assumed to be known. During the experiments, normalization took approximately 20 s on a SPARCStation 10–512 with a 50 MHz processor, and the system identified face position and scale correctly in approximately 99% of the images.

The simple algorithm proposed by the authors achieves 90% success recognition rate. However, this result can be reached only on databases smaller than 30 individuals. This limitation is caused by Toeplitz matrices, since they do not perform well on large databases. Algorithm such as PCA, ICA, and LDA can achieve 83% success rate [84], but tests performed with these algorithms were performed on databases that contained data for more than 1,000 individuals. If we compare PCA and EBGM algorithms [85] on similar database, we can see that results are quite similar. These results may vary based on different variables used in algorithms.

Authors' algorithm based on this size of database performed much worse. Because of that, further research on Toeplitz matrices must be performed to achieve good results on large databases.

2.5 Conclusions

Rapid progress and development of new technologies which increased the computational power of computers created possibility to build systems more complex and adjusting to the environment. During the past 20 years of constant development of new algorithms, researchers were able to create systems able to detect faces in images and recognize them. However, these systems are far from being perfect. They are still vulnerable to unconstrained environment, changes in facial expressions, or possibility of stealing a biometric key. These challenges show direction in which researchers should follow.

The algorithm for feature points detection presented by authors is very simple. However simple, it is able to work under different lighting conditions and it is robust to elements of environment because feature points are not being searched for outside the face area. Unfortunately the efficiency of a face descriptor based on Toeplitz matrices is not very high, which is not surprising. Based on the results we can notice that as the number of classes increases, the recognition rate drops. Currently, research on Toeplitz matrices focuses on maintaining recognition rate while increasing the size of the database.

Acknowledgement This work was partially supported by AGH University of Science and Technology in Cracow, grant no. 11.11.220.01. The authors are indeed indebted to Marcin Rogowski for his constructive remarks and thorough proofreading of the chapter.

References

1. Hietmeyer R (2000) Biometric identification promises fast and secure processing of airline passengers. Int Civ Aviat Organ J 55(9):10–11
2. Machine Readable Travel Documents (MRTD). http://www.icao.int/Security/mrtd/Pages/default.aspx. Accessed 23 May 2012
3. Kanade T (1973) Picture processing by computer complex and recognition of human faces. Ph.D. thesis, Kyoto University
4. Kohonen T (1989) Self-organization and associative memory. Springer, Berlin
5. Kirby M, Sirovich L (1990) Application of the Karhunen-Loeve procedure for the characterization of human faces. IEEE Pattern Anal Mach Intell 12(1):103–108
6. Turk M, Pentland A (1991) Eigenfaces for recognition. J Cog Neurosci 3(1):71–86
7. Fukunaga K (1990) Introduction to statistical pattern recognition, 2nd edn. Academic, Boston
8. Sirovich L, Kirby M (1987) Low-dimensional procedure for the characterization of human faces. J Opt Soc Am A 4(3):519–524
9. Bichsel M, Pentland A (1994) Human face recognition and the face image set's topology. CVGIP Image Understand 59:254–261
10. Turk M (2001) A random walk through eigenspace. IEICE Trans Inf Syst E84-D (12):1586–1695
11. Face Recognition Vendor Tests (FRVT). http://www.nist.gov/itl/iad/ig/frvt-home.cfm. Accessed 25 May 2012
12. Phillips PJ, Moon H, Rizvi SA, Rauss PJ (2000) The FERET evaluation methodology for face-recognition algorithms. IEEE Trans Pattern Anal Mach Intell 22(10):1090–1104
13. Chellappa R, Wilson C, Sirohey S (1995) Human and machine recognition of faces: a survey. Proc IEEE 83:705–740
14. Valentin D, Abdi H, O'Toole AJ, Cottrell GW (1994) Connectionist models of face processing: a survey. Pattern Recogn 27(9):1209–1230
15. Zhao W, Chellappa R, Phillips P, Rosenfeld A (2003) Face recognition: a literature survey. ACM Comput Surv 35(4):399–458. doi:10.1145/954339.954342
16. Caltech database. http://www.vision.caltech.edu. Accessed 10 Dec 2011
17. Moses Y, Adini Y, Ullman S (1994) Face recognition: the problem of compensating for changes in illumination direction. In: Proceedings of the European conference on computer vision, Stockholm, Sweden, vol A, pp 286–296
18. Sirovich L, Kirby M (1987) Low-dimensional procedure for the characterization of human faces. J Opt Soc Am A 4(3):519–524
19. Bartlett MS, Lades HM, Sejnowski TJ (1998) Independent component representations for face recognition. In: Proceedings of the SPIE, conference on human vision and electronic imaging III, San Jose, California, USA, vol 3299, pp 528–539
20. Belhumeur PN, Hespanha JP, Kriegman DJ (1997) Eigenfaces vs. fisherfaces: recognition using class specific linear projection. IEEE Trans Pattern Anal Mach Intell 19(7):711–720
21. Brunelli R, Poggio T (1993) Face recognition: features versus templates. IEEE Trans Pattern Anal Mach Intell 15(10):1042–1052
22. Goldstein AJ, Harmon LD, Lesk AB (1971) Identification of human faces. Proc IEEE 59(5):748–760
23. Kanade T (1973) Picture processing by computer complex and recognition of human faces. Ph.D. thesis, Kyoto University
24. Samal A, Iyengar PA (1992) Automatic recognition and analysis of human faces and facial expressions: a survey. Pattern Recogn 25:65–77
25. Cox IJ, Ghosn J, Yianilos P (1996) Feature-based face recognition using mixture-distance. In: Proceedings of IEEE computer society conference on computer vision and pattern recognition, San Francisco, USA, pp 209–216
26. Scholkopf B, Smola A, Muller KR (1999) Nonlinear component analysis as a kernel eigenvalue problem. Neural Comput 10:1299–1319

27. Mika S, Ratsch G, Weston J, Scholkopf B, Mller KR (1999) Fisher discriminant analysis with kernels. Neural Netw Signal Process IX:41–48
28. Guo GD, Li SZ, Chan KL (2000) Face recognition by support vector machines. In: Proceedings of fourth IEEE international conference on automatic face and gesture recognition, Grenoble, France, pp 196–201
29. Li Y, Gong S, Liddell H (2001) Recognising trajectories of facial identities using kernel discriminant analysis. In: Proceedings of British machine vision conference, Manchester, UK, pp 613–622
30. Moghaddam B (1999) Principal manifolds and Bayesian subspaces for visual recognition. In: International conference on computer vision (ICCV'99), Corfu, Greece, pp 1131–1136
31. Yang MH, Ahuja N, Kriegman D (2000) Face recognition using kernel eigenfaces. In: Proceedings of the IEEE international conference on image processing, Vancouver, BC, Canada, vol 1, pp 37–40
32. Penev P, Atick J (1996) Local feature analysis: a general statistical theory for object representation. Neural Syst 7(3):477–500
33. Lades M, Vorbruggen J, Buhmann J, Lange J, Malsburg C, Wurtz RP, Konen W (1993) Distortion invariant object recognition in the dynamic link architecture. IEEE Trans Comput 42:300–311
34. Wiskott L, Fellous J, Kruger N, Malsburg C (1997) Face recognition by elastic bunch graph matching. IEEE Trans Pattern Anal Mach Intell 19(7):775–779
35. Liu C, Wechsler H (2002) Gabor feature based classification using the enhanced fisher linear discriminant model for face recognition. IEEE Trans Image Process 11(4):467–476
36. Ahonen T, Hadid A, Pietikainen M (2004) Face recognition with local binary patterns. In: Proceedings of the European conference on computer vision, Prague, Czech, pp 469–481
37. Gordon GG, Lewis ME (1995) Face recognition using video clips and mug shots. In: Proceedings of office of national drug control policy (ONDCP) international technical symposium, Nashua, NH
38. Lengagne R, Tarel JP, Monga O (1996) From 2d images to 3d face geometry. In: Proceedings of IEEE international conference automatic face and gesture recognition, Killington, USA, pp 301–306
39. Atick JJ, Griffin PA, Redlich AN (1996) Statistical approach to shape from shading: reconstruction of 3Dface surfaces from single 2Dimages. Neural Comput 8(6):1321–1340
40. Yan Y, Zhang J (1998) Rotation-invariant 3D recognition for face recognition. In: Proceedings of IEEE international conference image processing, Prague, Czech, vol 1, pp 156–160
41. Zhao WY, Chellappa R (2000) 3D model enhanced face recognition. In: Proceedings of IEEE international conference on image processing, Nashua, NH
42. Yang P, Shan S, Gao W, Li SZ, Zhang D (2004) Face recognition using ada-boosted gabor features. In: Proceedings of international conference on automatic face and gesture recognition, Killington, USA
43. Zhang G, Huang X, Li SZ, Wang Y (2004) Boosting local binary pattern (LBP)-based face recognition. In: Li SZ, Lai J, Tan T, Feng G, Wang Y (eds) Advances in biometric personal authentication, vol 3338, Lecture notes in computer science. Springer, Berlin, pp 180–187
44. Zhang L, Li SZ, Qu Z, Huang X (2004) Boosting local feature based classifiers for face recognition. In: Proceedings of first IEEE workshop on face processing in video, Washington, DC
45. Chen W, Er M, Wu S (2005) PCA and LDA in DCT domain. Pattern Recogn Lett 26:2474–2482
46. Chen W, Meng JE, Shiqian W (2006) Illumination compensation and normalization for robust face recognition using discrete cosine transform in logarithm domain. IEEE Trans Syst Man Cybern B: Cybern 36(2):458–466
47. Tan X, Triggs B (2007) Preprocessing and feature sets for robust face recognition. In: IEEE conference on computer vision and pattern recognition, CVPR '07, Minneapolis, Minnesota, USA, pp 1–8

48. Xie X, Zheng W, Lai J, Yuen PC (2008) Face illumination normalization on large and small scale features. In: IEEE conference on computer vision and pattern recognition, CVPR '08, Anchorage, AK, USA, pp 1–8

49. Abbas A, Khalil MI, Abdel HS, Fahmy HMA (2009) Illumination invariant face recognition in logarithm discrete cosine transform domain. IEEE ICIP'2009, Cairo, Egypt, pp 4157–4160

50. Shao M, Wang Y (2009) Joint features for face recognition under variable illuminations. In: Fifth international conference on image and graphics, ICIG'09, Xi'an, Shanxi, China, pp 922–927

51. Liau HF, Isa D (2010) New illumination compensation method for face recognition. Int J Comput Netw Secur 2(3):308–321

52. Han H, Shan S, Qing L, Chen X, Gao W (2010) Lighting aware preprocessing for face recognition across varying illumination. LNCS 6312/ECCV 2010, Crete, Greece, pp 308–321

53. Goel T, Nehra V, Vishwakarma VP (2010) Comparative analysis of various illumination normalization techniques for face recognition. Int J Comput Appl 28(9):1–7

54. Saeed K (2004) Image analysis for object recognition. Bialystok Technical University Press, Bialystok

55. Kocjan P, Saeed K (2011) A feature based algorithm for face image description. In: Proceedings of IEEE-ICBAKE, IEEE CS Press–CD, Takamatsu, 19–21 Sep 2011, Japan, pp 175–178

56. Kocjan P, Saeed K (2011) Algorithm for extraction feature points from human face and their use in Toeplitz matrices. Faculty of Biomedical Engineering, Silesian University of Technology, Gliwice

57. Gao Y, Leung MKH (2002) Face recognition using line edge map. IEEE Trans Pattern Anal Mach Intell 24(6):764–779

58. Ivanevic V, Kaine AK, Mclindin BA, Sunde J (2003) Factor analysis of essential facial features. In: 25th international conference on information technology interfaces, Cavtat, Croatia, pp 187–191

59. Cootes TF, Edwards GJ, Taylor CJ (1998) Active appearance models. In: Computer vision – ECCV'98, Freiburg, Germany, vol 2, pp 484–498

60. Huang CL, Huang YM (1997) Facial expression recognition using model-based feature extraction and action parameters classification. J Vis Commun Image Represent 8:278–290

61. Kobayashi H, Hara F (1992) Recognition of six basic facial expression and their strength by neural network. In: IEEE international workshop on robot and human communication, Tokyo, Japan, pp 381–386

62. Pantic M, Rothkrantz LJM (2004) Facial action recognition for facial expression analysis from static face images. IEEE Trans Syst Man Cybern 34(3):1449–1461

63. Valstar M, Pantic M (2006) Fully automatic facial action unit detection and temporal analysis. In: Proceedings of the 2006 conference on computer vision and pattern recognition workshop (CVPRW'06) NY, USA

64. Cohn JF, Zlochower AJ, Lien JJ, Kanade T (1998) Feature-point tracking by optical flow discriminates subtle differences in facial expression. In: Proceedings of third IEEE FG, Nara, Japan, pp 396–401

65. Zhang Z, Lyons M, Schuster M, Akamatsu S (1998) Comparison between geometry-based and Gabor-wavelets-based facial expression recognition using multi-layer perceptron. In: Proceedings of third IEEE FG, Nara, Japan, pp 354–459

66. Cohn J, Zlochower A, Lien JJ, Kanade T (1999) Automated face analysis by feature point tracking has high concurrent validity with manual FACS coding. Psychophysiology 36:35–43

67. Tian YI, Kanade T, Cohn JF (2001) Recognizing action units for facial expression analysis. IEEE Trans Pattern Anal Mach Intell 23:97–115

68. Donato G, Bartelett MS, Hager JC, Ekman P, Sejnowski TJ (1999) Classifying facial actions. IEEE Trans Pattern Anal Mach Intell 21:974–989

69. Essa IA, Pentland AP (1997) Coding, analysis, interpretation, and recognition of facial expressions. IEEE Trans Pattern Anal Mach Intell 19:757–763

70. Fasel B, Luettin J (2002) Automatic facial expression analysis: a survey. Pattern Recogn 36:259–275
71. Pantic M, Rothkrantz LJM (2000) Expert system for automatic analysis of facial expressions. Image Vision Comput 18:881–905
72. Pantic M, Rothkrantz LJM (2000) Automatic analysis of facial expressions: the state of the art. IEEE Trans Pattern Anal Mach Intell 22:1424–1445
73. Bartlett MS, Movellan JR, Sejnowski TJ (2002) Face recognition by independent component analysis. IEEE Trans Neural Netw 13(6):1450–1464
74. Lu J, Plataniotis KN, Venetsanopoulos AN (2002) Face recognition using LDA-based algorithms. IEEE Trans Neural Netw 14(1):195–200
75. Kim KI, Jung K, Kim HJ (2002) Face recognition using kernel principal component analysis. IEEE Signal Process Lett 9(2):40–42
76. Baudat G, Anouar F (2000) Generalized discriminant analysis using a Kernel approach. Neural Comput 12(10):2385–2404
77. Bell AJ, Sejnowski TJ (1995) A non-linear information maximization algorithm that performs blind separation. Adv Neural Inf Process Syst 7:467–474
78. Phillips PJ (1999) Support vector machines applied to face recognition. Adv Neural Inf Process Syst 11:113–123
79. Li SZ, Lu J (1999) Face recognition using the nearest feature line method. IEEE Trans Neural Netw 10(2):439–443
80. Krüger N, Pötzsch M, Malsburg C (1997) Determination of face position and pose with a learned representation based on labeled graphs. Image Vision Comput 15(8):665–673
81. Images from public domain. http://www.totallyfreeimages.com. Accessed 10 May 2012
82. Images from public domain. http://www.publicdomainpictures.net. Accessed 10 May 2012
83. Kukharev G, Kuzminski A (2002) Biometric techniques: methods of face recognition. Szczecin Technical University Press, Szczecin, Poland (in Polish: Techniki Biometryczne: Metody rozpoznawania twarzy)
84. Delac K, Grgic M, Grgic S (2006) Independent comparative study of PCA, ICA, and LDA on the FERET data set. Int J Imag Syst Technol 15(5):252–260
85. Katadound S (2004) Face recognition: study and comparison of PCA and EBGM algorithms. Master thesis, Western Kentucky University

Chapter 3
Iris Pattern Recognition with a New Mathematical Model to Its Rotation Detection

Krzysztof Misztal, Emil Saeed, Jacek Tabor, and Khalid Saeed

Abstract The work deals with the iris pattern recognition as one of the most popular automated biometric ways of individual identification. It is based on the acquired eye images in which we localize the region of interest – the iris. This extremely data-rich biometric identifier is stable throughout human life and well protected as internal part of the eye. Moreover, it is genetic independent, so that we can use it to identify or verify people among huge population. This chapter will present the human vision nature focusing on defects and diseases that change the surface information of the iris. Also will be shown the main stream and the historical background of mathematical research resulting in a new algorithm for automatic iris feature extraction. A special attention is paid to the method developed to detect the iris rotation for accurate success rate under different destructive problems and environmental conditions. The obtained results after using the new mathematical model have proved the algorithm high success rate in iris pattern recognition.

K. Misztal (✉)
AGH University of Science and Technology, Kraków, Poland
e-mail: krzysztof.misztal@gmail.com

E. Saeed
Medical University in Bialystok, Bialystok, Poland

J. Tabor
Jagiellonian University, Kraków, Poland

K. Saeed
AGH University of Science and Technology, Faculty of Physics and Applied
Computer Science, Al. Mickiewicza 30, Kraków PL-30059, Poland
e-mail: saeed@agh.edu.pl

K. Saeed and T. Nagashima (eds.), *Biometrics and Kansei Engineering*,
DOI 10.1007/978-1-4614-5608-7_3, © Springer Science+Business Media New York 2012

3.1   History of Iris Recognition

The idea of using iris patterns for personal identification is very old [1]. However, the idea of automating this process was originally suggested in 1936 by ophthalmologist Frank Burch. In 1987 two American ophthalmologists, Aran Safir and Leonard Flom, patented Bruch's idea. Their belief that one can identify people based on individual iris features was supported by their clinical experience. However, they were unable to develop such a process.

In 1989 John Daugman [2], a Harvard mathematician, constructed algorithms for iris recognition upon request of A. Safir and L. Flom. These algorithms, patented by Daugman in 1994, form the basis for all basic iris recognition systems and products currently being used. The first commercial products became available in 1995 [3]. Nowadays companies in several countries are using such variety of products [2], for example, IBM; IrisGuard, Inc.; Securimetrics, Inc.; Panasonic; London Heathrow Airport; and Amsterdam Schiphol Airport.

Moreover, the idea of using iris in biometrics is also popular in science-fiction movies. We should mention the scene in Demolition Man (1993), where a bad character played by Wesley Snipes used gouged eye to gain access through a security door, and other movies like Angels and Demons (2000) and The Simpsons Movie (2007).

As we observe, the field of iris recognition is relatively young, and therefore one may hope for much progress in this field.

3.2   Human and Computer Vision

This chapter will start with an introduction about human vision. You may ask why, why human vision and what it would do with computer vision. What benefits will the computer engineers have from having this knowledge? The answer is that actually whenever we deal with a natural concept or a real event, we should always study it from inside before going further with the automatic process. The physical nature of the eye and the medical knowledge about it will give the engineer wide understanding about its iris. Researchers study the iris from computer vision point of view, but they always need to check what may affect their results. The iris has an exceptional pattern with trillions of shape and texture distribution combinations. And it is this fact that makes it one of the most reliable biometric features to distinguish between people.

The reliance on iris in biometric identification based on wide range of advantages of this human body characteristic [4]. Table 3.1 contains comparisons among biometric identifiers on the seven criteria, which can represent their basic properties – iris achieved good results in this comparison. Iris pattern and structure evidence is long-term – structural formation that is fixed about 1 year in age. It is an internal organ that is well protected against damage and worn by a highly

Table 3.1 Comparisons among biometrics based on different factors – high (H), medium (M), low (L) [5]

Biometric identifier	Universality	Distinctiveness	Permanence	Collectability	Performance	Acceptability	Circumvention
DNA	H	H	H	L	H	L	L
Face	H	L	M	H	L	H	H
Fingerprint	M	H	H	M	H	M	M
Hand geometry	M	M	M	H	M	M	M
Iris	H	H	H	M	H	L	L
Keystroke	L	L	L	M	L	M	M
Signature	L	L	L	H	L	H	H
Voice	M	L	L	M	L	H	H

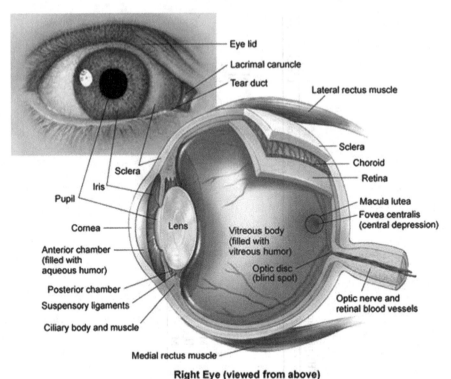

Right Eye (viewed from above)

Fig. 3.1 Eye anatomy [6]

transparent and sensitive membrane (the cornea, see Fig. 3.1). The iris is mostly flat, and its geometric configuration is only controlled by two complementary muscles that control the diameter of the pupil. This makes the iris shape far more predictable than, for instance, that of the face. An iris scan is similar to taking a photograph and can be performed from about 10 cm to a few meters away [7]. Moreover, the identification speed through iris scanning is very fast and cannot be compared with that of any other technology.

Additional important medical facts about the iris are the following:

- Every iris is different, even left and right or between identical twins.
- It is worn by easy to damage the iris by external factors, because of its deep location and because iris is worn by the cornea.
- Iris does not change during the whole life unless there is a diseaseor a mechanical damage.
- It is naturally destroyed few seconds after death.
- The physiological reaction of the iris toward the light and thenatural movement of the pupil make it impossible to replace the iris tissue with a photograph, by spoofers, for example.

Usually, the problems of the eye reflect on its iris shape, pattern, and texture – simply what affects its information code that it has behind its structure and construction. Therefore, in order to study what affects the success rate of iris classification and recognition, researchers should study the iris nature. They should know these and other environmental conditions and geometrical changes (with the light effects as their main factor). Any disturbance in the pattern information the iris supplies the automatic machines with is of importance and worth studying. This is because every single defect that hits the iris and makes its shape or pattern changed/ deformed would affect the results.

Considering all this information, the authors found it of great importance and benefit to introduce the problems with iris automatic recognition, particularly those of medical type and nature. With these concerns, the chapter will present first the medical effects. Then the geometrical factors and the other changes that may also affect the iris pattern will be given.

3.3 Iris Anatomy

The iris arises from the anterior portion of the eye ciliary body. It divides the space between the cornea and lens into anterior and posterior chambers. It contains variable amounts of pigment:

- Heavy pigmentation in the anterior layer results in brown eyes.
- If pigment is limited to the posterior layer, the iris appears blue or gray because light refracts within the unpigmented anterior layer. The iris contains primitive myoepithelial cells surrounding central aperture, the pupil [8].

3.3.1 The General Structure of the Iris

There are two layers building the iris: stroma – the front pigmented fibrovascular tissue – and, below the stroma, the pigmented epithelial cells.

The stroma adheres to the sphincter pupil which contracts it in a circular motion and a dilator which pulls the iris radially to extend the pupil, pulling it in folds – alike the camera shutter. The iris is divided into two major parts: pupillary and ciliary zone.

3.3.2 Histological Features

The first layer of the iris, from front to back, is anterior limiting layer. The second one is the stroma. The sphincter and dilator muscles are next. Then anterior pigment myoepithelium and posterior pigment epithelium close the structure of the iris.

Iris is a very important element of human vision. It is kind of a camera shutter, which is automatically regulated. It is responsible for controlling the size of the pupil and the amount of light reaching the retina; on the other hand it cuts circles of dispersal because of the imperfection of the optical system of the eye.

3.4 Iris Pathology and Diseases

This section will be shown in a table. It will contain full information about the iris diseases that affect its shape and pattern, or at least it may disturb the information collected from the iris. Table 3.2 will give information about such diseases – their names with a short description to show what exactly it does to cause a defect. A full eye image with the iris defect shown in it is given.

3.5 Iris Recognition Process: A Review of Selected Existing Algorithms

The automatic iris scanning systems make use of the visible features of the iris. After taking iris scan, a unique entry in the database is created. Thanks to this, for individual verification the person is required to look at an equipped camera that scans and verifies the iris in a few seconds.

The process of capturing an iris and projecting it into a biometric template is made up of three major steps:

- Capturing the image – one of the main challenges of automated iris recognition is to capture a high-quality image to include as many features of the iris as possible. The image should have sufficient resolution and sharpness, high contrast ratio, etc. The system should eliminate artifacts. Images are generally acquired in near infrared illumination. The distance between the eye and the camera can vary between 4 and 50 cm. There is an iris recognition system which works at a distance of about 3 m [18]. Iris diameter needs typically about 100–200 pixels for the extraction of good texture.
- Localizing the iris and optimizing its image – an iris recognition algorithm first has to identify the approximately concentric circular outer boundaries of the iris and the pupil in a photo of an eye. One has often to deal with additional problems caused by the eyelids which can reduce the surface of the iris. To deal with these problems along with the iris template, the mask template is also formed which makes sure that the noisy or less significant parts of the image are not encoded. Sensitivity to a wide range of edge contrast and insensitivity to irregular borders are the desired characteristics of localization algorithms.
- Storing and comparing of the images – the set of pixels covering the iris is transformed into a bit pattern that preserves the information essential for a comparison between two irises. To perform authentication, which includes identification or verification, an iris template is compared to stored template values in a database.

Table 3.2 Iris diseases – names, images, and defect description

Disease		Eye image	Description
1.	Melanocytic tumors	(a) Nevus	Nevus is a benign tumor. It can involve any portion of the iris, and it is mainly flat. An iris nevus rarely can lead to an irregular pupil. This would cause some changes in the iris structure and hence its pattern [9]
(b)	Melanoma		An iris melanoma is a malignant tumor. It usually concerns elder people, mostly with bright irises and occurs unilaterally. An iris melanoma is an elevated and variable pigmented neoplasm. Melanoma most often is larger than an iris nevus and can induce an irregular pupil [9]
2. Iritis	(a) Nongranulomatous		Hypopyon (arrow) – level of exudative fluid covers a part of the iris [10]
	(b) Granulomatous		Koeppe nodules appear at the pupil margin and changes iris structure [11]
			Busacca nodules on the periphery of the iris [12]
3. Iris defects	(a) Coloboma iridis		Congenital absence in the low part of the iris. It destroys part of the iris [10]

(continued)

Table 3.2 (continued)

Disease	Eye image	Description
(b) Aniridia		Congenital absence of the iris – it occurs bilaterally [13]
4. Glaucoma (a) Rubeosis iridis		New abnormal blood vessels, known as neovascularization, on the surface of the iris. This is caused by hypoxia, which involves retina. This happens when there is a lack of blood in the area, for example, in diabetic retinopathy [14]
(b) Axenfeld-Rieger syndrome (a defect that affects teeth, eyes, and abdomen, characterized by three types, but only two of them affect the iris)		Axenfeld syndrome – the most typical feature of the eye is a posterior embryotoxon and prominent Schwalbe's line (arrows) [15]
		Rieger syndrome – it contains hypoplasia of the iris stroma, displacement of the pupil, and full-thickness colobomas of the iris [16]
(c) Von Recklinghausen disease (Neurofibromatosis type I)		Iris pattern destroyed by Lisch nodules (nodular changes in the iris shape) [17]
		Congenital ectropion uvuae – it means the iris pigment epithelium is on the anterior surface of the iris [12]
5. Hyphema		Blood in anterior chamber. It is usually caused by a mechanical eye injury. Arrow shows the iris blood coverage [10]

Many methods have been developed for automatic iris recognition [19, 20]; they can be divided due to their feature encoding algorithms:

- The Gabor wavelet approach by Daugman [21]
- The Laplacian parameter approach by Wildes [22]
- Zero-crossings of the wavelet transform at various resolution levels by Boles et al. [23]
- The independent component analysis approach by Huang et al. [24]
- The texture analysis using multichannel Gabor filtering and wavelet transform by Zhu et al. [25] and many others

However, the existing algorithms are in many cases not successful enough to solve some basic problems. The commercial iris recognition systems usually cannot distinguish between high-quality photograph of a person's face and the real face [26]. And this is a big security problem, for example. To solve this problem, a human may supervise the use of an iris recognition system. Another solution is to track the movement of the eye in order to verify that the iris is alive.

There are free distributed iris image databases on the Internet, for example, the database provided by the Chinese Academy of Sciences' Institute of Automation (CASIA) [27] includes 756 iris images from 108 eyes – images are stored as BMP format with a 320×280 resolution.

3.6 Daugman's Classical Algorithm

The classical algorithm proposed by John Daugman is the most popular approach to individual identification by iris pattern recognition. The main steps in this algorithm are presented as follows:

- Iris localization
- Normalization
- Feature encoding
- Matching

3.6.1 Localizing and Segmentation

John Daugman's algorithm uses integrodifferential operator for determining the localization of the circular iris and pupil in addition to the areas of the upper and lower eyelids. The operator is defined as follows:

$$\max_{(r,x_0,y_0)} \left| G_\sigma(r) * \frac{\partial}{\partial r} \oint_{r,x_0,y_0} \frac{I(x,y)}{2\pi r} ds \right|,$$

Fig. 3.2 Example iris
localization and
segmentation. The area
between the *two circles* would
define the iris while the arcs
define the eyelids edge

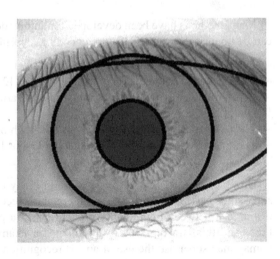

where:

$l(x,y)$ – image (containing the eye) pixel color

$G_\sigma(r)$ – the Gaussian smoothing function with scale (σ) is given by the following
    formula

$$G_\sigma(r) = \frac{1}{\sqrt{2\pi}\sigma} \exp\left(-\frac{(r-r_0)^2}{2\sigma^2}\right),$$

r – searching radius

s – contour given by circle with r, x_0, y_0 parameters

The smoothed image is scanned for a circle that has the maximum gradient
change that indicates an edge. To obtain a precise localization, the operator is
applied iteratively. During this operation, the smoothing function scale is changed
to increase the accuracy. Eyelids are localized in a similar way – the contour s is
changed from a circular into an arc (Fig. 3.2).

This approach uses the first derivative of the image and performs a search to
locate geometrical elements at it. However, one has to be careful with using it,
because the algorithm uses local scale, so it can perform badly, if the image
contains reflection or other types of noise.

The above method assumes that the iris has a circular boundary; nowadays
research shows that we can reject this assumption and give better algorithm for
iris segmentation [28].

3.6.2 Normalization

Given an iris region, we need to extract a fixed number of features based on this
region. We should be able to do this regardless (if possible) of the image resolution.

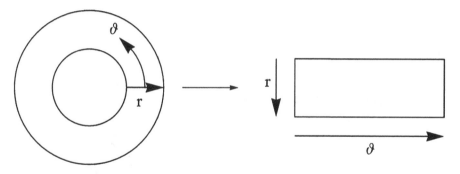

Fig. 3.3 Daugman's rubber-sheet model – Daugman normalization model

Fig. 3.4 Iris after normalization (based on Fig. 3.2)

Hence, we need to transform the given iris region into a fixed reference system. This transformation forms the normalization process; it is achieved by varieties of methods. For example, the Cartesian to polar coordinate transform suggested by J. Daugman converts the region of interest into a rectangular representation introducing an interesting method of normalization (Fig. 3.3).

This way we unfold the frequency information contained in the localized region in order to next simplify the feature extraction (Fig. 3.4).

Daugman's rubber-sheet model of iris normalization can be described as follows: Let θ ($\theta \in [0, 2\pi]$) and r ($r \in [0, 1]$) parameters describe the polar-coordinate system. Then the rubber sheet is modeled as

$$I(x(r, \theta), y(r, \theta)) \rightarrow I(r, \theta),$$

where

$$x(r, \theta) = (1 - r)x_p(\theta) + rx_i(\theta)$$
$$y(r, \theta) = (1 - r)y_p(\theta) + ry_i(\theta)$$

where r_p and r_i are, respectively, the radii of the pupil and the iris, while $(x_p(\theta), y_p(\theta))$ and $(x_i(\theta), y_i(\theta))$ are the coordinates of the pupillary and limbic boundaries in the direction θ.

This model introduces the normalized nonconcentric polar representation of the iris, which is size and translation invariant. It should be noted that the previous steps have a big influence on this stage, which in particular implies that the wrong recognition of the center or the radius of the iris can have profound consequences.

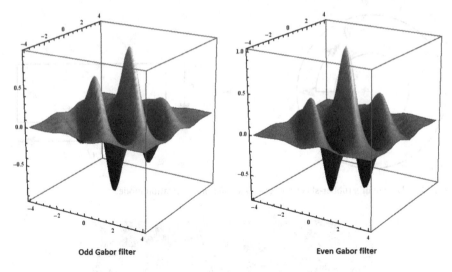

Odd Gabor filter   Even Gabor filter

Fig. 3.5 Odd and even Gabor filter

3.6.3 Feature Encoding

It has been shown by Oppenheim and Lim [29] that phase information rather than amplitude information provides the most significant information within an image. Taking only the phase will allow encoding of discriminating information in the iris while discarding the redundant information such as illumination, which is represented by the amplitude component. Therefore, it is required to transform the iris feature points into a domain where phase information is available. We need a domain where we have information about localization of pixels and frequency changing, with good ability of local measurement – that is why we use Gabor filters.

Gabor filters (Fig. 3.5) are the products of a Gaussian filter with oriented complex sinusoids. They come in pairs (decomposition of a signal is accomplished using a quadrature pair of Gabor filters), each consisting of a symmetric filter (a cosine modulated by a Gaussian)

$$G_S(x, y) = \cos(k_x x + k_y y) \exp\left(-\frac{x^2 + y^2}{2\sigma^2}\right)$$

and antisymmetric filter (a sine modulated by a Gaussian)

$$G_A(x, y) = \sin(k_x x + k_y y) \exp\left(-\frac{x^2 + y^2}{2\sigma^2}\right),$$

where (k_x, k_y) determines the spatial frequency and the orientation of the filter and σ determines the scale of the filter. A filter bank is formed by varying the frequency,

Fig. 3.6 The quantization
of the phase information into
four levels

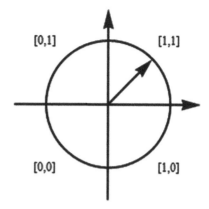

the scale, and the filter orientation. The center frequency of the filter is specified by
the frequency of the sine/cosine waves, while the bandwidth of the filter is specified
by the width of the Gaussian.

Daugman's algorithm uses two-dimensional version of Gabor filters in order to
encode iris pattern data:

$$h_{\{Re,Im\}}(r, \theta) = sgn_{\{Re,Im\}} \int\limits_{\rho} \int\limits_{\phi} I(\rho, \phi) e^{-i\omega(\theta-\phi)} e^{-\frac{(r-\rho)^2}{\alpha^2}} e^{-\frac{(\theta-\phi)^2}{\beta^2}} \rho d\rho d\phi$$

where

- $h_{\{Re,Im\}}(r, \theta)$ is the iris code at a feature point (iris feature) with r to be its distance
  from the pupil boundary and θ angle from the horizontal axis
- $I(\rho, \theta)$ is the raw iris image in the dimensionless coordinate system
- α, β is the width of the Gaussians used in modulation

Daugman demodulates the output of Gabor filters in order to compress the data.
This is done by quantizing the phase information into four levels, for each possible
quadrant in the complex plane (Fig. 3.6).

In fact the iris region (after normalization) is divided into 8×128 sectors, and
then for each we apply Gabor filters (Fig. 3.7). Hence, as an outcome we obtain
2,048 bits of code which can be understood as a compressed representation of the
current iris features – this is what we commonly understand by IrisCode.

3.6.4 Verification and Identification Methods

For image feature matching, the Hamming distance is chosen as a metric for
recognition. The Hamming distance is calculated using only the bits generated
from the true iris region – the calculations do not take into account the nonessential
parts of the iris. The modified Hamming distance formula is given as

Fig. 3.7 Iris divided into
sectors

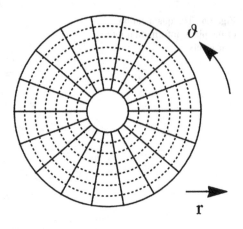

$$HD = \frac{\|(codeA \oplus codeB) \cap maskA \cap maskB\|}{\|maskA \cap maskB\|}$$

where *codeA* and *codeB* are two bit-wise templates to compare and *maskA* and
maskB are the corresponding noise masks. Masks allow to deal with iris surface
distortion, such as presented in Table 3.2, light reflections, visible eyelashes, etc.

In theory, Hamming distance of two iris templates generated from the same iris
image equals 0. However, since the normalization is not perfect, this will usually
not occur in practice. We commonly obtain noise that goes undetected, and hence, a
nonzero difference will usually appear.

The method proposed by Daugman corrects the misalignment in the normalized
iris pattern. In order to cope with rotational inconsistencies, when the Hamming
distance of two templates is calculated, one template is shifted to one bit left and
right. This operation is interpreted as a rotation of a specific angle of the input
image. Then the Hamming-distance values are calculated. This bit offset in the
horizontal direction corresponds to the starting area of the iris angle indicated by the
rubber-sheet model. For the iris distance we choose only the smallest which
corresponds to the best match between two templates.

The number of bits transferred during each shift equals two times the number of
filters used, since each filter will generate two bits of information from one pixel-
normalized region. The real number of changes necessary to normalize rotational
inconsistencies will be determined by the maximum angle difference between two
pictures of the same eye. One change is defined as one shift to the left and one shift
to the right. The example of the shifting process is presented in Fig. 3.8.

In practice the maximum number of shifts is fixed to the left and to the right. This
"brute force" rotation-angle estimation is performed with each element of the
database causing one of the main disadvantages of this method.

Moreover, in the case of iris recognition under relatively unfavorable conditions,
using images acquired at different distances and by different optical platforms,
Hamming distance can give wide range of images which can be classified as the
same (Fig. 3.9).

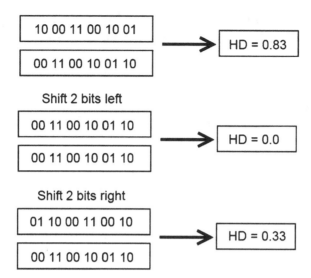

Fig. 3.8 The shifting process for one shift to the left and one to the right

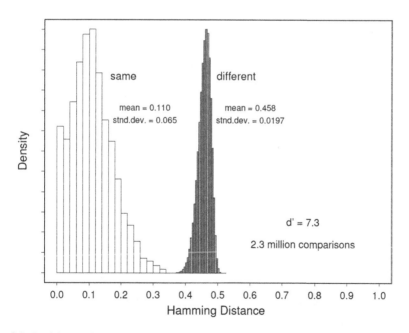

Fig. 3.9 Decision environment for iris recognition [30]

3.7 The Modified Fourier Descriptor Method: A New Approach to Rotation Detection in Iris Pattern Recognition

As we have seen, there is a strong need for rotation invariant iris recognition methods. This task can be obtained by, as classically, rotating by a fixed angle the iris pattern as can be seen, for example, in [31]. Another more advanced approach is applied in [32] where the use of directionlets (wavelets specialized in representation of elongated and oriented features along edges or contours) is used.

In this section we present another different approach (a method worked out by the first author) for recovering the angle in the iris images using some modification to the classical Fourier descriptor method [33]. An example of such images is shown in Fig. 3.10.

The classical Fourier descriptor method applied is not suitable for the case of iris pattern recognition because the iris is represented as concentric circles – the rotation of circles cannot be recovered basing on the rotation of the edges (Fig. 3.11). Moreover, the difference in illumination in various photographs can cause errors in edge detection.

To deal with such inconveniences we propose the following procedure:

3.7.1 Algorithmic Idea

Assume that we already applied classical Daugman's algorithm. After normalization with rubber-sheet model, two normalized iris images I_{Org} and I_{Rot} are obtained for original and rotated images, respectively. We can reduce our investigations to images in gray scale where each pixel is coded by a number from the set $\{0, ..., 255\}$. Afterward, in order to reduce complexity of calculations, resize the images, for example, set the new size to 8×256(image height $\times$ width). In this case an angle recover accuracy error of $360/256 \approx 1.5$degree is obtained.

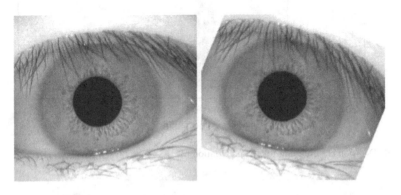

Fig. 3.10 Iris images: original (non-rotated) and rotated

Fig. 3.11 Example of two shapes with digital boundary. The rotation of the second does not allow to estimate the angle of rotation

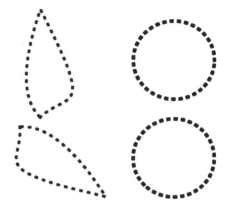

Now, the following two matrices are dealt with

$$\tilde{I}_{Org} = \left(c_{kn}^{Org}\right)_{k,n} \in M_{8\times256}(Z),$$

$$\tilde{I}_{Rot} = \left(c_{kn}^{Rot}\right)_{k,n} \in M_{8\times256}(Z)$$

where c_{kn}^{Org} and c_{kn}^{Rot} are integer numbers for $k \in \{0, ..., 7\}$ and $n \in \{0, ..., 255\}$.

Next construct the vectors of features describing $\tilde{I}_{Org}$ and $\tilde{I}_{Rot}$ by Fourier descriptors which allow to compare both images.

Calculate the first Fourier descriptor

$$C_{k1}^{Org} = \frac{1}{16} \sum_{n=0}^{255} c_{kn}^{Org} \exp\left(-i\frac{\pi n}{128}\right), \quad k = 0, ..., 7 \ and$$

$$C_{k1}^{Rot} = \frac{1}{16} \sum_{n=0}^{255} c_{kn}^{Rot} \exp\left(-i\frac{\pi n}{128}\right), \quad k = 0, ..., 7,$$

where k changes for each row of these matrices.

Denote

$$x_{Org} = \left(C_{0,1}^{Org}, ..., C_{7,1}^{Org}\right), \ and$$

$$x_{Rot} = \left(C_{0,1}^{Rot}, ..., C_{7,1}^{Rot}\right).$$

It is easy to see, by properties of Fourier transform, that those vectors are in the form $x_{Rot} = e^{i\varphi}v$ and $x_{Org} = w$, for some $v, w \in C^8$.

3.7.1.1 Remark

We can look at our problem from the mathematical point of view and formulate it as follows:

Let nontrivial vectors $v, w \in C^n$be fixed. Define a function$f$as follows:

$$f_{v,w} : [0, 2\pi] \ni \varphi \rightarrow \left\| e^{i\varphi}v - w \right\|^2 \in R_+.$$

To solve the problem of estimating rotation angle, we have to find the minimum of this function – it describes the rotation one of the vectors relatively to the second one; the optimum is reached when vectors are reduced to the same one-dimensional linear subspace. This will reduce the difference between them. It is easy to calculate that the minimum of the function f is obtained for

$$\varphi = Arg \frac{\overline{\langle v, w \rangle}}{|\langle v, w \rangle|}.$$

Based on this, we get

$$\varphi = Arg \frac{\overline{\langle x_{Org}, x_{Rot} \rangle}}{|\langle x_{Org}, x_{Rot} \rangle|} \tag{3.1}$$

where φ is the desired angle. Thus, we obtain a closed formula for the rotation angle (3.1), which gives us an advantage in terms of computation speed.

The formula used in (3.1) is also somewhat reminiscent of the widely used spectral angle mapper (SAM) [34, 35], which measures the angle between the spectral vector $r = (r_1, r_2, ..., r_L)^T$ and $s = (s_1, s_2, ..., s_L)^T$. It is given by

$$SAM(r, s) = \cos^{-1} \left(\frac{\langle r, s \rangle}{\|r\|_2 \times \|s\|_2} \right).$$

Summarizing, the new rotation angle-estimation algorithm can be stated as follows:

3.7.2 Algorithm

1. Perform Daugman's rubber-sheet model standardization for I_{Org} and I_{Rot}.
2. Determine the second Fourier descriptor from each rubber row and construct the vectors x_{Org} and x_{Rot}.
3. Estimate the angle of rotation using (3.1).
4. Compare irises by Hamming distance using the estimated angle.

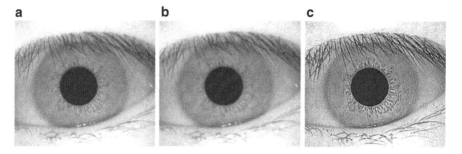

Fig. 3.12 Iris image modification: (**a**) original image, (**b**) blurring, (**c**) sharpening

Table 3.3 Angle detection in different image modifications (angle in degrees)

| Method | Angle | Algorithm results | | | |
| | | Classical approach | | Authors' Fourier-based approach | |
		Recognized	Error	Recognized	Error
None	5	5.00	0.00	4.22	0.78
Blur		0.00	5.00	3.69	1.31
Sharpen		0.00	5.00	3.66	1.34
None	23	23.00	0.00	22.50	0.50
Blur		3.00	20.00	21.87	1.73
Sharpen		0.00	23.00	23.10	0.10

The above algorithm was tested by comparing the efficiency with the classical shifting method. The images were noised by performing standard "destructive" operation on images (Fig. 3.12) such as brightness correction, contract reduction, gamma correction, blurring, and sharpening. Table 3.3 contains comparison of recovered angle between the classical and the proposed Fourier transform–based method.

The error level in both examples suggests that the new method is less affected by the proposed image modifications then the classical one.

Obviously, one can also apply other approaches to translation-, rotation-, illumination- and scale-invariant iris recognition systems [36].

3.8   Other Alternatives

As mentioned before, there still are other approaches for automatic iris recognition. The most important and widely used is Wildes [22] system, which was developed at Sarnoff Labs. There are some advantages to Wildes' design. This system has a less-intrusive light source designed to eliminate specular reflections. Moreover it can be more stable to noise perturbations.

The Wildes et al. algorithm performs localization and segmentation in two steps [37]. Firstly, the image is converted into edge map – we extract information about the edge points in the image. One possible method to do this is thresholding the magnitude of the image intensity gradient considering smoothed image. We can alternatively use various other methods in this step, for example, Roberts Cross, Sobel, or Canny [33].

Second step allows us to select circles describing, for example, pupil using voting procedure on parametric definitions of the iris boundary contours, which can be realized via Hough transforms [38]. Hough transform can be described in following steps:

- Find all the desired (edge) feature points in an image – by applying edge detection we can produce a set of boundary descriptions.
- Transform each feature point into a set of parameters – we find the space parameter, from which feature points are obtained as local maxima.
- The transformed feature point "votes" in the parametric space – for each point we calculate the most appropriate parameters describing desire object.
- The votes are accumulated and the local maxima are extracted – we choose the most likely object, the one on which most of the points chose.

Basic idea behind this transform is to transform the pattern detection problem into a parametric space and perform the easier pattern detection problem (e.g., peak detection) in the parametric space. There are a number of problems with the Hough transform method. The most important issue is that it requires threshold values to be chosen for edge detection, and this may result in critical edge points being removed, resulting in failure to detect circles/arcs (Fig. 3.13).

Hough Transform is also employed by Kong and Zhang [39], Tisse et al. [40], Ma et al. [41].

The Wildes et al. system uses an image-registration technique to compensate for both scaling and rotation [22]. The acquired image is rotated and scaled to obtain minimal differences with original image. For feature encoding, we use an isotropic bandpass decomposition derived from application of Laplacian of Gaussian filters to decompose the image data. Next, we represent image as a Laplacian pyramid which is able to compress data – details can be found in [42].

Proper verification and identification is based on normalized correlation between the acquired image and database template. This allows to account for local variations in image intensity that corrupt the standard correlation calculation.

3.9   Conclusions

The iris identification and verification process is complex, and the construction of a reliable automatic system requires addressing a number of problems. The chapter presents one of the most popular algorithms developed by John Daugman in detail. Moreover, a new method is applied to recover iris rotation detection. The algorithm is based on Fourier descriptor analysis of normalized iris images. The numerical experiments show that the authors' algorithm is better than classical Daugman

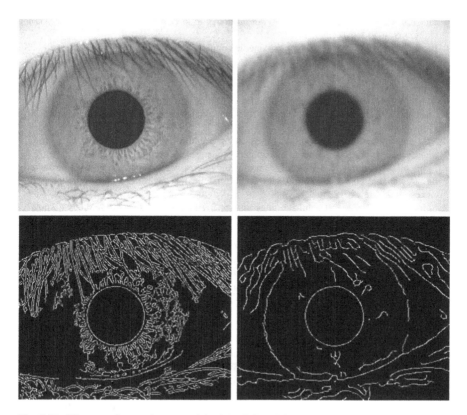

Fig. 3.13 Edge-map for two images: original (*on left*) and blurred (*on right*)

"brute force" approaches. Furthermore, it is relatively insensitive to rotation, contrast modification, illumination-level modification, blurring, and sharpening of the acquired input iris images. The last part of this chapter contains a brief knowledge about Wildes' algorithm concept for iris recognition – the most popular alternative for Daugman approach.

Acknowledgment This work was partially supported by AGH University of Science and Technology in Cracow, grant no. 11.11.220.01.

References

1. Bertillon A (1885) La couleur de l'iris. Rev Sci 36(5):65–73
2. John Daugman's webpage, Cambridge University, Faculty of Computer Science & Technology, Cambridge. http://www.cl.cam.ac.uk/~jgd1000/. Accessed 28 May 2012
3. Iridian Technologies: about Iridian. In: Historical timeline. http://www.iriscan.com/about.php?page=4. Accessed 28 May 2012
4. Iris ID – Iris Recognition Technology. http://www.irisid.com. Accessed 28 May 2012

5. Jain AK, Ross A, Prabhakar S (2004) An introduction to biometric recognition. IEEE Trans Circuits Syst Video Technol 14(1):4–20
6. BioGraphix. http://www.biriaographixmedia.com/human/eye-anatomy.html. Accessed 28 May 2012
7. Stamp M, Wiley J (2006) Information security: principles and practice. Wiley Online Library, Hoboken, NJ
8. April E (1997) Clinical anatomy. Williams and Wilkins, Baltimore
9. Tasman W, Jaeger EA (2007) Duane's clinical ophthalmology. Williams and Wilkins, Philadelphia
10. Medscape reference. In: Drugs, diseases and procedures, image no. 3, 6, and 13. http://reference.medscape.com/features/slideshow/iris-changes. Accessed 28 May 2012
11. London NJS, Cunningham ET (2012) Prompt and aggressive treatment might have preserved this mechanic's vision. http://www.aao.org/publications/eyenet/200804/am_rounds.cfm. Accessed 28 May 2012
12. Shiuey Y (2012) General ophthalmology quiz 6, Digital Journal of Ophthalmology – knowledge review. http://www.djo.harvard.edu/site.php?url=/physicians/kr/459&page=KR_AN. Accessed 28 May 2012
13. Digital reference of ophthalmology, review, Columbia University, New York. At: http://dro.hs.columbia.edu
14. Fulk G (2012) Ocular disease I: glaucoma, uveitis and lens disorders, photo no. 38, Northeastern State University. http://arapaho.nsuok.edu. Accessed 28 May 2012
15. Children network – disease research and education network, fig. 3. http://childrennetwork.org/physicians/ags.html. Accessed 28 May 2012
16. Jonathan T (2012) A systemic problem, Bascom Palmer Eye Institute Grand Rounds. http://media.med.miami.edu. Accessed 28 May 2012
17. Cackett P, Vallance J, Bennett H (2005) Neurofibromatosis type 1 presenting with Horner's syndrome. Nat Eye 19:351–353. doi:10.1038/sj.eye.6701478, Published online. Available (19.04.2012) at: http://www.nature.com/
18. Dong W, Sun Z, Tan T (2009) A design of iris recognition system at a distance. In: Chinese conference on pattern recognition 4–6 November 2009, Nanjing, China, (CCPR 2009). http://avss2012.org/2009papers/gjhy/gh99.pdf. Accessed 21 September 2012
19. Masek L (2003) Recognition of human iris patterns for biometric identification. Master's thesis, University of Western Australia
20. Farag AA, Elhabian SY (2012) Iris recognition. http://www.cvip.uofl.edu/wwwcvip/education/ECE523/Iris%20Biometrics.pdf. Accessed 28 May 2012
21. Daugman J (1993) High confidence visual recognition of persons by a test of statistical independence. IEEE Trans Pattern Anal Mach Intell 15(11):1148–1161
22. Wildes RP (1997) Iris recognition: an emerging biometric technology. Proc IEEE 85(9):1348–1363
23. Boles W, Boashash B (1998) A human identification technique using images of the iris and wavelet transform. IEEE Trans Signal Process 46(4):1185–1188
24. Huang YP, Luo SW, Chen EY (2002) An efficient iris recognition system. In: Proceedings of 2002 international conference on machine learning and cybernetics, 4–5 November 2002, Beijing, China, vol 1, pp 450–454
25. Zhu Y, Tan T, Wang Y (2000) Biometric personal identification based on iris patterns. In: Proceedings of 15th international conference on pattern recognition, 3–7 September 2000, Barcelona, Spain, vol 2, pp 801–804. http://www.cbsr.ia.ac.cn/publications/yzhu/Biometric%20Personal%20Identification%20Based%20on%20Iris%20Patterns.pdf. Accessed 21 September 2012
26. Harowitz S (2007) Faking fingerprints and eying solutions. Secur Manage Mag
27. Center for Biometrics and Security Research. http://www.cbsr.ia.ac.cn. Accessed 28 May 2012

28. Daugman J (2007) New methods in iris recognition. IEEE Trans Syst Man Cybern B: Cybernetics 37(5):1167–1175
29. Oppenheim AV, Lim JS (1981) The importance of phase in signals. Proc IEEE 69(5):529–541
30. Daugman J (2004) How iris recognition works. IEEE Trans Circuits Syst Video Technol 14(1):21–30
31. Takano H, Nakamura K (2009) Rotation independent iris recognition by the rotation spreading neural network. In: IEEE 13th international symposium on consumer electronics, 25–28 May 2009, Kyoto, Japan. ISCE'09, pp 651–654
32. Velisavljevic V (2009) Low-complexity iris coding and recognition based on directionlets. IEEE Trans Inf Forensics Secur 4(3):410–417
33. Gonzalez RC, Woods RE (2002) Digital image processing. Prentice Hall, Upper Saddle River
34. Du Y, Chang CI, Ren H, Chang CC, Jensen JO, D'Amico FM (2004) New hyperspectral discrimination measure for spectral characterization. Opt Eng 43:1777
35. Chang CI (2003) Hyperspectral imaging: techniques for spectral detection and classification. Springer, New York
36. Du Y, Ives RW, Etter DM, Welch TB (2006) Use of one-dimensional iris signatures to rank iris pattern similarities. Opt Eng 45:037201
37. Wildes RP, Asmuth JC, Green GL, Hsu SC, Kolczynski RJ, Matey JR, McBride SE (1994) A system for automated iris recognition. In: Proceedings of the second IEEE workshop on applications of computer vision, 5–7 December 1994, Sarasota, FL, USA pp 121–128
38. Illingworth J, Kittler J (1988) A survey of the Hough transform. Comput Vision Graph Image Process 44(1):87–116
39. Kong WK, Zhang D (2001) Accurate iris segmentation based on novel reflection and eyelash detection model. In: Proceedings of 2001 international symposium on Intelligent multimedia, video and speech processing, 2–4 May 2001, Hong Kong, China pp 263–266. http://www3.ntu.edu.sg/home/AdamsKong/publication/ISIM.pdf. Accessed 21 September 2012
40. Tisse C, Martin L, Torres L, Robert M (2002) Person identification technique using human iris recognition. In: Proceedings of vision interface, pp 294–299. http://citeseerx.ist.psu.edu/viewdoc/download?doi=10.1.1.5.3130&rep=rep1&type=pdf. Accessed 21 September 2012
41. Ma L, Wang Y, Tan T (2002) Iris recognition using circular symmetric filters. In: Proceedings of 16th international conference on pattern recognition, 11–15 August 2002, Quebec City, QC, Canada vol 2, pp 414–417. http://hci.iwr.uni-heidelberg.de/publications/dip/2002/ICPR2002/DATA/05_2_25.PDF. Accessed 21 September 2012
42. Burt P, Adelson E (1983) The Laplacian pyramid as a compact image code. IEEE Trans Commun 31(4):532–540

Chapter 4
Human Identification by Vascular Patterns

Jan Kosmala and Khalid Saeed

Abstract This chapter introduces an interesting laboratory method for human identification by finger vein patterns. For image capture, a simple webcam is used. The electronic circuit (the hardware part) is built from simple components with a low cost. The whole device is of small size and can be used in the laboratory for student laboratory application. The implemented algorithm and hence the testing software have shown very high success rate. For finger vein image denoising and binarization, a method worked out in the authors' team is applied. For easier feature extraction and data reduction, the authors make the necessary thinning by universal algorithms like Zhang or K3M. A big challenge is still to get efficient connection between image processing, securing data, and database exploration.

4.1 Introduction

Since many years ago, people have been working on how to secure information. In the past, the used passwords and ciphers were more or less complex. Today, having computer grids and rainbow tables, security specialists are able to break any given code. With time, people discovered that they can use their bodies as a unique key. This fact gave rise to biometrics of which two types can be distinguished behavioral and physiological.

Behavioral biometrics deals with the way people do certain basic activities, for example, writing, walking, typing, or even the way they move their hands or fingers.

J. Kosmala (✉)
ABB, Kraków, Poland
e-mail: jan.kosmala@gmail.com

K. Saeed
AGH University of Science and Technology, Faculty of Physics and Applied Computer Science, Al. Mickiewicza 30, Kraków PL-30059, Poland
e-mail: saeed@agh.edu.pl

K. Saeed and T. Nagashima (eds.), *Biometrics and Kansei Engineering*,
DOI 10.1007/978-1-4614-5608-7_4, © Springer Science+Business Media New York 2012

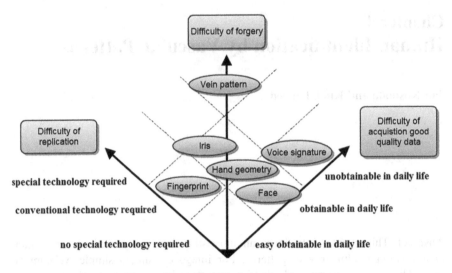

Fig. 4.1 Difficulty in spoofing, redrawn from [1] after authors' modification

Generally speaking, a human behavior cannot be easily recreated. The best example is the way how someone speaks. It is a unique trait and the voice can be recorded, mixed, and replayed in a very high quality. However, the possibility of reproduction in the same way even for the same speaker is the very weak point of this kind of security.

Physiological biometrics is strictly about how a body was built during pregnancy (e.g., palm veins) and the first years of the growing up (e.g., fingerprints). The value of the physiological biometric patterns is especially visible when the pattern contains the best traits according to [1]: uniqueness, permanence, universality, collectability, acceptability, performance, and resistance to circumvention.

All these conditions are satisfied by the human blood vessel pattern which is constructed on the embryo stage. The shape of vein patterns including ratio does not change with aging [1]. As for the spoofing, it is also very hard to perform (Fig. 4.1). So veins and blood vessels are unique biometric feature patterns.

The beginning of finger vein pattern usage can be found in the early 1990s. In 1992, Professor K. Shimizu presented the basis of this idea. During the next 5 years, the research became more known in the scientific world. In 1997 Hitachi started their works on finger vein pattern technology. The first presented to public Hitachi prototype device was built in 2000 [2].

Gathering vein patterns is not as easy as other features (Fig. 4.1). The veins are exposed under the skin and however are still well visible. To register the vein pattern, a time of less than 1 s is required, while the retina pattern registration can take up to 30 s. Comparing veins with fingerprints, every person has veins but 2–5% of human populations do not have fingerprints.

The vein patterns traits invoked a significant growth of the interest in this subject. Since the first half of the twenty-first century, the number of publications has risen each year. The publications meet the interest of security managers who introduce finger vein patterns in the international market of biometric technologies.

Fig. 4.2 Steering wheel with authentication system based on finger vein pattern (Image courtesy of Hitachi)

The majority available research is focused on the veins in palms and fingers. However, the research on veins in other parts of the body is also carried out. The veins in the hand are visible from both sides, but the patterns on the top and the bottom sides are different. This means that the near and far infrared can only be used in the palms. The amount of veins in the hand image is smaller, yet their thickness is more noticeable than in the image of blood vessels of the fingers.

A typical capturing device is composed of a camera and a source of light. When it comes to cameras used for palm image acquisition, they should be much bigger than the ones used for the fingers. Thanks to the small size of the finger devices, they might be hidden, for example, behind a car door handle or the steering wheel (Fig. 4.2).

Each finger has a different pattern; thus, in terms of research, it is easier to build a bigger pattern database. This is a big advantage because the number of people using such systems increases, so the testing database of samples must be much larger than in the past. An increased database gives opportunities to test algorithm performance before commercial implementation.

Devices based on hand vein patterns are installed, for example, in banks and datacenters [1], mainly in places where the device size is not taken into account. In 2005, banks in Japan started to use finger vein pattern to protect ATMs (Fig. 4.3), as a security key instead of PINs [1].

Since 2006, thanks to the miniaturization, the access to some mobile devices can be controlled with vein patterns [2]. An example of such a device is the computer mouse (Fig. 4.4).

4.2 Image Acquisition

To understand why the infrared light is used for finger vein pattern acquisition, let us start from the basic traits of blood vessels. Human blood vessels are hidden under the skin (0.3–1.0 mm). They are sensitive to the temperature of the environment and body conditions (e.g., blood pressure, diseases of the circulatory system). Any cut of vein or vascular causes immediately a change in the pattern. Moreover, alcohol circulating in the blood widens the vessels and changes the images of the patterns. The human body is mainly composed from water. Also blood might contain

Fig. 4.3 ATM with finger vein reader (Image courtesy of Hitachi)

Fig. 4.4 Mouse with hand vein pattern reader by Fujitsu (Image courtesy of Fujitsu)

oxygenated and deoxygenated hemoglobin which has different absorption factors concerning the wavelength. This is presented in Fig. 4.5.

From the technological point of view, we can acquire an image in near- and far-infrared bands. The preferred way is to use the near infrared due to absorption and costs. The devices and sources of light working in far-infrared band are less useful, more expensive, and less available.

As for the background, it should differ clearly; therefore, the black background would be most suitable in order to distinguish a finger in the image. Hence, as stated above, image acquisition is not easy in non-laboratory conditions.

To acquire the image, noncontact way of the acquisition might also be used. An example of such a device is presented in Fig. 4.6.

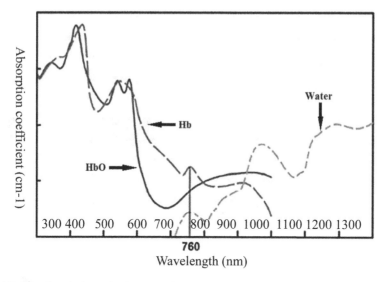

Fig. 4.5 Wavelength absorption by water, hemoglobin (*Hb*), and oxygenated hemoglobin (*HbO*) [3]. The *wavelength 760 nm* was marked as the best wavelength for image acquisition

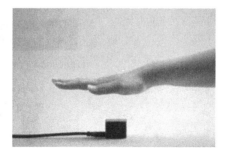

Fig. 4.6 Fujitsu contactless device (Image courtesy of Fujitsu)

For fingers, the image of the veins and vessels can be taken only from the bottom side of the finger. The top side does not show many vessels, so from this side, the camera cannot be placed. The image sensor can be placed on the bottom side. The lighting can be placed in three ways:

– Under the finger – reflection (Fig. 4.7a)
– From both sides of the finger – transition (Fig. 4.7b)
– Over the finger – transition (Fig. 4.7c)

The transition method is an easier way to get a good contrast of the image, but it also increases the size of the device. The problem might also involve the reflection of the light in the image sensor if the diodes' directional characteristic is too wide or the lighting direction is set improperly. Most of the commercial solutions use methods based on the reflection, but in some cases the transition method is used.

Fig. 4.7 Different lighting methods [2] (**a**) light source under the finger, (**b**) light source from both sides, (**c**) light source over the finger

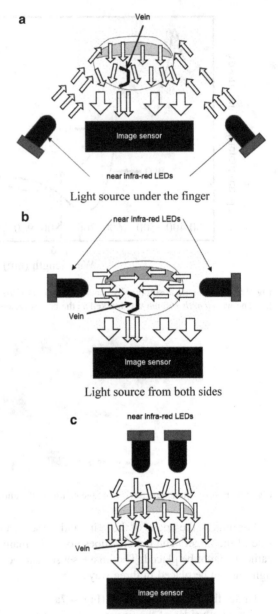

As a source of light, the infrared transmitters (LEDs) which emit the waves between 740 and 1,000 nm are recommended to use (for near-infrared image capturing). Somehow according to certain authors, the best wavelength is 760 nm. This was marked in Fig. 4.5. As an effective source of light, LED with

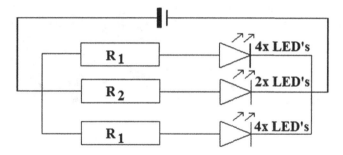

Fig. 4.8 Electronic circuit of the device built by the first author, used in the team research [4, 5] as a light source

peak in 850 nm is the most popular one. It is widely available and relatively cheap. The electronic circuit is built from a three diode-resistor series combination connected in parallel to a 9-V battery as shown in Fig. 4.8.

Typically, for experiment purposes, the internet camera without the infrared filter can be used as a sensor. Considering the sensor quality, the image can posses a lot of noises. Some of the less often dedicated cameras, including security cameras with a far-infrared reflector, can be used. It is important to mention that the infrared images are always in gray scale.

4.3   Vein Recognition by Others, How They Do It

4.3.1   Repeated Line Tracking

The repeated line tracking algorithm [6] is one of the best known and operating ones when it comes to finger vein patterns in today's world. The first interesting element of the system is the lighting controlled by the designed software. As to the luminosity of the image, its intensity changes to get the best possible contrast. The authors of the algorithm used two-dimensional normalization to keep the same position of the finger in the image for all cases. The acquired sample image, after normalization, is presented in Fig. 4.9a.

The authors of the method invented the repeated line tracking algorithm. At the beginning some start points were drawn using Monte Carlo algorithm. The decision to pass from one point to another and in which direction depends on the gray profile. If the next point is darker and the minimum can be found in the environment, the point is moved forward. Otherwise, it is treated as a noise. In such a situation, the tracking is started from a new point.

The number of visits in each pixel is saved in the matrix. Based on the number of visits, veins are marked in the image as it is presented in Fig. 4.9b. If the point is

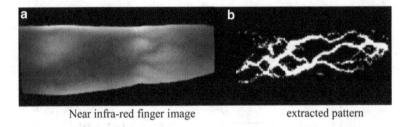

| Near infra-red finger image | extracted pattern |

Fig. 4.9 Images (**a**) and their extracted patterns (**b**) according to the algorithm of [6]

more frequently visited, the probability that this is a vein and not a noise increases significantly.

The acquired images have the resolution 240 × 180 pixels. Before the classification the images were scaled down three times. In this process the algorithm based on image template and correlation was used.

4.3.2 Wide Line Detector

The authors of this algorithm [7] built a vast database (about 800,000 images) and selected 50,700 images to prove the solution efficiency. Original images were acquired in resolution 512 × 384 px, but in preprocessing they were scaled down to 128 × 96 px. The proposed algorithm was based on a wide line detector. For each region, based on complicated set of equations, up to the equation solutions, some pixels were set as white (presence of the line) or black (background). The authors of this method used pattern normalization during which images were rescaled to 128 × 80 px. The results are presented in Fig. 4.10.

4.3.3 Moment Invariants

The authors of this method [8] acquired images with low contrast with 320 × 240 px resolution, which, during normalization, were rescaled to 256 × 256 px. In order to denoise the images, the use of the soft thresholding had been essential, and to extract vein pattern, the wavelet transform was used. Finally, the modified moment invariant helped describe the shapes.

The database was relatively small. It was then possible to use the Hausdorff distance as a classifier. This algorithm works very well on small and medium data sets. In this research the database contained 256 images acquired from 32 persons. Original image and the extracted pattern are presented in Fig. 4.11.

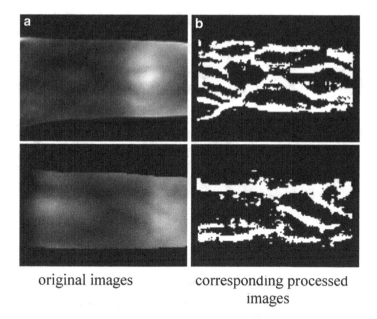

original images   corresponding processed
                                           images

Fig. 4.10 Wide line detector algorithm [7] (**a**) original images, (**b**) corresponding processed images

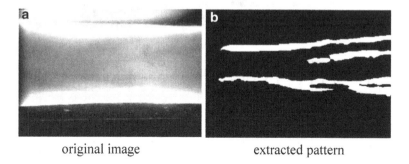

original image   extracted pattern

Fig. 4.11 Moment invariants algorithm [8] (**a**) original image, (**b**) extracted pattern

4.3.4   Repeated Line Tracking with LSH

Algorithm of the repeated line tracking was proposed in [7]. In the presented solution [9], the researchers used the same database as in [7]. The main difference is in the extraction of the characteristic points based on LSH algorithm [10]. Few samples are presented in Fig. 4.12.

The processed image is split into smaller parts (32 × 24 parts). In each square, created in this way, the numbers of black and white pixels are counted. If the

Fig. 4.12 Vein extracted patterns for image samples in repeated line tracking algorithm [9]

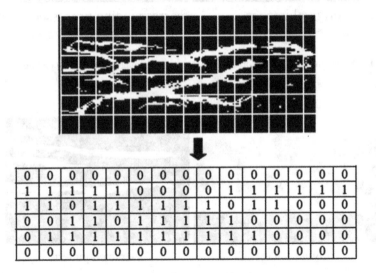

Fig. 4.13 Finger vein pattern hashed with LHS algorithm [9]

number of white pixels is bigger than the threshold, then the whole square is white, else it is black. The result of such processing is a feature vector with a length of 768 bits. The process is presented in Fig. 4.13.

The above way of compression has one big disadvantage. When database enlarges and becomes wider, the probability of finding two similar patterns with the proposed data compression is very high.

4.4   Authors' Algorithm

The algorithm was worked out at the AGH University of Science and Technology in Kraków by the first author in his MSc thesis [4] under the supervision of the second author. The thesis was awarded the first prize as the best MSc thesis at the AGH University in 2011. In its simplest summarized version, the work was introduced in [5]. The main reason for this solution was to create a person identification system based on a low-cost laboratory device. The designed system is composed of three parts:

– A device for collecting images
– Algorithm to extract characteristic points
– A classifier for verification

The constructed database contains 348 images from 29 persons; three fingers of each hand were scanned twice. The whole collection was divided into two data sets (training and testing). The images were taken from young people (the average age was about 25 years). A sample of the acquired image is presented in Fig. 4.14.

4.4.1   Preprocessing

One of the important steps is the preprocessing stage where the image is denoised and the unused borders are removed. The best primary results were obtained by

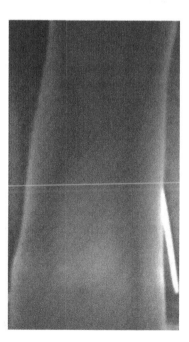

Fig. 4.14 Source image sample within the suggested algorithm [4]

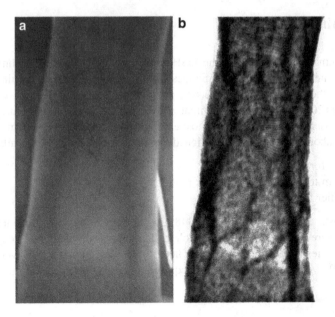

Fig. 4.15 (**a**) Image after median filtering [4], (**b**) further denoising by Godzwon Lee algorithm [11]

Table 4.1 Gradient magnitude mask	$a(i-1, j-1)$	$b(i-1, j)$	$c(i-1, j+1)$
	$d(i, j-1)$	$e(i, j)$	$f(i, j+1)$
	$g(i+1, j-1)$	$h(i+1, j)$	$l(i+1, j+1)$

median filter with a 3 × 3 pixel mask. Currently, our team is working on methods of improving the images for better feature extracting. One of these methods is the one worked out by Godzwon in her MSc thesis [11]. The result is given in Fig. 4.15b.

4.4.2 Edge Detection

The edge detection is performed to find the finger position and to remove the redundant data from the image (the whole area which flows over the finger). The authors used the fast estimate of the gradient magnitude given in [12] to separate the edges.

Table 4.1 presents how pixels were selected for (4.1) and (4.2). The rows were marked by i; the columns by j:

$$Grad(i, j) = \max(|d - e|, |f - e|, |h - e|, |b - e|, val) \qquad (4.1)$$

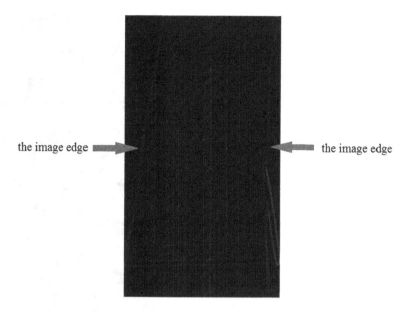

the image edge ➡   ⬅ the image edge

Fig. 4.16 The image after gradient magnitude [4]

with

$$val = \frac{\max(|a - e|, |c - e|, |l - e|, |g - e|)}{\sqrt{2}} \qquad (4.2)$$

4.4.3 Thresholding

The resulting image (Fig. 4.16) contains multiple gray lines which are invisible to the human eye because of the low image contrast. To designate the borders of the image, the thresholding is necessary. Throughout the experiments, for the collected images, the best threshold value was proved to be 7. The sample result of this step is given in Fig. 4.17.

Having the original image (Fig. 4.15a) and already extracted edges (Fig. 4.17), the removing area outside the finger is performed. For each line from both edges of the image up to its center, the last white pixel is taken as a point of the finger edge (left or right). Then the coordinates of the points are saved and the area between the edge of the image and the edge of the finger is removed. The following pseudocode presents its implementation:

Fig. 4.17 The image after gradient magnitude and threshold [4]

```
pixelR = array[len(image_lines)]
pixelL = array[len(image_lines)]

for each transverse_line in image_lines
begin
   for i = 0; i < len(transverse_line)/2; i++
   begin
     if transverse_line(i) = white
        pixelL(transverse_line_number) = i
   end
   for  i = len(transverse_line)-1;  i > len(transverse_
line)/2; i-
   begin
     if transvers_line(i) = white
        pixelR(transverse_line_number) = i
   end
end
for i = 0; i < len(images_lines); i++
begin
   for j = 0; j < pixelL(i); j++
     SetPixelWhiteOnDenoisedImage(i,j)
   for j = last pixel in line index; j > pixelR(i); j-
     SetPixelWhiteOnDenoisedImage(i,j)
end
```

4.4.4 Vein Extraction

Having prepared the image, the vein pattern can now be extracted. For this purpose, the proposed solution used the approximation of the gray-profile curve with the functions (4.3) and (4.4) instead of using randomly selected points or analyzing the image from different angles. Additional benefit of this solution is noise reduction:

$$
LineL(i) = \frac{n\frac{\sum_{k=i}^{i+val-1} Line(k)}{val} + \frac{\sum_{k=i-1}^{i+val-2} Line(j)}{val}}{n+1}
\tag{4.3}
$$

where

$$
i \in [2, size(Line) - val - 1]; n, val \in N^+
$$

$$
LineR(i) = \frac{n\frac{\sum_{k=i-val+1}^{i} Line(k)}{val} + \frac{\sum_{k=i-val}^{i-1} Line(j)}{val}}{n+1}
\tag{4.4}
$$

where Line(point) indicates gray intensity, $i \in [size(Line) - 1, val]; n, val \in N^+$

The following pseudocode shows how to implement this part of the algorithm:

```
Set values n, val
for each transverse_line in image_lines
begin
   for i = 1; i < len(transverse_line)-val; i++
   begin
     LineL(i);
   end
   for i = len(transverse_line)-1; i > val; i-
   begin
     LineR(i);
   end
   Find minimums
   Remove impair minimums
end
```

The continuous line in Fig. 4.18 indicates the original intensity levels in one of the image lines. The second line, the dotted one, indicates LineL; the last line (dash-dotted) indicates LineR. Letters L and R indicate from which image edge (Left, Right) the calculations start.

When pattern is extracted, some interruptions in the pattern can be observed. To remove them keeping the original structure the following blur mask is used.

1	2	1
1	4	1
1	2	1

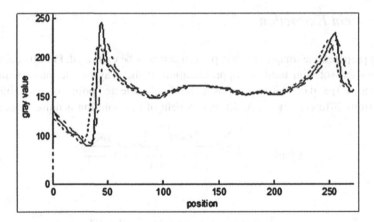

Fig. 4.18 Sample chart of the position-gray-profile curve (continuous line) with results of calculations of (4.3) as *dotted line* and (4.4) as *dash-dotted line* [5]

Fig. 4.19 The vein pattern image after blur [4]

The result is presented in Fig. 4.19. The matrix was selected accordingly to get the best results on the entire image set.

The next operation is the static thresholding with a threshold equal to 128. The authors believe that this value based on experiments is the best possible for the used data set. In another set it is possible that the value of threshold may differ. The result of the operation is presented in Fig. 4.20.

Fig. 4.20 The vein pattern
image after blur and
thresholding with threshold
equal to 128 [4]

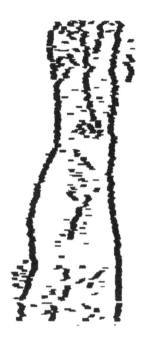

4.4.5 Thinning

Thinning reduces the number of data in the next steps of analysis. In this context, the extraction of the characteristic points is easier and more accurate. Let us follow some thinning algorithms. The authors mainly experienced Guo-Hall [13–15], Zhang-Suen [16], K3M [17], and KMM [18] algorithms for thinning and skeletonization.

After skeletonization the pattern is 1 pixel wide, but it still has redundant data. To avoid saving all pixel values, only the essential characteristic points are selected. They can be terminations in horizontal and vertical directions, bifurcations, bends, narrowing, etc.

In the presented algorithm, the extraction of the characteristic points is done with the following masks:

– Terminations of the vertical directions

0	0	0	0	1	0
0	1	0	0	1	0
0	1	0	0	0	0

– Terminations of the diagonals

1	0	0	0	0	0	0	0	1	0	0	0
0	1	0	0	1	0	0	1	0	0	1	0
0	0	0	1	0	0	0	0	0	0	0	1

– Bifurcations

1	1	0	0	1	0	0	1	1	0	1	0
0	1	1	0	1	1	1	1	0	1	1	0
0	1	0	1	1	0	0	1	0	0	1	1
1	0	0	0	0	1	0	1	0	0	1	0
0	1	1	1	1	0	1	1	0	0	1	1
0	1	0	0	1	0	0	0	1	1	0	0
0	1	0	0	1	0	0	0	0	0	1	0
0	1	1	1	1	0	1	1	1	1	1	1
0	1	0	0	1	0	0	1	0	0	0	0
1	0	1	0	1	0	1	0	0	0	0	1
0	1	0	0	1	0	0	1	1	1	1	0
0	1	0	1	0	1	1	0	0	0	0	1

Horizontal points were excluded because very often they were parts of noises which were not removed in the preprocessing stage. The identification results are given in the section following the discussion of the classification stage.

4.5 Classifiers

The last stage in all algorithms is the classification for authentication. At this point some well-known algorithms like kNN (k-nearest neighbors) [19], artificial neural network [20–26], and Hausdorff metric [27, 28] were verified.

In authors' experiments the neural network was built from three layers with backward propagation. The efficiency was close to 100%. In [23], for palm veins, the authors achieved 100% efficiency.

Algorithm kNN is based on comparing training feature set with sample values. For each sample in training set and checked sample, the distance between them is calculated. Typically, Mahalanobis or Euclidean distances are used. Also in some cases, Manhattan distance can be used. In the next step, the results are sorted ascendingly. K-nearest values (nearest samples) are selected. The value of k can be selected heuristically by calculating the root-mean-square error. The disadvantage of kNN is getting good results only if the database is small and the data are not very noised. Otherwise, the efficiency is 0% as the author proved it in [4]. The biggest advantage of the kNN algorithm is its easy implementation. Sample implementation is shown below:

```
SetK()
for each sampleTraining in sampleTraingingSet
   calculateDistance(sample,sampleTraining)
sortDistances()
selectKDistances()
selectTheBestSolution()
```

Table 4.2 Sample methods efficiency comparison by classifier

	Neural network	Hausdorff
[4, 5]	100%	51.44%
[8]	N/A	92.7%
[23]	100%	N/A

Hausdorff metrics is a shape matching algorithm. It is based on calculating distances between two sets of points (e.g., characteristic points) and looking for the best match. The distance between two sets of points (A, B) is defined as

$$d_H(A, B) = \max\{d_{H1}(A, B), d_{H2}(A, B)\} \tag{4.5}$$

where

$$d_{H1}(A, B) = \max\{ d(a, B) : a \ A)\} \tag{4.6}$$

$$d_{H2}(A, B) = \max\{ d(b, A) : b \ B)\} \tag{4.7}$$

$$d(v, W) = \min\{ d(v, w) : w \ W \} \tag{4.8}$$

Equations (4.5, 4.6, 4.7, and 4.8) in such forms are valid only for one dimension. The efficiency of the identification was 51.44%. In [8] the authors got the efficiency of 92.7%. In [3] authors also used this algorithm, but the exact results were not given.

In Table 4.2 sample identification results are given. Comparison is done between different algorithms of the vein extraction and classification.

4.6   Conclusions

At the end of twenty and beginning of the twenty-first century, vein pattern became significantly tested by many researchers [8, 9, 25, 29–34]. First, they proved the uniqueness of the biometrics pattern; next the speed of the acquisition and its efficiency. With technological progress, the finger vein pattern acquisition became easier, the device became smaller, and the images had better quality and higher resolution. Also the number of invented applications has significantly increased.

With more and more scientific work, the number of proposed systems mounted up. Among them some solutions found commercial application, the most significant in banking systems (ATMs).

Researchers are still working on the development of this pattern in order to put it into common use. Our algorithm shows a different approach where we could prove that with low costs the innovative solution might be still invented.

The suggested algorithm is based on the analysis of the gray-profile curve which when combined with the series of the approximations gives the required extracted pattern. However, the entire system is fragile on noises in characteristic points. The selection of the classifier that should be resistant to noises in data sets is very important when constructing the biometric system on the basis of finger vein patterns.

The further research is concentrated on image denoising and parallelism in image processing. In this area we are working on threads and parallelism with CPU and processing on Nvidia GPUs which support CUDA. It should give much better performance.

A comparison with other known algorithms has shown high efficiency. It was achieved though the high noises in the source images. The authors have proved the importance of the classifier selection for better results.

A big challenge is still to get efficient connection between image processing, securing data, and intensive searching. This still is a young technology and is waiting for much more intensive work for public use.

Acknowledgment This work was partially supported by AGH University of Science and Technology in Kraków, grant no. 11.11.220.01.

References

1. Wilson C (2010) Vein pattern recognition. CRC Press, USA
2. Hashimoto J (2006) Finger vein authentication technology and its future. In: Symposium on VLSI circuits. Digest of technical papers, Honolulu, pp 5–8
3. Hong J, Shuxu G, Xueyan L, Xiaohua Q (2009) Vein pattern extraction based on the position-gray-profile curve. In: 2nd international congress on image and signal processing, Tianjin, China, pp 1–4
4. Kosmala J (2011) Vascular pattern as an access key: algorithm and implementation. M.Sc. thesis, Kraków, Poland (in Polish)
5. Waluś M, Kosmala J, Saeed K (2011) Finger vein pattern extraction algorithm. In: HAIS 2011 – international conference on hybrid artificial intelligent systems, Wrocław, 23–25 May 2011. LNCS 6678, Springer, Berlin, pp 404–411
6. Miura N, Nagasaka A, Miyatake T (2004) Feature extraction of finger-vein patterns based on repeated line tracking and its application to personal identification. Mach Vision Appl 15(4):194–203
7. Huang B, Dai Y, Li R, Tang D, Li W (2010) Finger-vein authentication based on wide line detector and pattern normalization. In: 20th international conference on pattern recognition (ICPR), Istanbul, Turkey
8. Ye L, Shuxu G, Fengli G, Ye L (2007) Vein pattern recognitions by moment invariants. In: The 1st IEEE international conference on bioinformatics and biomedical engineering, Wuhan, China, pp 612–615
9. Tang D, Huang B, Li R, Li W (2010) A person retrieval solution using finger vein patterns. In: 20th international conference on pattern recognition (ICPR), Istanbul
10. Gionis A, Indyk P, Motwani R (1999) Similarity search in high dimensions via hashing. In: Proceedings of the 25th international conference on very large data bases, Edinburgh, Scotland
11. Godzwon M, Saeed K (2012) Biometrics image denoising algorithm based on contourlet transform. In: LNCS proceedings of 6th international conference on computer vision and graphics – ICCVG'2010, Warsaw, 224, Springer-Verlag, Heidelberg, 26 May 2012 (accepted)

12. Discussion on gradient magnitude algorithm (2011). http://www.thbcomponents.com/image/ Sobel_operator_implementation_b9b9300e_0e92_44d4_a6a5_7cbd76414e.html.   Accessed 24 March 2012
13. Couprie M (2006) Note on fifteen 2D parallel thinning algorithms. Internal report, Université de Marne-la-Vallée, IGM2006-01
14. Guo Z, Hall RW (1989) Parallel thinning with two-subiteration algorithms. Commun ACM 32(3):359–373
15. Guo Z, Hall RW (1992) Fast fully parallel thinning algorithms. CVGIP 55(3):317–328
16. Zhang TY, Suen CY (1984) A fast parallel algorithm for thinning digital patterns. Commun ACM CACM 27(3):236–239
17. Saeed K, Tabedzki M, Rybnik M, Adamski M (2010) K3M: a universal algorithm for image skeletonization and a review of thinning techniques. Appl Math Comput Sci 20(2):317–335
18. Saeed K, Tabedzki M, Rybnik M (2001) Implementation and advanced results on the noninterrupted skeletonization algorithm. In: Proceedings of the 9th international conference on computer analysis of images and patterns, Springer-Verlag, Berlin, LNCS 2124, pp 601–609
19. kNN algorithm description. http://en.wikipedia.org/wiki/K-nearest_neighbor_algorithm. Accessed 1 April 2012
20. Saropourian B (2009) A new approach of finger-print recognition based on neural network. In: 2nd IEEE international conference on computer science and information technology, Beijing, China, pp 158–161
21. Mao J, Jain AK (1995) Artificial neural networks for feature extraction and multivariate data projection. IEEE Trans Neural Netw 6(2):296–317
22. Jain A K, Mao J (1991) A k-nearest neighbor artificial neural network classifier. In: IJCNN-91-seattle international joint conference on neural networks, Seattle, USA, vol 2, pp 515–520
23. Malki S, Spaannenburg L (2010) CBAS: a CNN-based biometric authentication system. In: 12th international workshop on cellular nanoscale networks and their applications, IEEE, Berkley, pp 1–6
24. Jinpeng D, Yanzhi Z (2010) Hand veins feature extraction based on morphology and cellular neural network. IEEE Int Conf Comput Appl Syst Modell 14:175–178
25. Zhang Z, Ma S, Han X (2006) Multiscale feature extraction of finger-vein patterns based on curvelets and local interconnection structure neural network. In: 18th international conference on pattern recognition, IEEE, Hong Kong, vol 4, pp 145–148
26. Malki S, Fuqiang Y, Spaanenburg L (2006) Vein feature extraction using DT-CNNs. In: 10th international workshop on cellular neural networks and their applications, IEEE, Istanbul, Turkey, pp 1–6
27. Rotter P, Skulimowski A, Kotropoulos C, Pitas I (2005) Fast shape matching using the Hausdorff distance. Mirage 2005: computer vision/computer graphics collaboration techniques and applications, INRIA Rocquencourt, France, 1–2 March 2005
28. Hausdorff distance. http://en.wikipedia.org/wiki/Hausdorff_distance. Accessed 3 April 2012
29. Hartung D, Busch C (2009) Why vein recognition needs privacy protection. In: 5th international conference on intelligent information hiding and multimedia signal processing, IEEE, Kyoto, Japan, pp 1090–1095
30. Lee EC, Park KR (2009) Restoration method of skin scattering blurred vein image for finger vein recognition. IEEE Electron Lett 21:1074–1076
31. Zhang H, Hu D (2010) A palm vein recognition system. In: International conference on intelligent computation technology and automation, IEEE, Changsha, China, pp 285–288
32. Nishiuchi N, Soya H (2011) Cancelable biometric identification by combining biological data with artifacts. In: International conference on biometrics and Kansei engineering, IEEE, Takamatsu, Japan, pp 61–64
33. Crisan S, Tarnovan I, Crisan E (2007) A low cost vein detection system using near infrared radiation. In: Sensors applications symposium, IEEE, San Diego, USA, pp 1–6
34. Qian S, Guo S, Li X, Zhong F, Shao X (2009) Finger-vein recognition based on the score level moment invariants fusion. In: International conference on computational intelligence and software engineering, IEEE, Wuhan, China, pp 1–4

Chapter 5
A Study on Touch Screen Devices: User Authentication Problems

Marcin Rogowski and Khalid Saeed

Abstract The focus of this chapter is on security of touch screen devices. The emphasis is placed on smartphones – such as Apple iPhone and Android phones – and tablets – such as Apple iPad. The chapter starts with the description how the touch screen devices are winning a significant share in the market. The current state of the security methods used on these devices is discussed. Deficiencies of prevailing approaches are pointed out, and the need for new authentication mechanisms is reasoned. The hardware available in modern touch screen devices is characterized, and the sensors providing biometric data are described.

In the last part of this chapter, some of the new security means using biometric features and potential new directions are discussed.

5.1 Introduction

First patents and inventions concerning touch screen devices can be dated as far back as 1965 [1]. HP-150 produced in 1983 is considered one of the earliest commercial touch screen computers. However, it was not sensitive to the actual touch but rather had infrared emitters and detectors around the screen which detected any objects that happened to be between the emitter and detector. With the technology theoretically present, it took years until touch screen devices really reached the market and became widely available to the customers.

M. Rogowski (✉)
King Abdullah University of Science and Technology, Thuwal, Saudi Arabia
e-mail: marcin.rogowski@gmail.com

K. Saeed
AGH University of Science and Technology, Faculty of Physics and Applied
Computer Science, Al. Mickiewicza 30, Kraków PL-30059, Poland
e-mail: saeed@agh.edu.pl

K. Saeed and T. Nagashima (eds.), *Biometrics and Kansei Engineering*,
DOI 10.1007/978-1-4614-5608-7_5, © Springer Science+Business Media New York 2012

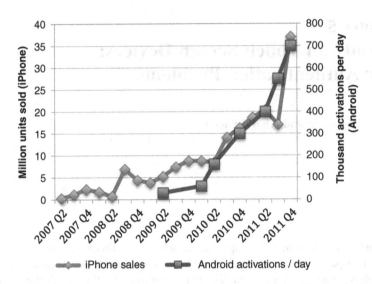

Fig. 5.1 iPhone sales (*left Y axis*) and Android activations per day as reported by Google (*right axis*)

Certainly, the years after 2000, when the required technology was getting more mature and reasonably priced, were the breakthrough years for the touch screen market. As reported in [2], 2007 sales of touch screens for mobile devices exceeded 2006 results by 91%. The same study expects the revenue from this particular market to reach $5 billion in 2009. It should be kept in mind that the report was written in 2008, just as Apple iPhone's popularity was exploding. It is even noted that at the time when the report was written, Samsung, Motorola, and Sony Ericsson controlled 90% of the market, and Apple was one of the niche players. Surely, $5 billion figure had to be corrected and touch screens are now a multibillion-dollar market.

The year 2007, when the first Apple iPhone was presented, can be considered a turning point for the touch screen market. Shortly followed by Google's Android system with the first commercial phone available in 2008, it can be certainly said that iPhone and Android brought the touch screens to the mass market. Apple sold over 183 million iPhones from 2007 until the end of 2011 [3]. Due to market fragmentation, it is difficult to say definitely how many Android devices there are on the market, but Google provides some data – 190 million Android devices in the market as of October 2011 with 60 million registered only between July and October! However, more than 370 million of iPhones and Android devices on the market are only a share of the total touch screen market. Android figures include tablets, but to calculate how widely available the technology is, we would need to add all the other touch screen-based smartphones and non-Android-based tablets. Apple has already sold over 67 million of their tablet device – iPad released only in 2010 – as of December 2011 and the market is booming. Cumulatively, we are most likely looking at more than 500 million of modern touch screen devices in the market.

Surely, after a close evaluation of Fig. 5.1, one can say that market is huge at the moment, and rather than stabilizing, it is exponentially growing.

In the following parts of this chapter, when particular solutions currently used by the manufacturers are discussed, Android or iPhone is used as an example as these two products dominate the market at the moment and any contender would have to match or exceed the options offered by the leading bands.

5.2   Current State of the Security of the Mobile Devices

Mobile devices are getting more powerful and are no longer used only as phones. They also serve purposes of personal information managers and web browsers and often contain amounts of private data and passwords comparable with that of a personal computer. Already in 2005, before the real smartphone revolution had even started, it was estimated that over 80% of new critical data is stored on a mobile device [4]. Increasingly, especially in post-2007 era, the exact same services and websites are used on mobile devices and on the personal computers. While security barriers were implemented on PCs for years, it is a relatively new trend on the mobile devices. Despite that, the need of securing aforementioned hundreds of millions of devices from unauthorized access is clear and not discussable.

Unfortunately, the mobility only makes the risks higher as compared to the personal computers. Obviously, the chance of an attempt of unauthorized access is higher when the device is carried to different locations. A few methods of securing a device do exist, but they mainly secure devices from the unauthorized access in the moments when the user leaves his phone or tablet unattended and another person tries to access his data during the few minutes when the owner is absent. These methods are not likely to ensure a good protection from a determined attempt to break the security barrier.

Certainly one cause of the deficiencies of authentication methods used on mobile devices is the required access time. In the case of PCs, the user authenticates and then uses the machine for extended time so he is more likely to accept more sophisticated security check that takes a little more time. On the other hand, for mobile devices, the user usually requires access quite often and for short periods of time, which makes it more difficult to use a very trustworthy verification method if it is time consuming. The ratio of time required to authenticate to the average time for which the device is used should always be taken into account and, for the comfort of the user, be minimized if possible.

5.2.1   Password

The most popular desktop securing method – a password – is also ported in the same form to smartphones. This, however, is not that straightforward to be accepted by a user. Due to the instant access to the device a user requires, it is unlikely that the user will voluntarily agree to have this instant access taken away in the name of security.

Many will easily agree for a minor discomfort of a few seconds of delay, but it is unlikely that they would agree for a password as difficult as the passwords we use nowadays on PCs. Even if the users agree, there has been a discussion going on for past years whether the passwords we are using ensure us a good level of security or not at all. There are some publications describing what characterizes a good password – for example, complexity, uniqueness, and secrecy rules proposed in [5] – but most would probably agree that users would choose to compromise one or more of these rules for their own comfort. On a smartphone or a tablet, as the device is designed to be comfortable to use, users are even more likely to jeopardize the complexity rule. Despite the numerous attempts, most researchers agree that because there is nothing better we can propose, passwords will stay there for some more time on the desktops. However, on mobile devices the approaches more comfortable for a user, which he would be more likely to use, should be evaluated first.

5.2.2   PIN

PIN – Personal Identification Number is a special case of a password we all know from ATM machines. In banking, it dates back to 1966 when James Goodfellow patented a PIN derivation scheme [6]. Despite contemporary standards requiring its length to be 4–12 digits, most often used numbers are still of the length of 4 digits only. This carries a clear disadvantage as it can be easily calculated – there are only 10,000 possible PINs, so the level of security proposed does not seem to be high. In banking, it is usually coupled with blocking the card after three failed attempts, and hence some level of security is ensured – probability of guessing a PIN within three attempts is only 0.06%. It also still remains relatively comfortable for the legitimate user.

PIN was also adopted by smartphone makers as a security measure. The length is no longer fixed to 4 with the newest Android system specifying the length of a PIN to be between 4 and 17 characters. Apple still uses the length of 4 for iPhone and iPad, but "Simple Passcode" mode may be turned off changing a PIN into a password, as discussed before. Regrettably, there should be no illusion that mobile users will actually use a long number. Most likely the biggest group will use four digits, and many of those will be birth dates, patterns on keyboard, or common passwords like "1234." Recent study has clearly shown these tendencies [7]. After analyzing 204,508 PINs from iPhones, it turned out that 46 of the possible combinations were not even used, and 4.3% of all the PINs were "1234."

Another problem with the use of a PIN on a mobile device is that it would not be acceptable, as in banking, to cause major discomfort for a user after he inputs a wrong number three times. The number can be entered numerous times during a day on a mobile phone, so mistakes, even many times in a row may happen. The solution used now by Android developers is locking the device for a predetermined period of time, so it protects the device from spontaneous brute-force attacks when

Fig. 5.2 Pattern lock on an Android phone

it is unattended for a few minutes. However, this simple lock is not going to protect the device if it can be accessed for a longer period of time. Apple included an option to erase all the data on the phone after the PIN is entered incorrectly for 10 times, but this solution may frustrate users, especially if they have kids or if a user with malicious intent gets access to their device even for a few minutes.

Another problem is that the PIN encourages users to pick the numbers that create a pattern on a keyboard and makes the password predictable. In general, a PIN can be considered a special case of a password that carries all of its deficiencies.

5.2.3 Pattern Locks

Another form of a security measure that can be used on contemporary touch screen devices is a pattern lock. Instead of a PIN, the user is required to connect dots in a predefined order, as shown in Fig. 5.2.

Surely, this kind of patterns may be easier to memorize and does not cause major discomfort for a user. The researchers from the University of Pennsylvania explored deficiencies of pattern locks in [8]. As calculated there, in general there are about one million possible patterns using nine points. However, if constraints of implementations are taken into account – for Android, if a point lays between two selected points, it also has to be selected – there are only 389,112 combinations left. If the user's comfort is also taken into account, it turns out, that more than a half of

Fig. 5.3 Unlikely stroke

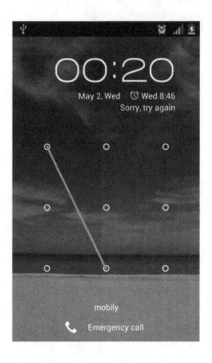

these combinations contain patterns that are not comfortable for the user to enter. One such case is illustrated in Fig. 5.3. When entering patterns like the one shown, it is very likely that also one of the points close to the actual stroke will be incorrectly selected. As the users pick convenient patterns, it is not likely that they will pick one of these special cases, and as a result search space can be narrowed down to 158,410 likely combinations.

Considering this size of search space, a brute-force approach surely is possible, but the main focus of the discussed paper exposes another drawback of using pattern locks on touch screen devices. Researchers analyzed the oily residue left behind by user's finger. Using photo-editing software, they were able to success-fully expose the trace of a finger, and in the report they state the method worked in 92% of the cases.

A solution to the problem was proposed by Whisper Systems with their product Whisper Core offering smudge-resistant screen unlock patterns [9]. The solution proposed is to force the user to replace pattern-smudge with another smudge – namely, wiping the entire screen with a finger. It is some solution to the problem, but the problem with wider adaptation of the method may be, again, the comfort of the user. This method adds at least two additional strokes of a thumb, so for some users it may double the effort of unlocking a screen.

Another risk of using a pattern lock is that it is quite easy to be compromised. It is usually a characteristic pattern, and it can be easily observed and memorized by a bystander.

5.2.4   Face Unlock

Face Unlock is a new feature added to Android system in late 2011. It is also the first biometric feature used there. It has to be admitted that this implementation of unlocking using face image works instantaneously. Unluckily, for this level of comfort, a price had to be paid.

When authenticating with a password, a PIN, or a pattern, the authentication is a binary problem – either the predetermined pattern matches or it does not. When using biometric features, the problem is more complex. Whether it is a fingerprint, a face image, or any other biometric feature, it is very unlikely that the obtained feature will exactly match the one collected while enrolling the user. There is always a trade-off between false acceptance rate and false rejection rate. Minimizing FAR makes the system more secure but at the same time causes discomfort to the users by making FRR higher and vice versa. Clearly, to achieve the speed and low "insult rate" as FRR may be called, developers of Android had to sacrifice FAR, therefore making Face Unlock less secure. It is even incorporated as a standard warning to the user that Face Unlock is less secure than other methods, and persons looking similar will be able to get access to the device. What is not mentioned is that also people having a picture of a person that looks similar to the user will be able to get access to the system as a simple camera will not be able to tell the difference between the actual face and the picture of the face being in front of it.

There are also a few different problems with Face Unlock. The lighting of the environment plays a big role, and the method will simply not work when it is too dark or too bright (*see* Chap. 2 *on face recognition in unconstrained environment*). Another fact is that the position of the device when taking a picture of a user's face is important, so it will not be possible to use this method to unlock a phone or a tablet lying flat on the desk or to do it discreetly in public without positioning a device in front of one's face. There is also a requirement for the device, as it has to be equipped with a front-facing camera to make it comfortable to use.

5.3   Collecting Biometric Features to Improve the Security

It can be noticed that despite the obvious need for securing mobile devices, most of the methods instead of being devised particularly for mobile devices were used elsewhere and were later adopted in the new environment. Also, as discussed before, due to the circumstances – mainly instantaneous access time expected by the user – they do not seem to work very well because they are used in their least secure form.

The key difference in the interaction with contemporary mobile devices and personal computers is the interface. We rarely see a physical keyboard and almost never see a mouse attached to a mobile device. Touch screens are used to interact with the device and replace both the mouse and the keyboard, which is now displayed on the screen and typed on using the embedded display in the device.

There is also another difference between a PC and a mobile device that was not mentioned before. Admittedly, the trend is decreasing, but still quite commonly PCs are shared by more than one person. Contrastingly, mobile devices are almost never shared and are much more personal than the bigger machines. Incidentally, it is even better for biometric user-specific features to be used to authenticate the user. The owner's information can be stored on the device and, if required, no one else will be authorized to use the particular device. As the usual case with the biometric features, not only would the password not be possible to steal but also, even if the legitimate user wanted to allow someone to access his device, it would be impossible to pass the biometric password. This characteristic of the biometric password has to be kept in mind while implementing the security barrier, and in specific cases, maybe another method of granting access to the device should be thought of.

It should also be noted that as any password, a biometric password can sometimes be lost. Certainly unpleasant situations as losing one's physical feature like a fingerprint might happen, and despite being unlikely, some backup method of authentication should be thought of.

Using a touch screen device, more features can be extracted than when interacting with a personal computer. Physical keyboard is replaced by a virtual one, and in addition to timing of keystrokes, also the size of each finger pressing a screen can be measured, pressure can be estimated, and the exact position of the finger pressing a key in relation to the position of this particular key pressed can be analyzed. In contrast to a PC, mobile devices – whether tablets or phones – produced these days also have a plethora of other sensors most often including an accelerometer, a gyroscope, a proximity sensor, an ambient light sensor, two microphones, one or two cameras, and sometimes even a magnetometer. Some of these sensors obviously can provide more information about the user and his behavior and help differentiate between users. Later in this chapter, it is discussed how each of these sensors works and how the data coming from it could be possibly used to authenticate users.

What is important is that most of the data coming from the aforementioned sensors can be collected transparently to the user. That creates two possibilities: either to use it alongside the traditional methods discussed before (i.e., to strengthen the password rather than replace it) or to continuously authenticate the user. In the second approach, data is collected and analyzed all the time as the user ordinarily uses the device. If a system like this was used, even if the device is stolen in the authenticated state (e.g., grabbed from the user's hand), an algorithm analyzing particular data may determine that the user using the device is no longer the legitimate one and may block the device.

In the following sections, we will discuss the most commonly encountered hardware and describe the biometric data associated with it.

Fig. 5.4 Resistive screen

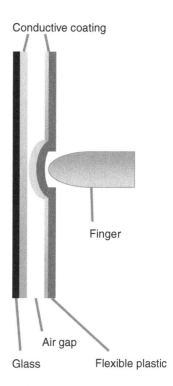

Conductive coating

Finger

Air gap

Glass   Flexible plastic

5.3.1 Screen

Most of the modern touch screen devices use one of the two leading technologies to implement the touch screen functionality – resistive or capacitive screens. A breakthrough point for the market was the debut of Apple iPhone in 2007 when capacitive screens started gaining popularity at the expense of resistive technology.

5.3.1.1 Resistive Screen

Screens produced in the resistive technology are based on the two flexible, resistive sheets separated with air gaps or another type of insulator (Fig. 5.4). When the pressure is put on the top sheet, it touches the bottom one causing a contact. Electric voltage generated when the two resistive layers come into contact indicates the place of touch.

The biggest advantage of this method is that the screen can be operated using any object. Usually, a special stylus is used, but anything that will cause the two layers to come into contact will work – whether it is a stylus, a finger, a gloved finger, a nail, or even a pen. Also, if the screen is operated using a stylus, it is assumed to be more accurate than a finger or other objects. Sharp-pointed stylus not only prevents creation of oily smudges on the screen that were discussed previously as a security

Fig. 5.5 Capacitive screen

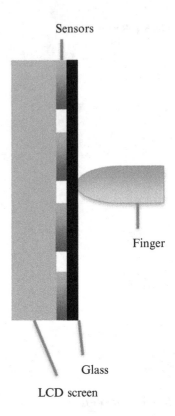

Sensors

Finger

Glass

LCD screen

threat but, what is more important, makes the input more precise and allows developers to create smaller user interface elements.

Ironically, using the stylus also accounts for a disadvantage of resistive touch screens. As mentioned before, users require instant access to their device. If they have to use the stylus, it creates an additional mini-barrier before they can fully use the device. It is also usually difficult to eject the stylus from its slot in the device and hold it in the same hand. Two hands are required, therefore creating discomfort for the user. There is another disadvantage that appears – a smaller, more condensed user interface is created. It is fine for users using a stylus, but when choosing to use the finger (too big compared with the interface elements), then the user may get frustrated trying to press the right button.

5.3.1.2 Capacitive Screen

Capacitive screens (Fig. 5.5) are based on the concept of capacitance. There is no longer a need for two layers of resistive sheet, as one is sufficient. This layer is usually glass (insulator) covered with indium tin oxide (conductor). When another conductor, like human body, touches the screen, distortion in the screen's electrostatic field (a change in the capacitance) occurs and touch is registered.

Similarly, as in the case of resistive screens, advantages and disadvantages of this type of the screen will have the same source. Because capacitance is used, any contact between a conductor and the screen, regardless of the pressure, will result in registering the touch event. That makes the screen really sensitive and convenient to use. Also, no additional objects are required as a finger can be used successfully. Obviously, the size of the finger makes it necessary to adjust the user interface so that all the elements are sufficiently big for the user not to make mistakes, although it is not really a problem. The biggest drawback is the requirement of the object touching the screen to be a conductor. That bans traditional styli (special capacitive styli are available), pens, and most importantly gloved fingers from using the screen. For some world regions, the fact that the device cannot be used with gloves on is a big drawback.

5.3.1.3   Other Technologies

Capacitive and resistive touch screens are the most common in the marketplace today, but there are also other technologies that allow the creation of a touch screen. This group includes screens that use:

– Surface acoustic wave, where ultrasonic wave passing over the panel is used and absorptions of the wave correspond to the touches.
– Infrared, where sensors are placed around the screen and touches are detected by disruptions in the pattern of the beams.
– Piezoelectricity, a technology developed by 3 M uses ordinary glass panel and analyzes piezoelectricity in the glass generated as a result of a touch.
– Sound, developed by Tyco International, the technology is based on unique sounds generated by each point of the plate of the glass.

In the case that capacitive touch screens are replaced by any of the mentioned technologies, they all do offer advantages specified afterward unless specified otherwise.

5.3.1.4   Biometric Features

Touch screen devices provide much more data on how they are used than traditional means of communication with a personal computer – the keyboard or the mouse.

On a physical keyboard, the only available information is whether the key is pressed or not. In the case of a virtual keyboard displayed on the touch screen, there is also the possibility to extract exact coordinates where the keys were pressed, the size of the user's fingers that touch the screen, and the pressure put on the display. Initial research has shown the finger size to be a very promising differentiating feature, while the pressure, on physical keyboards, was shown to be as effective as latency information [10]. A huge advantage was clear when the latency and the pressure information were combined – accuracy was significantly improved.

Different paradigm of interaction does not only create new options in security but also gives opportunities to improve human interaction in general. Using the example of a music player, n7player [11] is surely a step in the right direction. Instead of the traditional media player interface – usually some form of a list – user is presented with a cloud of text tags or a wall of album covers. In this form, picking a wanted album is not only easier but also more "fun." User applications can also make use of extra biometric features that were not available on traditional interfaces. Here, even creators of n7player have a room for improvement – for example, the wall that is shown to the user could vary in size depending on the size of user's finger so that the process is more comfortable.

Some research has been done on the mouse dynamics, as will be introduced in 5.4.3, trying to distinguish people based on how they interact with a computer using a mouse. On a touch screen device, the user's finger takes the role of the mouse. Similarly as in physical/virtual keyboard comparison, using a touch screen provides all the same information and a few features more. Not only XY coordinates in time can be recorded, but additionally there is also the information about the size and the pressure. What may be important for some concepts, like gesture recognition, the most modern touch screens support multi-touch, that is, more than one finger may interact with the screen at the same time.

5.3.2 Accelerometer and Gyroscope

Accelerometers and gyroscopes are both becoming the standard equipment of a modern smartphone and tablet. They both measure similar features; however, they differ.

Accelerometer, as the name suggests, measures acceleration along three axes – the acceleration that the device experiences compared to free fall. That means a device laid on the table will have upward acceleration of 9.81 m/s^2. A phone in free fall toward the center of the Earth would register acceleration of zero in every direction. This principle has been used in some of the hard disks, which turn off when the event of falling occurs. This way, data is better protected. This, however, is not the most common use of accelerometers. They are widely used in digital cameras and mobile devices to tell, based on the changes in acceleration, in what position the user is holding the device. They are widely used in mobile phones to implement the pedometer functionality, for image stabilization in cameras and camcorders, as well as in game controllers for steering (Sony PlayStation 3 with DualShock 3 remote). The accelerometer is also used in Nike + sensors and mounted on one's shoe helps to detect the speed and distance when one is running.

The gyroscope measures angular velocity – that is, the extent and the speed of rotation along three axes (X, Y, Z or roll, pitch, yaw). Gyroscopes measuring one- or two-axes also exist.

A gyroscope is based on the principle of angular momentum. Historically, they were usually constructed using a rotating sphere or a disk as shown in Fig. 5.6.

Fig. 5.6 Gyroscope [12]

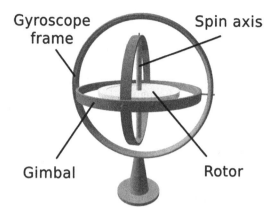

Gyroscope frame · Spin axis · Gimbal · Rotor

The goal of the mechanism, which most important elements are the rotor and two gimbals, is to allow the axle of the gyroscope to be in any orientation. The outer gimbal has 1° of freedom, while, mounted in it, inner gimbal has two. The innermost rotor has 3° of freedom. The effect of this construction is that when the rotor is spinning, the gyroscope resists attempts to change its position. It allows to register all the rotations. Nowadays, gyroscopes are built with microelectromechanical technology and are available as small chips. They are deployed in many electronic devices, often alongside accelerometers.

The most important difference between data that can be provided by accelerometer and gyroscope is that using only the accelerometer, one cannot distinguish moves around gravity. Usually, both types of sensors at the same time not only enable distinguishing those moves, but they also improve the accuracy.

It has also been shown that using the accelerometer and the gyroscope can help distinguish between similar touch events – soft versus hard taps as well as gentle swipe to scroll between displays versus hard drag to rearrange items on the screen [13].

In another approach, Derawi et al. [14] have used the data from the mobile phone accelerometer to distinguish between users based on the way they walk (gait dynamics). The achieved equal error rate of 20.1% is higher than in some other works on the subject, but only a standard mobile phone was used and not specialized equipment or video recording like in other cases.

5.3.3 Microphones

Most of the modern phones are equipped with two microphones. One is used to register the user's voice when he talks and is placed in the bottom part of the phone, and the other one is often placed next to the speaker in the upper part of the phone and is used for the purpose of noise-canceling.

With the ability to use data from two microphones, an obvious realization is that the speaker recognition system could be employed to allow the mobile device to authenticate the user.

Not many people would expect any connection between the microphone and the user's typing pattern on the touch screen. However, recent research has shown otherwise. Scientists from Carnegie Mellon Human-Computer Interaction Institute developed TapSense [15] – a system which, based on the sound resulting from an object impact on the screen, is able to determine what kind of object it is. Not only are they able to distinguish between a fingernail and a finger but also between different parts of a finger – a tip, a pad, or a knuckle. The goal of TapSense is to enhance the interaction with the device. So far the following ideas were presented:

– Replacing a fixed backspace key with a fingernail tap anywhere
– Calling contextual menu using a knuckle
– Entering numbers and symbols with a tip of the finger instead of the pad in contrast to the typical requirement of a long press to do that

There are some doubts as to ambient noise and how accurate differentiating based on the sound really is – Carnegie Mellon team used the iPod Touch screen with a stethoscope attached and achieved an accuracy of classification of 88.3–94.7% (for four and five input types, respectively). They suggest the same technique may be potentially achieved using standard microphones if raw access to the data from them is provided, but no tests were performed using a standard microphone instead of a stethoscope.

Considering the results of TapSense, its high accuracy, and a very small difference between fingertip and palm, it is conceivable that the sound generated allows not only to discriminate between the parts of the finger used but also may help identify different users.

5.3.4 Proximity Sensor, Ambient Light Sensor, Cameras

There are also other sensors in modern touch screen devices. Many phones include a proximity sensor, which is able to tell whether a phone is held next to one's ear or within a distance which is used to prevent from unknowingly interacting with the screen by one's ear or face. Usually, proximity sensor is implemented using a light sensor. Based on the changes of light intensity that it registers, conclusions about user's proximity to the phone are drawn. Unfortunately, in smartphones this information is often binary and only changes from "far" to "near." The change occurs once the distance is smaller than a set threshold – approximately 5 cm. Most likely this limited distinction will not be of great use for authentication purposes.

An ambient light sensor is also often included and used for adjusting the screen brightness to the changes in the user's environment. This output of this sensor is the characterization of the intensity of the light that it registers in lux units. It is not clear how those sensors would be used for security purposes, but it cannot be definitely stated that they cannot be useful.

Another sensor type is a camera. All the modern phones and tablets include one or two digital cameras. Nowadays, at least one of these cameras is a high-quality unit, and the standard resolution seems currently to be 8 megapixels. There is virtually no limitations on what data can be collected using a camera. As discussed before, Face Unlock already uses a camera to authenticate the user based on his face image. Other ideas used in traditional biometrics also come to mind: hand geometry, fingerprint, iris image, etc. There are also surprising applications. One well-known Android application – Azumio Instant Heart Rate [16] – promises to measure one's heart rate using a camera. The finger has to be placed immediately on the camera, flash is turned on, and based on changes in the color of the finger, the pulse is measured.

5.4   Sample Applications in Security

After discussing plenty features that can be collected on almost any modern device equipped with a touch screen, it comes as a sad realization that almost none of these additional characteristics are exploited by the developers to provide users with higher level of security. Not only can they be used instead of a conventional security precaution, but thanks to their transparency, they can also enable the developer to enhance the existing methods and provide raised level of security to the user. Many of the discussed characteristics do not require the user's cooperation or even their knowledge and can be collected in the background. That gives the ability to create a system that will continuously authenticate the user based on his action without even the legitimate user knowing about it. The goal of this system would be to block the access to the device immediately after it detects that the user's behavior changed enough to suspect an impostor is using the device. This may not only prevent an unauthorized access to the device when it is stolen in authorized state but would also make compromising or breaking the password using brute-force methods virtually impossible. There is also the potential to use some of the biometric methods at the same time as the conventional authentication techniques, that is, asking the user for a password or a pattern and not only checking if it matches the recorded data but also verifying if the change in biometric features is as expected or not. The following sections will discuss some of the possible approaches that use biometric features in addition to or instead of the conventional security mechanisms. Most of the ideas or systems described here combine data from different sensors to achieve better performance.

5.4.1   Keystroke Dynamics

The user's typing style was shown to be a feature differentiating well between users. The idea first came as early as 1975 when it was mentioned by R. J. Spillane [17] and has since then been modified and improved on multiple occasions with the results reported as high as 99–100% correct classification. In general, in almost all the works on keystroke dynamics, the user is asked to type a particular password multiple times. Then specific timing data – the single key depression time, the time between consecutive key pairs, etc. – is extracted. Based in this data, user is authenticated not only based on the fact if the password is correct but also how closely it matches the timing data obtained during the enrollment phase.

There is no obstacle that would prevent the same characteristics that were used on a physical keyboard to be used on the touch screen keyboard. As discussed before, not only the same properties can be registered but also many more including the pressure, the size, and the changes in position coming from both the accelerometer and the gyroscope. This gives a huge potential for keystroke dynamics to be used as an additional security barrier. The same approaches as in traditional keystroke dynamics can be used – a fixed-text authentication and a free-text authentication.

In the case of the fixed-text authentication, the user will perform the verification procedure as usual – whether it is a pattern lock, a PIN, or a password – and not only correctness of the combination would be evaluated but also how they did it. There are a number of features that can be extracted to help determine if a user is a legitimate one. For traditional keystroke dynamics, the dwell time of a single key press is universally used. Most commonly it is combined with the so-called flight time – time from releasing a key to pressing a subsequent one in the password. These characteristics proved to be reliable, and there are no significant improvements over these results if additional features are extracted. It has to be considered if the problem is exactly the same on a small touch screen – usually around 4 in. in diameter for a phone and around 10 in. for a tablet – as on a full-sized physical keyboard.

Some preliminary research was done a few years ago on mobile phones when touch screens were not prevalent in the market. A device with a small, thumb-typed physical keyboard was used by Karatzouni and Clarke [18], and some interesting observations were made. In contrast to the full-sized physical keyboard, in this case, the dwell time of any single key did not prove to be a reliable differentiating characteristic, and the resulting error rate was near 50%. Using the flight time between pairs of keys resulted in a much better 12.2% error rate on a group of 50 participants. The results obtained point out that the fact that the depression time of a key is not a good discriminating feature may be caused by the use of thumb-typed keyboard. On the full-sized keyboard, however, different number of fingers, ranging from 1 to 10 depending on the user, is made use of. If that is the reason for this phenomenon, then it will be interesting to see if on a medium-sized touch screen phone and a bigger tablet the same observation holds or not and how it varies with the keyboard size.

Initial research done on a device with 4.3-in. touch screen device shows that there is no big difference between the discriminating power of the dwell and the flight times, but they both give an error rate higher than 10% if not combined with additional features. The results obtained combining different characteristics, for example, the dwell time and the size of the finger, are very promising, but as the area is relatively fresh, comprehensive results are not yet available. Using data from a gyroscope or an accelerometer also improves the classification accuracy significantly.

Another interesting approach that can be used for keystroke dynamics was also evaluated for a conventional full-sized physical keyboard [19] but may be even more relevant to mobile devices. Free-text authentication approach can be used in the form of an algorithm running in the background monitoring the user's behavior as he uses the devices as usual. The reason of this approach being invented was the risk that an impostor gets the access to the computer when the user is logged in and will continue working as if he was authorized. Because of the very nature of mobile devices, this risk is amplified and, if implemented well, the continuous authentication approach may prove to be very relevant and useful in the new area. Later in this chapter, the speaker recognition is discussed as a method that may prevent an attacker from using the device that he gained access to. Almost certainly, if the impersonator is not naïve enough to make a phone call from the device, he will need to type something to benefit from his actions, and then the continuous authentication keystroke dynamics algorithm can come into action and block access to the device.

5.4.2 Gestures

Recently a study of biometric-rich gestures was conducted by a team led by Prof. Nasir Memon and published in [20]. The authors used tablets and asked users to perform particular gestures such as closing, opening, and various rotations, all in many different versions with different fingers fixed. The user-defined gesture was also allowed, and in this case the movement of five fingertips while the user was signing his signature was recorded. In the verification phase, the input is compared to the stored template, and based on the similarity, the user is authenticated or not. A time warping algorithm is used to compare the similarity of the two sequences. Thirty-four users were asked to participate. From the predetermined methods, counterclockwise rotation of all five fingers gave the best results with 7.21% equal error rate, while the average was 10%. The researchers also evaluated the performance when two gestures were used. In this case the error rate was significantly lower and as low as 2.58% for clockwise rotation of five fingers followed by counterclockwise rotation of four fingers with fixed thumb. This result indicates that different gestures make different characteristics of hand or the user's interaction style stand out. The user-defined gesture was also very effective, and the error rate was 2.88% in this case. It is important that most of the users said that the gestures are pleasant to use, and a good number said they were "excited" to use them. Twenty-five out of 29 users preferred this method over a text password, and all 29 users thought it would be faster.

5.4.3 Touch Screen Dynamics and Mouse Dynamics

Mouse dynamics is a method of evaluating the user's specific style of moving a mouse. Different researchers analyzed different characteristics, often including deviation from the straight line, a user-specific ratio of dragging, clicking, average speed, etc. Detailed solutions will be discussed later in the section.

It may not seem intuitive to evaluate mouse dynamics methods on mobile devices, where there is no mouse at all. Despite the initial impression, mouse dynamics algorithms can be adapted, in some cases with only minor changes, and applied on touch screen devices. It may turn out that mouse dynamics is even more relevant to touch screen devices than the much better researched keystroke dynamics. Perhaps the similarities will become more apparent when specific solutions used by researchers are explained.

One of the interesting and relevant approaches was introduced in 2005 by Hashia et al. [21]. The team's system asks users to connect some dots. Dots are shown one at a time, and the user is simply required to move the mouse from one dot to another. The coordinates of the mouse are recorded every 50 ms, and the speed, the deviation from a straight line, and the angle are calculated. In the verification phase, these values are compared to the ones recorded during the enrollment phase. The resulting error rate is 15%, which is not that bad considering how simple the statistical model is. It is quite easy to notice the similarities between this method and the pattern lock used in Android phones. Authenticating using a pattern lock is basically the same task – connecting dots, but only the order in which the dots are connected is evaluated. It is a very simple extension to also include some statistical information about the speed, the angle, or the deviation from a straight line, as in the work discussed, to the same system. The change will be transparent to the user but may result in increasing the security level.

Hashia et al. also discuss the continuous authentication introduced before or as they call it – passive authentication. Instead of requiring the user to move the mouse over dots, whole regions of screen are treated as dots. They record the movements, and every 2 min analyze them and authenticate the user. No detailed performance characteristics are provided, but an average time of 2 min for which the intruder was allowed to use the computer and 5 min after which the actual user was considered an intruder which suggests that false rejection rate may be alarmingly high. Passive authentication could be implemented on a mobile touch screen as well.

Slightly different approach was evaluated in [22]. Only the speed of the mouse between predetermined points was analyzed, and using minimal eigenvalues of a Toeplitz matrix for classification resulted in accuracy of almost 70%. On a touch screen, data about pressure and size of the fingers could also be used, giving more discriminative features, and the result would be most likely improved.

Another approach was presented by Gamboa et al. [23]. They required users to type a username and PIN using a mouse on a virtual keyboard displayed on the webpage. Numbers on a numeric keyboard were ordered randomly to protect from automated attacks. The data collected is divided into strokes – mouse movements performed between the mouse clicks; therefore, there is as many strokes as there are digits in the PIN. Then, for each user, the best performing subset of features is selected, and only these features are later used to authenticate the user using the researchers' statistical model. Depending on the number of strokes used, the performance of the system varies between 17% equal error rate (5 strokes) and 6% (15 strokes).

The method introduced by Gamboa et al. not only does seem suitable to touch screen devices but might even be a better fit than in the original version. Typing using a mouse on a virtual keyboard is neither convenient nor natural, while on the touch screen device, it is not only natural but usually the only way to type.

5.4.4   Graphic Passwords

Replacing PIN with a graphic password is another idea of using the nature of touch screens to improve upon the security of the PIN. One of the ideas was introduced by J. Citty in [24]. Instead of using a four-digit sequence, 16 images partitioned into four parts are used. To verify the user, they are required to select the correct parts of the correct images in the right order. This change increases the number of possible password combinations from 10^4 for a four-digit PIN to over 10^7. The sequence entry time is initially about two times that of a PIN, but as users practice, it gets very close to it.

The main problem of this method is also pointed out by the researchers. As they checked, it is possible that the users forget their passwords after some time, especially if they are randomly generated. In the study, 13% of the users forgot their sequences after a week of not using them. Another problem with this particular paper is that the study was conducted on a group of 15 students. The group is not only quite small, but as they were students and regular touch screen users, they might have been more tech-savvy, and in the general population, even more than 13% of users might forget their password.

5.4.5   Voice Unlock

There are two approaches for speaker recognition – text dependent and text independent. Both could be used on the mobile device, especially a phone. Considering text-dependent approach, a system analogous to Face Unlock may be implemented – Voice Unlock. It has to be admitted that this approach may not be perfect, as probably many users will feel awkward whispering their password to the phone in public. Environmental noises as well as the user's physical and mental state are also always a concern for a system like that. There is an obvious risk of a determined impostor recording a password being pronounced and accessing the device. Comfort provided by a method like this is debatable but in fact may not be higher than that of other systems. Another approach could be the text-independent solution, and the most apparent solution will be analyzing the user's voice while he speaks on the phone. This will eliminate other people, even if authorized, from talking on the particular phone.

Many of the modern touch screen devices are smartphones, and more or less often, their conventional function is used. In this case, it is possible to let the user unlock the device using any method he wishes to use, but then if the voice analyzed during the conversation does not match the pattern stored beforehand, an additional authentication may be required. This method will protect users from the impostors that managed to come into possession of the primary password. However, there is the condition that an impostor must make a phone call from the device, so the scope of the method is not only limited to phones but it also requires a thief to behave in a certain way. Then we can safely assume if someone steals an expensive smartphone, it is not for the sake of free calls. These limitations do not render the speaker recognition as a very good method to be used standalone, but it may be useful for multi-biometric systems discussed later. The performance of speaker recognition systems is estimated to be similar to those of signature at error rate of about 2% [25].

5.4.6   Enhanced Pattern Lock

The authors in [26] proposed an approach to authenticate users on the basis of the correctness of the pattern they enter and the way they do it. This is a direct translation of keystroke dynamics enhanced password to a pattern lock. Similarly as in Memon's work [20], a dynamic time warping algorithm is used to compare the similarity between the reference and the current input while the procedure of verification is taking place. Here, x–y coordinates, time, size, pressure, and speed are collected. Based on the data set of 31 users, researchers have achieved 77% accuracy with 19% false rejection rate and 21% false acceptance rate. Modifying the threshold used for some of the users helped to further improve the accuracy. It also suggests that machine learning approach can be evaluated for the same problem, and it should be checked how its performance compares to simple thresholds based on the dynamic time warping algorithm.

5.4.7   Face and Voice Recognition

Certainly, the abundance of sensors providing various, also biometric data, allows to create some kind of a system that will combine these inputs and authenticate the user based on the combination of features. One such system was proposed by the researchers from MIT in 2003 [27] using a personal digital assistant device with a resistive touch screen but no phone option. Their system investigates the usage of two-way multi-biometric authentication combining the face image and the speaker recognition. The image of the face is taken using the embedded 640 × 480 resolution camera. For the speaker recognition, a built-in microphone is used which registers user's voice pattern when pronouncing a password consisting of three two-digit numbers. The results obtained are promising with the error rate below 1% when analyzing both the face and the voice. It is important to note that despite the very good results achieved, this particular approach will not serve well as a replacement for passwords used nowadays. As mentioned, an important factor is the user's comfort. Efficient enrollment is also important, and it is unlikely that users will choose to replace their PINs and patterns with a multimodal system which takes an average of 30 min to set up – MIT researchers required users to take 25 face images in different lighting settings and to recite 16 generated pass phrases.

5.5   Conclusions

This chapter described how mobile touch screen devices are becoming ubiquitous and what challenges it brings into the security aspect. Security measures used currently by the leading players in the market were discussed, and their deficiencies were clearly shown. The authors have concluded that the fact that biometric features are not made use of by the iPhone and Android developers does not serve neither convenience of the users nor the security provided. Face Unlock introduced in late 2011 is the first biometric security measure available on those devices.

Hardware of the touch screen devices was then described, and biometric data possible to collect from it was discussed. Systems employing these features in other context have been shown, and hence the potential of this data on touch screen devices was demonstrated.

In the last part of this chapter, possible application of the biometric data available on touch screen devices in new authentication systems is discussed. Some of the new methods already experimentally implemented are described, others mentioned as possible research directions. Relevant approaches on different hardware, like mouse dynamics, were reviewed to assess their usability on the new type of devices. Hopefully, for the sake of security and the comfort of the users, the new security measures employing biometric features will be adapted widely and eventually become available as a part of the mobile operating systems.

Acknowledgement This work was partially supported by AGH University of Science and Technology in Cracow, grant no. 11.11.220.01.

References

1. Johnson EA (1965) Touch display: a novel input/output device for computers. Electron Lett 1(8):219–220. doi:10.1049/el:19650200
2. ABI Research (2008) Touch screen in mobile devices to deliver $5 billion next year. http://www.abiresearch.com/press/1231-Touch+Screens+in+Mobile+Devices+to+Deliver+$5+Billion+Next+Year. Accessed 14 May 2012
3. Earnings Releases. http://investor.apple.com/results.cfm. Accessed 29 May 2012

4. Allen M (2005) A day in the life of mobile data. Mobile security, British Computer Society. http://www.bcs.org/server.php?show=conWebDoc.2774. Accessed 14 May 2012
5. Burnett M, Kleiman D (2005) Perfect passwords. Syngress, Rockland, MA
6. Ivan A, Goodfellow J (1966). Improvements in or relating to customer-operated dispensing systems. UK patent #GB1197183. doi:10.1049/el:19650200
7. Bonneau J, Preibusch S, Anderson R (2012) A birthday present every eleven wallets? The security of customer-chosen banking PINs. Financial cryptography and data security. http://www.cl.cam.ac.uk/~jcb82/doc/BPA12-FC-banking_pin_security.pdf. Accessed 14 May 2012
8. Aviv AJ, Gibson K, Mossop E, Blaze M, Smith JM (2010) Smudge attacks on smartphone touch screens. Workshop on offensive technology. http://static.usenix.org/event/woot10/tech/full_papers/Aviv.pdf. Accessed 14 May 2012
9. Whisper Systems WhisperCore. http://whispersys.com/screenlock.html. Accessed 14 May 2012
10. Loy CC, Lim CP, Lai WK (2005) Pressure-based typing biometrics user authentication using the fuzzy ARTMAP. In: Neural network international conference on neural information processing. http://www.eecs.qmul.ac.uk/~ccloy/files/iconip_2005.pdf. Accessed 14 May 2012
11. n7player. http://www.n7mobile.com/. Accessed 15 Jun 2012
12. Gyroscope. http://en.wikipedia.org/wiki/Gyroscope. Accessed 15 May 2012
13. Hinckley K, Song H (2011). Sensor synaesthesia: touch in motion, and motion in touch. In: Proceedings of the 2011 annual conference on human factors in computing systems (CHI'11). ACM, New York, pp 801–810. doi:10.1145/1978942.1979059
14. Derawi MO, Nickel C, Bours P, Busch C (2010) Unobtrusive user-authentication on mobile phones using biometric gait recognition. In: Sixth international conference on intelligent information hiding and multimedia signal processing (IIH-MSP), Darmstadt, Germany, pp 306–311. doi: 10.1109/IIHMSP.2010.83
15. Harrison C, Schwarz J, Hudson SE (2011) TapSense: enhancing finger interaction on touch surfaces. In: Proceedings of the 24th annual ACM symposium on user interface software and technology, New York, pp 627–636. http://chrisharrison.net/projects/tapsense/tapsense.pdf. Accessed 15 May 2012
16. Azumio Instant Heart Rate. http://www.azumio.com/apps/heart-rate/. Accessed 14 May 2012
17. Spillane R (1975) Keyboard apparatus for personal identification. IBM Techn Disclosure Bull 17(3346). doi:10.1109/MSP.2004.89
18. Karatzouni S, Clarke NL (2007) Keystroke analysis for thumb-based keyboards on mobile devices. In: Proceedings of the 22nd IFIP international information security conference (IFIP SEC 2007), Sandton, South Africa, 14–16 May, pp 253–263. doi:10.1007/978-0-387-72367-9_22
19. Rybnik M, Tabędzki M, Saeed K (2008) A keystroke dynamics based system for user identification. In: Proceedings of the 7th international conference on computer information systems and industrial management applications: CISIM'08. IEEE Computer Society, pp 225–230. doi: 10.1109/CISIM.2008.8
20. Sae-Bae N, Ahmed K, Isbister K, Memon N (2012) Biometric-rich gestures: a novel approach to authentication on multi-touch devices. In: Proceedings of the 2012 ACM annual conference on human factors in computing systems (CHI'12). ACM, New York, pp 977–986. Doi:10.1145/2207676.2208543
21. Hashia S, Pollet C, Stamp M, Hall MQ (2005) On using mouse movements as a biometric. In: Proceedings of the international conference on computer science and its applications. http://www.cs.sjsu.edu/faculty/pollett/papers/shivanipaper.pdf. Accessed 15 May 2012
22. Tabędzki M, Saeed K (2005) New method to test mouse movement dynamics for human identification. In: KBIB 2005 conference, Tom I, computer science telemedicine systems, Czestochowa Technical University Press, Poland, pp 467–472 (in Polish). http://home.agh.edu.pl/~saeed/arts/2005%20KBIB.pdf. Accessed 15 May 2012
23. Gamboa H, Fred ALN, Jain AK (2007) Webbiometrics: user verification via web interaction. Biometrics Symp. doi:10.1109/BCC.2007.4430552

24. Citty J, Tapi DRH (2010) Touch-screen authentication using partitioned images. Elon University Technical Report. http://facstaff.elon.edu/dhutchings/papers/citty2010tapi.pdf. Accessed 15 May 2012
25. Myers L (2004) An exploration of voice biometrics. GSEC practical assignment. http://www.sans.org/reading_room/whitepapers/authentication/exploration-voice-biometrics_1436. Accessed 15 May 2012
26. De Luca A, Hang A, Brudy F, Lindner C, Hussmann H (2012) Touch me once and i know it's you!: implicit authentication based on touch screen patterns. In: Proceedings of the 2012 ACM annual conference on human factors in computing systems (CHI'12). ACM, New York, pp 987–996. doi:10.1145/2207676.2208544
27. Hazen TJ, Weinstein E, Park A (2003). Towards robust person recognition on handheld devices using face and speaker identification technologies. In: Proceedings of the 5th international conference on multimodal interfaces (ICMI'03). ACM, New York, pp 289–292. doi:10.1145/958432.958485

Chapter 6
New Proposals for Biometrics Using Eyes

Nobuyuki Nishiuchi and Masayuki Daikoku

Abstract Biometric identification using modalities based on the human body is being actively studied. For physical biometrics, such as fingerprints, veins, irises, and faces, which have been widely used for identification, spoofing is recognized as a serious vulnerability. In an attempt to prevent spoofing, here, we have proposed three new biometrics approaches based on various features of the eyes, namely, the behavioral characteristics of eye movement, three-dimensional shape of the iris surface, and a combination of measuring the contour of the upper eyelid during blinking, respectively. All three proposed methods have high accuracy of identification and are resistant to spoofing. In this chapter, the respective characteristics, experimental devices, algorithms of image processing, evaluative experiments, and summary of each proposed method are described. In the final section, the characteristics and accuracy of each method are compared and discussed.

6.1 Introduction

In recent years, in areas of financial security, immigration control, and the user management of personal computers, biometric identification based on features of the human body has attracted attention in place of conventional control systems, such as personal ID numbers and ID cards. The opportunity to use biometric identification increases exponentially due to the rapid development and spread of information and communication technologies. Numerous types of modalities based on the human body can potentially be used for biometric identification, which can be roughly divided into two types depending on the modality. The first type is physical biometrics, such as fingerprints, veins, irises, and the face, while the second is behavioral biometrics, such as hand motions, gate, voice, handwriting,

N. Nishiuchi (✉) • M. Daikoku
Faculty of System Design, Tokyo Metropolitan University, Tokyo, Japan
e-mail: nnishiuc@sd.tmu.ac.jp

K. Saeed and T. Nagashima (eds.), *Biometrics and Kansei Engineering*,
DOI 10.1007/978-1-4614-5608-7_6, © Springer Science+Business Media New York 2012

Table 6.1 Attributes of physical and behavioral biometrics

	Physical biometrics	Behavioral biometrics
Main advantage	High accuracy	Difficult to spoof
Main disadvantage	Easy to spoof	Low accuracy (low repeatability)

and keystroke [1]. Although the measurement of physical biometrics allows for high accuracy, they are relatively easy to spoof; in contrast, behavioral biometrics are resistant to spoofing but have low repeatability and accuracy (Table 6.1).

Physical biometrics are widely used as forms of identification; however, spoofing is recognized as a serious vulnerability of these systems. Yamada et al. [2], Hirabayashi [3], and Matsumoto et al. [4] pointed out this limitation of physical biometrics and demonstrated that existing technology can be used to obtain biological information from adhered surface residues and artificially replicate the biological information.

In this chapter, we propose three novel biometric approaches to identification that are effective against spoofing. The first approach is based on the concept of traditional behavioral biometrics, the second uses three-dimensional shapes, and the third combines physical biometrics with motion.

We have proposed and evaluated various methods of biometric identification based on the above ideas in an attempt to develop methods that are resistant to spoofing [5–8]. In this chapter, we introduce the following biometrics approaches that are based on human eyes:

1. Biometric identification using the behavioral features of eye movement.
2. Biometric identification using the three-dimensional shape of the iris surface.
3. Biometric identification combining the shape of the eyelid with blinking.

In the following sections, an outline of the features, algorithms for image processing and comparison, and evaluation of each proposed methods are described. Finally, the characteristics and accuracy of the three methods are compared and discussed.

6.2 Biometric Identification Using the Behavioral Features of Eye Movement

In this section, eye movement was applied as a behavioral feature for biometric identification. Specifically, eye movement was measured while the user followed a moving target. The frequency distribution of eye movement speed, which is considered to include individual behavioral features, such as saccades, was determined and compared. The saccade is a type of rapid eye movement that occurs when a user is unable to smoothly track the motion of a target. As saccades are not consciously controlled, it is impossible to mimic the motions of another individual's eye, making spoofing quite difficult.

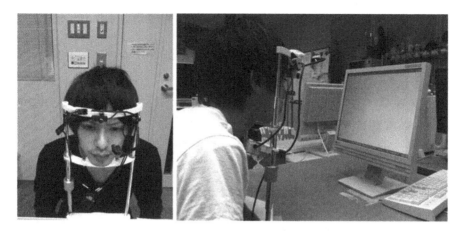

Fig. 6.1 The Eye Mark Recorder and retainer used to track eye movement (*left*) and a snapshot image of a user performing the measurement (*right*)

Previous research has shown that the appearance frequency of saccades changes in response to stress [9, 10]. Thus, in this study, a series experiments were first conducted under nonstress conditions in an attempt to extract individual biometric features and validate the possibility of using eye movement for behavioral biometric identification.

6.2.1   Experimental Device Configuration

An Eye Mark Recorder (EMR-8B; NAC Image Technology, Inc., Japan) was used to measure users' eye movement at a sampling frequency of 60 Hz and detection resolution of 0.1°. The Eye Mark Recorder was fixed to a retainer that was set on the user's face (Fig. 6.1). The moving target followed by users was developed independently using Microsoft Visual C++ software (Ver. 6). As shown in Fig. 6.2, the target moved in the shape of a saw waveform from the left to right side of the monitor (17-in. FlexScanL565; Eizo, Japan) for three cycles. The distance between the monitor and user's face was 40 cm. In the preliminary experiment, the movement speed of the target was fixed at 70°/s, as this is the optimal speed for the appearance of representative features of individual users (as described in Sect. 6.2.2).

6.2.2   Algorithm

From the obtained eye movement data, the frequency distribution of eye speed movement (class intervals: 30°/s) was determined. A representative graph is shown in Fig. 6.3, in which the horizontal and vertical axes represent the distribution of eye

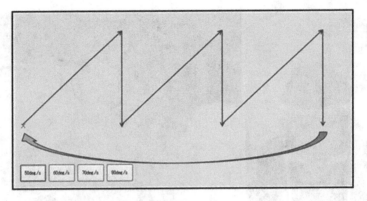

Fig. 6.2 Movement pattern of the target followed by users

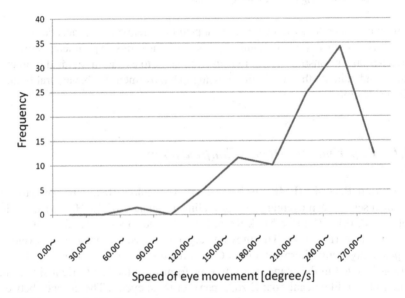

Fig. 6.3 Frequency distribution of eye movement speed

movement speed and appearance frequency, respectively. The data shown in Fig. 6.3 was used for the reference and probe data during the identification process, which determines whether a user is genuine or an imposter. For the comparison step, the correlation coefficient is used to compare the reference and probe data.

To detect the suitable target speed, a preliminary experiment was conducted. The frequency distribution of eye movement speed was compared among six subjects (A–F) using target speeds ranging from 50°/s to 80°/s (Fig. 6.4). Based

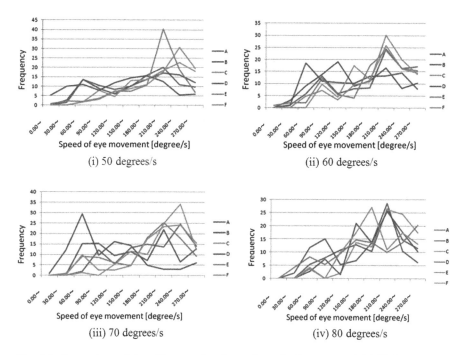

(i) 50 degrees/s (ii) 60 degrees/s

(iii) 70 degrees/s (iv) 80 degrees/s

Fig. 6.4 Comparison of six subjects used to detect the optimal target speed (**a**) 50°/s, (**b**) 60°/s, (**c**) 70°/s, (**d**) 80°/s

on this analysis, a target speed of 70°/s was used for all subsequent experiments, as this appeared to provide the most representative individual features of users.

6.2.3 Evaluative Experiment

To evaluate the proposed biometric identification method based on the behavioral features of eye movement, an evaluative experiment was conducted. Ten trials were conducted for each of the ten subjects, and the averaged of data of five randomly selected trials were used for the reference data, while the averaged data of the other five trials were used for the probe data.

The results of the comparisons for the data of all combinations of the ten subjects are shown in Fig. 6.5. In genuine trials, the minimum value of the correlation coefficient was 0.74, which is reasonably high for biometric identification.

The receiver operating characteristic (ROC) curve shown in Fig. 6.6 was plotted using the FRR (false rejection rate) and FAR (false acceptance rate) with the threshold value adjusted by units of 0.01. Using the ROC curve, the EER (equal error rate) value at which FAR becomes equal to FRR determined to be 0.17, which is close to the security level reported for behavioral biometric identifications. [1].

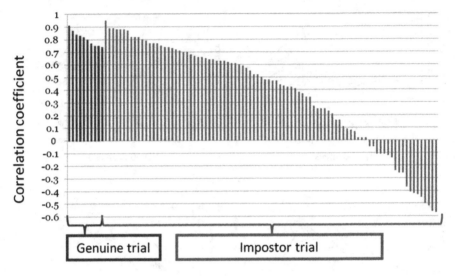

Fig. 6.5 Results of the comparisons of genuine and impostor trials

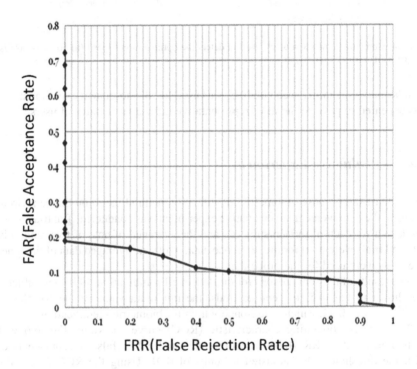

Fig. 6.6 ROC curve

6.2.4 Summary

A biometric identification method using eye movement was proposed and evaluated. As this method is based on the concept of traditional behavioral biometrics, it provides strong resistance to spoofing. Although there remains room for improvement with respect to accuracy, positive identification results were obtained in the evaluation experiments, showing the potential effectiveness of the proposed method. One of the reasons for the lower accuracy is the low repeatability of motion, which is an unavoidable limitation of behavioral biometrics. As mentioned above, measurements of motion as a behavioral characteristic may be susceptible to fluctuations as a result of stress or daily conditions. It is necessary to perform further analyses under different measurement conditions, days, and time zones.

6.3 Biometric Identification Using the Three-Dimensional Shape of the Iris Surface

Iris identification is a personal identification method that identifies unique patterns of the iris. Although this approach has the notable advantage of high accuracy, iris identification is vulnerable to spoofing [11]. Evaluation of commercially available iris identification systems using a genuine user's iris image printed on paper revealed that most identification systems registered the artificial iris, with several also able to identify it. This finding demonstrates that spoofing is possible with current iris identification systems.

In this section, we describe a novel biometric identification method based on the pattern of wrinkles resulting from the concavity and convexity of the iris surface, which forms a unique three-dimensional shape. As such, the pattern of shadows present on the iris differs according to the lighting angle, as shown in the images presented in Fig. 6.7. For current iris identification systems, when the gaze angle exceeds the device tolerance, an error occurs and identification must be reattempted. However, the method proposed here can be used to evaluate iris patterns from various angles (all images in Fig. 6.7). Although it is possible with present technology to generate an artificial iris using a two-dimensional image, it is impossible to produce a three-dimensional artificial iris. Therefore, the proposed method has strong resistance to spoofing.

6.3.1 Experimental Device Configuration

As described in Sect. 6.2.1, an Eye Mark Recorder was used to capture images of irises and was fixed on a retainer to set on the user's face. Using a monitor that was positioned 40 cm in front of the user, nine targets were shown consecutively in

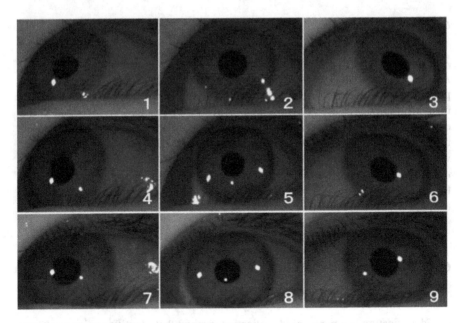

Fig. 6.7 Captured iris images oriented in nine directions

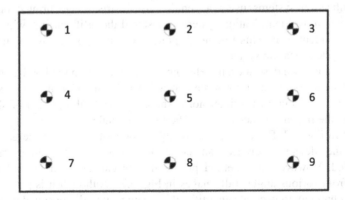

Fig. 6.8 The nine targets that appeared on the monitor, shown here in numerical order

numerical order (Fig. 6.8), and images of the iris were captured at nine different angles (trials) while the user gazed at each of the nine targets.

Although iris images were captured for nine trials in this experiment, if multiple devices are used, it would be possible to install nine cameras to simultaneously capture iris images from nine different angles. As an alternative configuration, a single camera could be used to capture images of the iris under lighting from different nine directions.

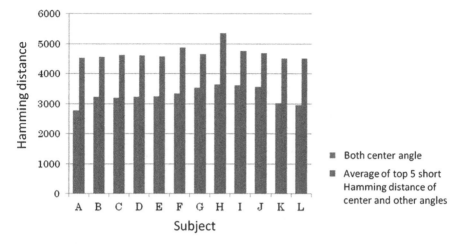

Fig. 6.9 Results of experiment 1: comparison of iris patterns determined from the center and eight other capture angles

6.3.2 Algorithm

First, eight iris images, excluding the center image (no. 5) shown in Fig. 6.7, were converted by projective transformation as a preprocessing step. Nine iris codes were then extracted using the general image processing for iris identification [12], which involved noise cancelation, polar coordinate transformation, and binarization. The Hamming distance was used for comparison of the reference and probe iris codes.

In the preliminary experiment, it was apparent that the shortest Hamming distance (representing the highest degree of similarity) differed among users depending on the gaze angle. Therefore, the five shortest Hamming distances were used for reference data out of the nine examined gaze angles.

6.3.3 Evaluative Experiment

Two experiments were conducted to evaluate the proposed biometric identification method. In experiment 1, two sets of iris images at nine gaze angles were captured for twelve different subjects (Fig. 6.9). The blue bars in Fig. 6.9 show the Hamming distance between the two iris patterns of the center angle (image no. 5), which is equivalent to a typical comparison of current iris identification systems. The red bars in Fig. 6.9 show the average of the five shortest Hamming distances for comparisons of iris patterns obtained from the center and other eight angles. When the threshold value for the identification was set at 3,640, which was based on the maximum Hamming distance of the center angle (Fig. 6.9, blue bars), the iris

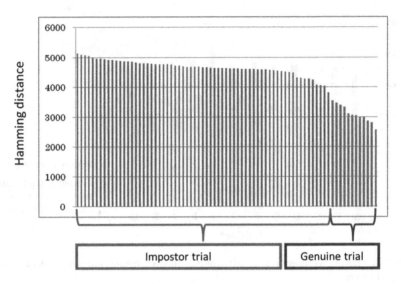

Fig. 6.10 Results of experiment 2: comparison of genuine and impostor trials for the proposed method based on the three-dimensional shape of the iris surface

patterns generated from the center and other capture angles were clearly divided. This finding indicates that the measurement of iris patterns from various eye angles, with the exception of the center angle, can be used as a novel iris identification method.

In experiment 2, the average of the five shortest Hamming distances (five highest degrees of similarity; Fig. 6.10, blue bars) for the iris patterns obtained using the same angles in the genuine trial were determined. The red bars in Fig. 6.10 show the results of the impostor trial. When the threshold value for identification was set at 3,537 based on the maximum Hamming distance of the genuine user (Fig. 6.10, blue bars), both FRR and FAR were 0%. Thus, the proposed method has reasonably high accuracy.

6.3.4 Summary

The proposed identification method is based on the analysis of the three-dimensional shape of the iris surface. As it is extremely difficult to generate a three-dimensional artificial iris, our proposed method has strong resistance to spoofing. Moreover, the evaluative experiment demonstrated that the method also has quite high accuracy. Despite these advantages, the users required considerable time and effort to gaze in several different directions during the image capture process, which are negative attributes compared with current iris identification systems. However, further improvements to our method can be achieved through the use of multiple cameras or lighting from various angles.

6.4   Biometric Identification Combining the Shape of Eyelid with Blinks

In addition to the two methods described above, we are actively developing a biometric identification method that combines physical characteristics and motion. Notably, only dynamic parameters – no behavioral characteristics – are extracted from the motion of a body part for use in identification. Practically speaking, biological data are compared only when the dynamic parameter of probe data is consistent with that of the reference data in the comparison process. Thus, the use of a dynamic parameter, represented by the motion of a body part, provides strength against spoofing, while the measurement of biological data, represented by physical characteristics, allows for high identification accuracy.

In the combined approach used here, the contour of the eyelid was collected as the biological data, while the process of blinking [13, 14] represented the dynamic parameter, specifically the degree of eye opening (length between top and bottom eyelids) during blinking. By using blinking for biometric identification, spoofing is difficult because it is beyond the impostor's capability to imitate the reflexive motion of blinking.

6.4.1   Experimental Device Configuration

The experimental system used to capture images of blinking is shown in Fig. 6.11. After the user's face was placed in the retainer, temporally continuous eye images during blinking were obtained using a high-speed camera (FASTCAM-PCI; Photron Inc., Japan) operating at 1,000 frames/s. A series of the images captured using this system is shown in Fig. 6.12.

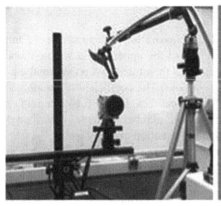

Fig. 6.11 Experimental setup for capturing eye images during blinking

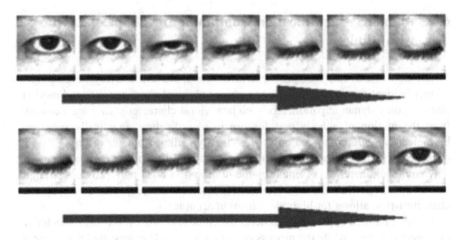

Fig. 6.12 Series of images showing the blinking of a subject's right eye (*the arrows* show time flow)

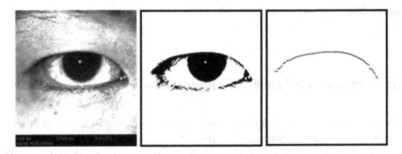

Fig. 6.13 Binarization and edge extraction of the upper eyelid

6.4.2　Algorithm

Obtained images were first processed using binarization to separate the eye and skin areas into a binary image. The edge pixels of the upper eyelid were obtained by edge extraction (Fig. 6.13), and the edge was then fitted to a polynomial equation that utilize quadratic and biquadratic equations. The coefficient of the polynomial equation was used for the analysis of biological data. Figure 6.14 is a graph based on the image processing described above, with number of frames described on the x-axis and the coefficient of the polynomial equation on the y-axis.

Given that the repeatability of blinking could not be confirmed, we were unable to use the original biological data of the eyelid contour in the comparison step. Therefore, these data (Fig. 6.14) were normalized using the degree of eye opening (dynamic parameter), which was determined by measuring the length between the upper and lower eyelids. Specifically, the x-axis (the number of frames) of the graph in Fig. 6.14 was ordered based on the degree of eye opening (Fig. 6.15).

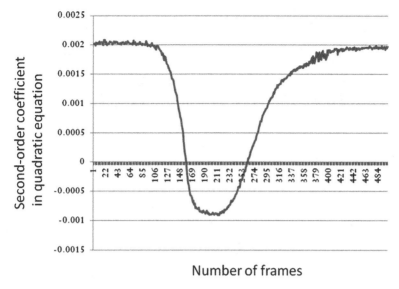

Fig. 6.14 Changes in the second-order coefficient of the quadratic equation for blinking

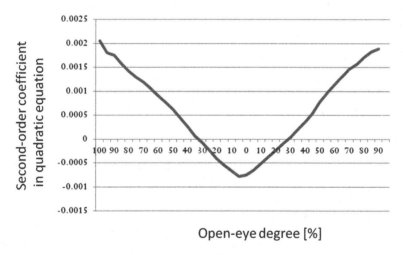

Fig. 6.15 Changes in the second-order coefficient of quadratic equation for degree of eye opening

The contour of the eyelid lacks sufficient uniqueness for identification at the individual level. However, given that the blinking reflex in humans is frequently unconscious, we proposed a verification system integrating data for several consecutive blinks, rather than a single blink. Normalized biological data from five trials were integrated based on the degree of eye opening, and these data were subsequently used in the comparison step. Without integration, the difference between the normalized data of genuine and impostor trials was not clearly was discernible, and less similarity across trials was observed for genuine data. By integrating the

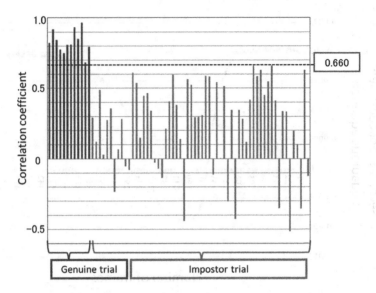

Fig. 6.16 Experimental results on identification combing the eyelid shape with blinks

data, a remarkable difference was discernible between the normalized data of genuine and impostor trials, and much greater similarity across trials was noted for genuine data. In the comparison step, the correlation coefficient between reference and probe data was used.

6.4.3 Evaluative Experiment

To evaluate the proposed biometric identification method, two experimental trials were conducted. Twelve data sets were obtained by collecting two samples for each of the six subjects. Two trials were conducted for twelve samples used as the reference and probe data.

The best comparative results were obtained using a fourth-order coefficient in the biquadratic equation. The analysis results for all possible combinations of the 12 sets of sample data are shown in Fig. 6.16. When the threshold value was set at 0.660, the genuine user and impostor were clearly discernible. In the genuine trials, the lowest correlation coefficient value was 0.68, which is considered reasonably high.

6.4.4 Summary

We developed a biometric identification method that combines measurements of an eyelid shape and blinking. This approach is based on the concept of evaluating

Table 6.2 Comparison of the EER of the three proposed biometric identification methods

	(1) Behavioral characteristics of eye movement	(2) 3-D shape of the iris surface	(3) Shape of eyelid during blinking
ERR	0.17	0	0
Number of subjects	10	12	12

biological data of a physical characteristic (eyelid contour) in combination with a dynamic parameter extracted from the motion of a body part (eyelid during blinking). On its own, the contour of the eyelid lacks sufficient uniqueness for identification. However, given that the blinking reflex in humans is predominantly unconscious, we proposed a verification system integrating data collected during several blinking events, rather than a single blink alone. Based on the findings of the evaluative experiment, the proposed method appears to have high accuracy and high resistance against spoofing.

6.5   Discussion and Conclusion

In this chapter, three new methods of biometric identification based on the following characteristics of the eye were proposed: (1) behavioral features of eye movement, (2) three-dimensional shape of the iris surface, and (3) contour of the eyelid during blinking.

Each proposed method has distinctive characteristics and advantages for identification. As the first method is based on traditional behavioral biometrics, it has lower accuracy than the other two methods due to the low inherent repeatability of behavioral characteristics. The second method is a trade-off between usability and hardware costs; however, it displayed high accuracy and was resistant spoofing. The basic concept of modeling the three-dimensional shape of the iris can be applied to other modalities, such as facial features, hand geometry, and the ear. The third method had the highest accuracy because of the nonuse of behavioral characteristics for identification; rather, the motion of the eyelid during blinking was measured as a dynamic parameter and was combined with data of the eyelid shape for use in identification. As the contour of the eyelid lacks sufficient uniqueness among individuals, in other words, it has low complexity compared with fingerprints or vein patterns; the data collected from multiple blinks were integrated for identification. The basic concept of this method can be applied to other combinations of physical characteristics and motion, such as the geometry and bending motion of fingers, vein patterns and rotating motion of the hand, and shape of the lip outline and speech.

Finally, the accuracies of each method are compared in Table 6.2, showing that methods (2) and (3) had the most promise, with an ERR rate of 0%. From the viewpoint of the accuracy of identification, proposed methods (2) and (3) are in the initial stages of development and are potential candidates for further development.

References

1. Yampolskiy RV, Govindaraju V (2008) Behavioural biometrics: a survey and classification. Int J Biometrics 1(1):81–113
2. Yamada K, Matsumoto H, Matsumoto T (2000) Can we make artificial fingers that fool fingerprint systems? Technical report of institute of electronics, information, and communication engineers, ISEC2000-45, pp 159–166
3. Hirabayashi M, Tanabe T, Matsumoto T (2004) Can we make artificial fingers that fool fingerprint systems? (Part VI). Technical report of institute of electronics, information, and communication engineers, IT2003-99, ISEC2003-139, WBS2003-217, pp 151–154
4. Matsumoto T (2006) Biometric authentication systems: vulnerability of biometric authentication – on the issue of physiological spoofing. Inform Process Soc Jpn (IPSJ Mag) 47(6):589–594
5. Nishiuchi N, Komatsu S, Yamanaka K (2010) Biometric verification using the motion of fingers: a combination of physical and behavioural biometrics. Int J Biometrics 2(3):222–235
6. Nishiuchi N (2010) Combining dynamic data with physical biometric verification counteract spoofing. J Med Inform Technol 15:11–18
7. Yamagishi M, Nishiuchi N, Yamanaka K (2008) Hybrid fingerprint authentication using artifact-metrics. Int J Biometrics (IJBM) 1(2):160–172
8. Nishiuchi N, Soya H (2011) Cancelable biometric identification by combining biological data with artifacts. Intech book, Chap 7, pp 125–142
9. Mizushina H, Sakamoto K, Kanako H (2011) The relationship between psychological stress induced by task workload and dynamic characteristics of saccadic eye movements. Technical report of institute of information, and communication engineers, J94-D(10), pp 1640–1651
10. Wright N, McGown A (2001) Vigilance on the civil flight deck: incidence of sleepiness and sleep during long-haul flights and associated changes in physiological parameters. Ergonomics 44(1):82–106
11. Mastumoto T, Sato K (2005) On the set of biometric test objects for security evaluation of iris authentication systems. IPSJ SIG Tech Rep 2005(122):55–60
12. Hosoya M (2006) Identification system by iris recognition. Trans Jpn Soc Med Biol Eng 44(1):33–39
13. Westeyn T, Starner T (2004) Recognising song-based blink patterns: applications for restricted and universal access. In: Sixth IEEE international conference on automatic face and gesture recognition, Seoul, Korea
14. Westeyn T, Pesti P, Park K, Starner T (2005) Biometric identification using song-based eye blink patterns. Hum Comput Interac Int (HCII), Las Vegas, NV

Chapter 7
Local Texture Descriptors on Biometric Detection: New Local Quaternary Pattern Descriptors and Case Study on Eye Detection

Jiayu Gu and Chengjun Liu

Abstract This chapter presents a new local texture descriptor, local quaternary patterns (LQP), and its extension, feature local quaternary patterns (FLQP). The LQP, which encodes four relationships of local texture, includes more information of local texture than the local binary patterns (LBP) and local ternary patterns (LTP). The FLQP which encodes both local and feature information is expected to perform better than the LQP for texture description and pattern recognition. To reduce the size of feature dimensions and histograms of both LQP and FLQP, a new coding schema is proposed to split the LQP and FLQP into two binary codes: the upper and lower binary codes. As a result, the total possible values of split LQP and FLQP are reduced to 512. The feasibility of the proposed LQP and FLQP methods is demonstrated on an eye detection problem. Experimental results using the BioID database show that both the FLQP and the LQP methods archive better eye detection performance than the feature LTP, the LTP, the feature LBP, and the LBP methods. Specifically, the FLQP method achieves by far the highest eye detection rate among all the competing methods. In addition, the FLQP method has the lowest average relative distance error γ, while the average γ of the LQP, the feature LTP, the LTP, the feature LBP, and the LBP methods are 5.8%, 7.5%, 9.7%, 6.9%, and 125.6% higher than the average γ of the FLQP method, respectively.

7.1 Introduction

Local binary patterns (LBP) have recently become a popular method in texture description for content-based image search and feature extraction for pattern recognition and computer vision. The most important properties of the LBP operator are its tolerance against illumination and computational simplicity, which makes it possible to analyze images in real world in real time.

J. Gu (✉) • C. Liu
New Jersey Institute of Technology, University Heights, Newark, NJ, USA

K. Saeed and T. Nagashima (eds.), *Biometrics and Kansei Engineering*,
DOI 10.1007/978-1-4614-5608-7_7, © Springer Science+Business Media New York 2012

Wang and He [1] introduced the concept of texture unit and texture spectrum. A texture unit of a pixel is represented by a 3×3 neighborhood with three possible values: 0, 1, and 2. The three values represent three possible relationships between the center pixel and its neighbors: "less than," "equal to," or "greater than." As a result, there are $3^8 = 6,561$ possible texture units in total. The large number of texture units poses a computational challenge. To reduce the computational burden, Ojala et al. [2–4] and Gong et al. [5] proposed a method that applies two relationships: "less than or equal to" or "greater than" that are represented by two possible values: 0 and 1. The method thus reduces the total number of texture units from 6,561 to 256. Ojala et al. [2] named the 256 possible texture units local binary patterns or LBP.

Tan and Triggs [6] argued that the original LBP tends to be sensitive to noise, especially in near-uniform image regions, because it thresholds exactly at the value of the central pixel. To solve the problem, they proposed 3-valued codes, called local ternary patterns (LTP). In LTP, neighbor pixels are compared with an interval $[-r, +r]$ around the value of the center pixel. A neighbor pixel is assigned 1, 0, or -1, if its value is above $+ r$, in the interval $[-r, +r]$, or below $-r$, respectively. Because the radius r is not changed with the gray scale, the LTP is no longer a strictly gray-scale invariant texture description and has less tolerance against illumination than LBP. Similar to the text unit method, the LTP has 6,561 possible values as well, which not only poses a computational challenge but also leads to sparse histograms. To solve these problems, a coding scheme is introduced to split a LTP code into two binary codes, the positive one (PLTP) and the negative one (NLTP). Therefore, the total number of possible values of two split binary codes is reduced to 512. The LTP doubles the size of feature dimensions and histograms. Some of experiments in [6, 7] show that LTP and LBP achieved similar results for face and facial expression recognition, although LTP has a higher computational cost than LBP.

To improve the performance of LTP, we present in this chapter a new local texture descriptor, local quaternary patterns (LQP), and its extension, feature local quaternary patterns (FLQP). The LQP encodes four relationships of local texture, and therefore, it includes more information of local texture than the LBP and the LTP. To reduce the size of feature dimensions and histograms of LQP, a coding scheme is introduced to split each LQP code into two binary codes, the upper LQP (ULQP) and the lower LQP (LLQP). The possible LQP values are reduced to 512. We [8, 9] have introduced a new feature local binary pattern (FLBP) method to improve upon the LBP approach. In this chapter, we further extend LQP to FLQP and demonstrate that FLQP improves upon LQP and other competing methods, such as LBP, FLBP, LTP, and feature LTP (FLTP). The FLQP which encodes both local and feature information is expected to perform better than the LQP for texture description and pattern analysis. We further show that the FLQP code can be split into two binary codes as well, the upper FLQP (UFLQP) and the lower FLQP (LFLQP). To demonstrate the feasibility of the proposed LQP and FLQP methods, we apply them to eye detection on the BioID database. Experimental results show that both FLQP and LQP achieve better eye detection performance than FLTP,

LTP, FLBP, and LBP. The FLQP method achieves the highest eye detection rates when the relative distance error $\gamma \leq 0.25, 0.1$, and 0.05. The FLQP method has the lowest average γ. The average γ of the LQP, FLTP, LTP, FLBP, and LBP methods are 5.8%, 7.5%, 9.7%, 6.9%, and 125.6% higher than the average γ of FLQP method, respectively.

7.2   Background

The local binary patterns (LBP) have been widely applied in many applications, such as face recognition [6, 10–12], face detection [13, 14], and facial expression analysis [15–19]. Many extensions of the original LBP have been proposed to improve the performance. Jin et al. [20] argued that original LBP might not include all the local structure information as the central pixel is not considered in the LBP coding. They presented an improved LBP (ILBP) for face detection, which compares all the pixels including the center pixel in a 3×3 neighborhood with the mean of the pixels in the same neighborhood. As a result, the ILBP can represent 511 patterns (2^9-1, as all zeros and all ones are the same). Huang et al. [21] proposed an active shape model that combines with an extended LBP representation for localizing and representing key facial points. The extended version of local binary patterns (ELBP) encodes on both facial images and the gradient magnitude images of the face images. A modified local binary pattern (MLBP) [22] is introduced for face detection by adding a set of spatial templates. Instead of comparing with each pixel of its neighborhood, the central pixel compares with two pixels in the neighborhood which are paired according to the spatial templates. Eight main spatial templates are defined in MLBP. Each of the spatial templates corresponds to one binary digit. If the value of center pixel is greater than the values of both pixels in a pair, their corresponding binary digit is assigned to 1, otherwise 0. A multi-block LBP (MB-LBP) is introduced for face recognition [23] and detection [24]. The MB-LBP compares the average intensity of the central subregion with its neighboring subregions. The original LBP can be regarded as a special case of the MB-LBP, where the central and neighboring subregions contain only one pixel. The neighboring pixels in the original LBP are defined on a circle. An elongated LBP [25] with neighboring pixels lying on an ellipse is introduced for face recognition. The experimental results demonstrate that the elongated LBP outperforms the original LBP for face recognition. Fu and Wei [26] introduced the centralized binary patterns (CBP). The CBP compares two neighbor pixels at the same diameter of the circle and also compares the central pixel with the mean of all the pixels (including the central pixel) in the neighborhood. The CBP needs only five binary digits which represent the relationships of four pairs of the neighbor pixels on the same diameter and the central pixel with the mean of all the pixels. The experiments for facial expression recognition show that the CBP has better performance than the LBP although it includes less relationships of local texture.

Tan and Triggs [6] argued that the original LBP tends to be sensitive to noise, especially in near-uniform image regions. They introduced the three-valued code, the LTP to solve the problem. They compared the performance of LBP and LTP on face recognition using different image preprocessing methods. Their results show that LTP yields best results using their proposed preprocessing method. However, their experiments also shows that the LBP archives better results than LTP using some other competing preprocessing methods. Gritti et al. [7] compared the performance of different local texture features, including LBP and LTP for facial expression recognition. Their results show that the LBP archived the best overall performance. The performance of LTP depends on r, the radius of the interval around the value of the central pixel. It is a challenging task to find a best r. Akhloufi and Bendada [27] proposed the local adaptive ternary pattern (LATP). The LATP computes r using the mean and the standard deviation of the local region. The results show the LATP performs better than LTP in face recognition. Liao et al. [28] proposed a scale invariant local ternary pattern (SILTP). In the SILTP, r is determined by the value of center pixel and is gray-scale invariant. The results show that SILTP is effective for handling illumination variations.

Eye detection plays an important role in automatic face recognition and eye tracking. Eyes have unique geometric and photometric characteristics, which provide important and reliable information for their localization. Some progress on eye detection has been made recently; however, eye detection is still a challenging research topic due to the difficult factors caused by occlusion, closed eye, illumination variation, eye size and orientations, etc. There are three major approaches for eye detection, template-based, distinctive feature-based, and photometric appearance-based. In the template-based approach [29–31], an eye template that is constructed based on the eye shape is used to search an eye in an image. The template-based methods are usually time consuming. The distinctive feature-based methods [32–38] aim to detect the eyes by a set of distinctive features around the eyes, including edges, the intensity of iris, and the color distribution. The photometric appearance-based approaches [39–41] usually collect a large amount of training data representing the eyes of different subjects, with different face orientations and under different illumination conditions. A classifier or regression model is then constructed for eye detection.

7.3 Local Binary Patterns and Local Ternary Patterns

Before we introduce our local quaternary patterns (LQP) and feature local quaternary patterns (FLQP), we briefly review LBP and LTP for comparison. Local binary patterns or LBP define a gray-scale invariant texture description by comparing a center pixel used as a threshold, with those pixels in its local neighborhood [2–4]. Specifically, for a 3×3 neighborhood of a pixel $\mathbf{p} = [x, y]'$, each neighbor is labeled by a number from 0 to 7 as shown in Fig. 7.1. The neighbors of the pixel $\mathbf{p}$ thus may be defined as follows:

Fig. 7.1 The 3 × 3 neighborhood of a pixel p and the label of its neighbors

0	1	2
7	p	3
6	5	4

Fig. 7.2 Computing the LBP code for the center pixel

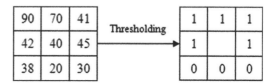

$$N(\mathbf{p}, i) = [x_i, y_i]^t, i = 0, 1, 2, \ldots, 7 \qquad (7.1)$$

where i is the number used to label a neighbor. The value of the LBP code of a pixel $\mathbf{p}(x, y)$ is calculated as follows:

$$LBP(\mathbf{p}) = \sum_{i=0}^{7} 2^i S_{lbp}\{G[N(\mathbf{p}, i)], G(\mathbf{p})\} \qquad (7.2)$$

where $G(\mathbf{p})$ and $G[N(\mathbf{p}, i)]$ are the gray levels of the pixel $\mathbf{p}$ and its neighbor $N(\mathbf{p}, i)$, respectively. S_{lbp} is a threshold function that is defined as follows:

$$S_{lbp}(g_i, g_c) = \begin{cases} 1, & \text{if } g_i \geq g_c; \\ 0, & \text{otherwise.} \end{cases} \qquad (7.3)$$

Figure 7.2 shows an example of computing the LBP code for the center pixel whose gray level is 40.

Tan and Triggs proposed a local ternary pattern or LTP operator [6]. In LTP, the threshold function S_{ltp} is defined as follows:

$$S_{ltp}(g_i, g_c, r) = \begin{cases} 1, & \text{if } g_i \geq g_c + r \\ 0, & \text{if } |g_i - g_c| < r \\ -1, & \text{if } g_i \leq g_c - r \end{cases} \qquad (7.4)$$

where r is the radius of the interval around the gray level of the central pixel. Figure 7.3 shows an example of the computation of the LTP. The gray level of the central pixel is 40, and r is 5. A neighbor pixel is assigned to 1, 0, or −1, if its gray

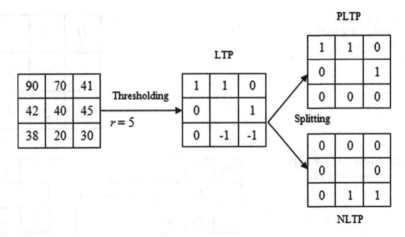

Fig. 7.3 Computing the *LTP* and splitting it to two binary codes, *PLTP* and *NLTP*

level is greater than or equal to 45, between 44 and 36, or less than or equal to 35, respectively. The total number of the possible LTP codes is 6561, which leads to a large size for the feature dimension and sparse histograms of the LTP codes. To solve the problem, an LTP code is split into two binary codes: the positive and negative halves as shown in Fig. 7.3. The positive half of LTP (PLTP) is obtained by replacing −1 with 0. The negative half of LTP (NLTP) is obtained by first replacing the 1 with 0 and then changing −1 to 1. Thus, an LTP code can be represented by two binary codes. As a result, the total number of the split LTP codes is reduced to 512.

7.4 Local Quaternary Patterns

We now present our new local quaternary patterns (LQP) which encode four relationships of local texture, and therefore, it includes more information of local texture than LBP and LTP. The threshold function of LQP is defined using two binary digits as follows:

$$S_{lqp}(g_i, g_c, r) = \begin{cases} 11, & \text{if } g_i \geq g_c + r \\ 10, & \text{if } g_c \leq g_i < g_c + r \\ 01, & \text{if } g_c - r \leq g_i < g_c \\ 00, & \text{if } g_i < g_c - r \end{cases} \tag{7.5}$$

where r is the radius of the interval around the value of the central pixel and may be defined as follows:

$$r = c + \tau g_c \tag{7.6}$$

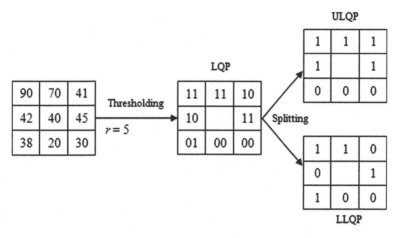

Fig. 7.4 Computing the *LQP* and splitting it to two binary codes *ULQP* and *LLQP*

where c is a constant and τ is a parameter to control the contribution of g_c to r. To reduce the total number of codes, an LQP code can be split into two binary codes, the upper and lower halves as shown in Fig. 7.4. The upper half of LQP (ULQP) is obtained by extracting the first digit of LQP code. The lower half of LTP (LLQP) is obtained by extracting the second digit of LQP code. Thus, the total number of LQP codes is reduced to 512.

From (7.5) we can derive the threshold functions of ULQP and LLQP, S_{ulqp} and S_{llqp} which may be formulated as follows:

$$S_{ulqp}(g_i, g_c) = S_{lbp}(g_i, g_c) \qquad (7.7)$$

$$S_{llqp}(g_i, g_c, r) = \begin{cases} 1, & \text{if } g_i \geq g_c + (-1)^{[1-S_{lbp}(g_i,g_c)]}r; \\ 0, & \text{otherwise.} \end{cases} \qquad (7.8)$$

The threshold function of ULQP S_{ulqp} is equal to the threshold function of LBP and does not depend on the r. The ULQP and LLQP are therefore defined as follows:

$$ULQP(\mathbf{p}) = LBP(\mathbf{p}) \qquad (7.9)$$

$$LLQP(\mathbf{p}) = \sum_{i=0}^{7} 2^i S_{llqp}\{G[N(\mathbf{p}, i)], G(\mathbf{p})\} \qquad (7.10)$$

Note that the ULQP is the same as the LBP. Figure 7.4 shows an example of the computation of the LQP. The 3 × 3 neighborhood is the same as the one shown in Fig. 7.2. The gray level of the central pixel is 40, and r is 5. The ULQP code is

1111001 that is equal to the LBP code shown in Fig. 7.2. For LLQP, a pixel is assigned 1 if it is greater than or equal to 45 or it is less than 40 and greater than or equal to 35, otherwise is assigned 0. The LLQP code is 11010010.

7.5 Feature Local Quaternary Patterns

Our new feature local quaternary patterns or FLQP can be split into two binary codes, the upper half of FLQP (UFLQP) and the lower half of FLQP (LFLQP) using the threshold functions defined in (7.7) and (7.8), respectively. The UFLQP is equivalent to our feature LBP or FLBP. FLBP generalizes the LBP approach by introducing feature pixels, which may be broadly defined by, for example, the edge pixels, the intensity peaks, or valleys in an image. FLBP, which encodes both local and feature information, has been shown more effective than LBP for texture description and pattern recognition, such as eye detection. Two new concepts, True Center (TC) and Virtual Center (VC), are used to define FLBP.

Definition 1 True Center (TC) is the center pixel of a given neighborhood.

Definition 2 Virtual Center (VC) is a pixel used to replace the center pixel of a given neighborhood.

Another important concept is distance vector [42], which is applied to determine the locations of TC and VC. In a binary image, each pixel assumes one of two discrete values: 0 or 1. While pixels of value 0 are called the background pixels, pixels of 1 are called feature pixels. Let $\mathbf{p}$ and $\mathbf{q}$ represent a pixel and its nearest feature point in a binary image, respectively. The distance vector of $\mathbf{p}$ pointing to $\mathbf{q}$ is defined below:

$$\mathbf{dv}(\mathbf{p}) = \mathbf{q} - \mathbf{p},$$
$$\mathbf{q} = \arg\min_{\mathbf{r} \in F} \delta(\mathbf{p}, \mathbf{r}) \tag{7.11}$$

where F is the set of feature pixels of the binary image and δ is a distance metric. Figure 7.5 shows an example of a binary image and its distance vector field (DVF) that is derived by assigning to each pixel $\mathbf{p}$ of a vector $\mathbf{dv}(\mathbf{p})$ that points to its nearest feature point $\mathbf{q}$. Note that the upper left pixel has coordinates $(1, 1)$ in a Cartesian coordinate system with a horizontal axis pointing to the right and a vertical axis pointing downward. In particular, the binary image in Fig. 7.5a has only one feature pixel at the location $(2, 2)$. Figure 7.5b displays the DVF where the numbers are derived using (7.11).

The TC, which may be any pixel on the path pointed by $\mathbf{dv}(\mathbf{p})$ from $\mathbf{p}$ to $\mathbf{q}$, is defined below:

$$C_t(\mathbf{p}) = \mathbf{p} + \alpha_t \mathbf{dv}(\mathbf{p}) \tag{7.12}$$

a

0	0	0	0
0	1	0	0
0	0	0	0
0	0	0	0

b

1,1	0,1	-1,1	-2,1
1,0	0,0	-1,0	-2,0
1,-1	0,-1	-1,-1	-2,-1
1,-2	0,-2	-1,-2	-2,-2

Fig. 7.5 (**a**) An example of a binary image with only one feature pixel at the location (2, 2); (**b**) distance vector field (DVF) where the numbers are derived using (7.11)

a

70	1	2	1	3	2	7
1	50	45	66	1	4	9
3	56	30	77	1	2	8
1	58	62	64	20	31	1
2	1	1	34	60	26	2
4	3	4	22	28	90	1
9	5	8	1	2	1	40

b

0	0	0	0	0	0	0
0	0	0	0	0	0	0
0	0	0	0	0	0	0
0	0	0	0	0	0	0
0	0	0	0	0	0	0
0	0	0	0	0	1	0
0	0	0	0	0	0	0

Fig. 7.6 (**a**) A gray-scale image; (**b**) the binary feature image

where $\alpha_t \in [0, 1]$ is a parameter that controls the location of the TC. The VC, which may be any pixel on the path pointed by **dv(p)** from **p** to **q** as well, is defined below:

$$C_v(\mathbf{p}) = \mathbf{p} + \alpha_v \mathbf{dv}(\mathbf{p}) \tag{7.13}$$

where $\alpha_v \in [0, 1]$ is a parameter that controls the location of the VC. The general form of FLBP is defined below:

$$FLBP(\mathbf{p}) = \sum_{i=0}^{7} 2^i S_{lbp}\{G[N(C_t(\mathbf{p}), i)], G[C_v(\mathbf{p})]\} \tag{7.14}$$

where $N(C_t(\mathbf{p}), i)$ represents the ith neighbors of the TC of **p**. $G[C_v(\mathbf{p})]$ and $G[N(C_t(\mathbf{p}), i)]$ are the gray levels of the VC and the ith neighbor of the TC, respectively.

Now, we demonstrate how to compute the FLBP code. Specifically, Fig. 7.6a shows a gray-scale image, and we assume that the upper left pixel is at location (1, 1) in a Cartesian coordinate system with a horizontal axis pointing to the right and a vertical axis pointing downward. Here we define the pixels whose gray level is greater than 80 as feature pixels. The binary feature image of Fig. 7.6a is

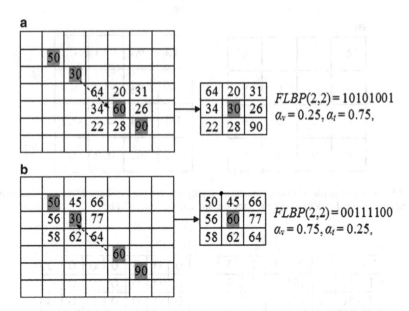

Fig. 7.7 (a) The TC ($\alpha_t = 0.75$), the VC ($\alpha_v = 0.25$), and the FLBP code for the pixel at (2, 2); (b) the TC ($\alpha_t = 0.25$), the VC ($\alpha_v = 0.75$), and the *FLBP* code for the pixel at (2, 2)

shown in Fig. 7.6b. The pixel with the coordinates (6, 6) is the only one with gray level greater than 80, and it becomes the only feature pixel in the binary image.

Next, we illustrate how to compute FLBP in Fig. 7.7. The gray-scale image and the feature pixel are the same as Fig. 7.6. In Fig. 7.7, we only display the gray levels of the pixels involved in the computation. We select the pixel **p** at (2, 2) to demonstrate FLBP computation. The nearest feature pixel of **p** is the one at (6, 6) as shown in Fig. 7.6b. First, we compute the distance vector **dv** of **p**. Note that we use **dv** to replace **dv(p)** for simplicity. Given $\mathbf{p} = [2, 2]^t$, $\mathbf{q} = [6, 6]^t$, we have $\mathbf{dv} = \mathbf{q} - \mathbf{p} = [4, 4]^t$. Then we determine the locations of TC and VC and compute FLBP. In Fig. 7.7a, given $\alpha_v = 0.25$ and $\alpha_t = 0.75$, we have $Cv(\mathbf{p}) = \mathbf{p} + \alpha_v\mathbf{dv} = [3, 3]^t$, $Ct(\mathbf{p}) = \mathbf{p} + \alpha_t\mathbf{dv} = [5, 5]^t$. Therefore, the VC is the pixel at location (3, 3), and the TC is the pixel at location (5, 5). According to (7.14), we replace the gray level 60 of TC at location (5, 5) by the gray level 30 of VC at location (3, 3) and threshed the neighbors of the TC. We have the binary FLBP code: FLBP(2, 2) = 10101001 when $\alpha_v = 0.25$ and $\alpha_t = 0.75$. Figure 7.7b shows another example of the FLBP(2, 2) computation when $\alpha_v = 0.75$ and $\alpha_t = 0.25$. Similarly, we locate the TC in the pixel at location (3, 3) and the VC in the pixel at location (5, 5). The binary FLBP code becomes FLBP(2,2) = 00111100 when $\alpha_v = 0.75$ and $\alpha_t = 0.25$.

As our FLBP method encodes both local and feature information, we present a new feature pixel extraction method, the LBP with relative bias thresholding (LRBT) method, to extract feature pixels from an image. The LRBT method first

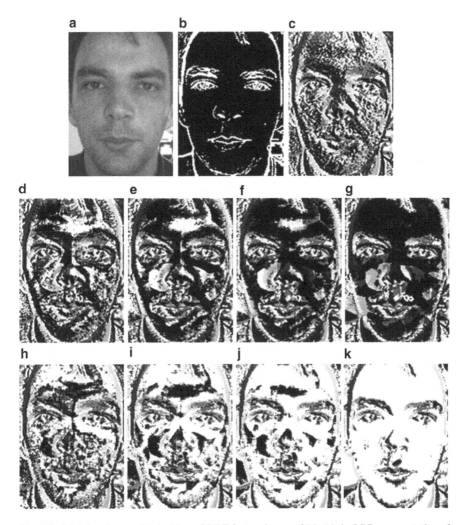

Fig. 7.8 (**a**) A face image; (**b**) the binary LRBT feature image of (**a**); (**c**) the LBP representation of the face image of (**a**); (**d–g**) the FLBP image when $\alpha_v = 0$ and $\alpha_t = 0.25$, 0.5, 0.75, and 1, respectively; (**h–k**) the FLBP image when $\alpha_t = 0$ and $\alpha_v = 0.25$, 0.5, 0.75, and 1, respectively

computes the LBP representation using the relative bias threshold function defined below:

$$S(g_i, g_c, \beta) = \begin{cases} 1, & \text{if } g_i \geq (1 + \beta)g_c; \\ 0, & \text{otherwise.} \end{cases} \qquad (7.15)$$

where β is a parameter that controls the contribution of g_c to the bias. An LBP image is defined by its corresponding LBP representation, and different β values

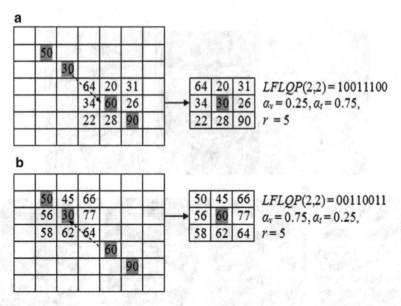

Fig. 7.9 (a) The TC ($\alpha_t = 0.75$), the VC ($\alpha_v = 0.25$), $r = 5$, and the LFLQP code for the pixel at (2, 2); (b) the TC ($\alpha_t = 0.25$), the VC ($\alpha_v = 0.75$), $r = 5$ and the LFLQP code for the pixel at (2, 2)

define different LBP images. Then the LRBT method derives the binary LRBT feature image by converting the LBP image to a binary image, whose feature pixels correspond to those whose LBP code is greater than 0, and the background pixels correspond to the pixels in the LBP image with the LBP code 0.

Figure 7.8 shows an example of the FLBP representations of a face image. Figure 7.8a, b displays a face image and its binary feature image. The feature pixel of the binary image is derived using our LRBT method when $\beta = 0.1$. Figure 7.8d shows the LBP image of the face image of Fig. 7.8a. Figure 7.8d–g exhibits the FLBP images when $\alpha_t = 0.25$, 0.5, 0.75, and 1, respectively, and $\alpha_v = 0$. Figure 7.8h–k exhibits the FLBP images when $\alpha_v = 0.25$, 0.5, 0.75, and 1, respectively, and $\alpha_t = 0$.

Our proposed FLQP consists of two binary codes: the upper half of FLQP or the UFLQP and the lower half of FLQP or the LFLQP. The general form of the UFLQP and the LFLQP is defined below:

$$UFLQP(\mathbf{p}) = FLBP(\mathbf{p}) \tag{7.16}$$

$$LFLQP(\mathbf{p}) = \sum_{i=0}^{7} 2^i S_{llqp}\{G[N(C_t(\mathbf{p}), i)], G[C_v(\mathbf{p})], r\} \tag{7.17}$$

Figure 7.9 shows the computation of FLQP when $r = 5$. The gray level image and the feature pixel are the same as Fig. 7.6. We use the same pixel $\mathbf{p}$ at (2, 2) and the same values of α_v and α_t as those in Fig. 7.7 to compute FLQP. Therefore, the

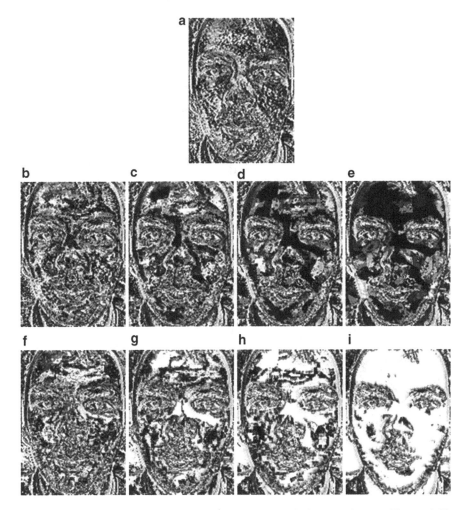

Fig. 7.10 (a) The LLQP image when $r = 10$; (**b–e**) the LFLQP images when $r = 10$, $\alpha_t = 0.25$, 0.5, 0.75, and 1, respectively, and $\alpha_v = 0$; (**f–i**) the LFLQP images when $r = 10$, $\alpha_v = 0.25$, 0.5, 0.75, and 1, respectively, and $\alpha_t = 0$

computation of **dv**, TC, and VC are the same as the examples in Fig. 7.7. Figure 7.9a shows the FLQP computation of the pixel **p** at (2, 2), when $\alpha_v = 0.25$ and $\alpha_t = 0.75$. Because the UFLQP is the same as the FLBP shown in Fig. 7.7a, only the LFLQP is shown in Fig. 7.9a. First, the gray level 60 of TC at (5, 5) is replaced by the gray level 30 of VC at (3, 3). For LFLQP, a neighborhood pixel is assigned 1 if it is greater than or equal to 35 or it is less than 30 and greater than or equal to 25 and is assigned 0 otherwise. Then we have LFLQP(2, 2) = 10011100. Figure 7.9b shows the FLQP computation of the pixel **p** at (2, 2) when $\alpha_v = 0.75$ and $\alpha_t = 0.25$. The UFLQP is the same as FLBP shown in Fig. 7.7b and not shown in Fig. 7.9b. First, the gray level 30 of TC at (3, 3) is replaced by the gray level 60 of VC at (5, 5).

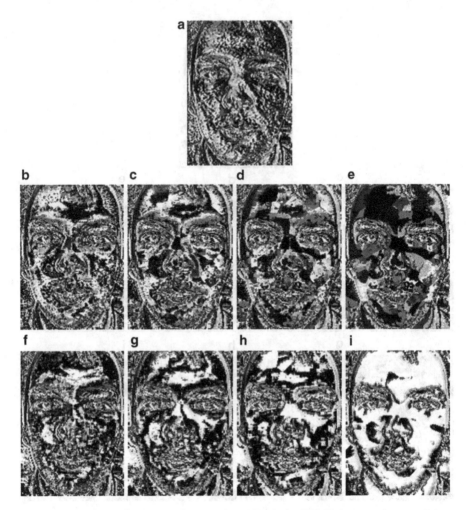

Fig. 7.11 (a) The LLQP image when $r = 0.1g_c$; (**b–e**) the LFLQP images when $r = 0.1g_c$, $\alpha_t = 0.25, 0.5, 0.75$, and 1, respectively, and $\alpha_v = 0$; (**f–i**) the LFLQP images when $0.1g_c$, $\alpha_v = 0.25, 0.5, 0.75$, and 1, respectively, and $\alpha_t = 0$

For LFLQP, a neighborhood pixel is assigned 1 if it is greater than or equal to 65 or it is less than 60 and greater than or equal to 55 and is assigned 0 otherwise. Then we have the LFLQP(2, 2) = 00110011.

Figure 7.10 shows an example of the FLQP and LQP representations of a face image when $r = 10$. The face image and the binary LRBT feature image are the same as Fig. 7.8a, b. Figure 7.10a shows the LLQP image. The ULQP image is the same as LBP image in Fig. 7.8c. Figure 7.10b–e show LFLQP images when $\alpha_t = 0.25, 0.5$, 0.75, and 1, respectively, and $\alpha_v = 0$. Their corresponding UFLQP are the same as Fig. 7.7d–g. Figure 7.10f–i shows LFLQP images when $\alpha_v = 0.25, 0.5, 0.75$, and 1, respectively, and $\alpha_t = 0$. Their corresponding UFLQP are the same as Fig. 7.7h–k.

Figure 7.11 shows another example of the FLQP representations when $r = 0.1$ g_c. The face image and the binary LRBT feature image are the same as Fig. 7.8a, b. Figure 7.11a shows the LLQP image. The ULQP image is the same as LBP image in Fig. 7.8c. Figure 7.11b–e shows LFLQP images when $\alpha_t = 0.25, 0.5, 0.75$, and 1, respectively, and $\alpha_v = 0$. Their corresponding UFLQP are the same as Fig. 7.7d–g. Figure 7.11f–i shows LFLQP images when $\alpha_v = 0.25, 0.5, 0.75$, and 1, respectively, and $\alpha_t = 0$. Their corresponding UFLQP are the same as Fig. 7.7h–k.

7.6   Application of FLQP to Eye Detection

Eye detection plays an important role in automatic face recognition [43–45], as many face recognition systems use eye centers to align faces [46, 47]. We introduce in this section an FLQP-based eye detection method. Figure 7.12 shows the system architecture of our FLQP-based eye detection method that consists of three major steps.

In the first step, a binary image, which contains the feature pixels of the gray-scale face image, is derived by applying our new feature pixel extraction method, namely, the LBP with relative bias thresholding method, or LRBT. Note that in our experiments we observe that the LRBT features perform better than the edge features derived by the Canny edge detector. The LRBT method first computes the LBP representation using the relative bias threshold function defined by (7.15).

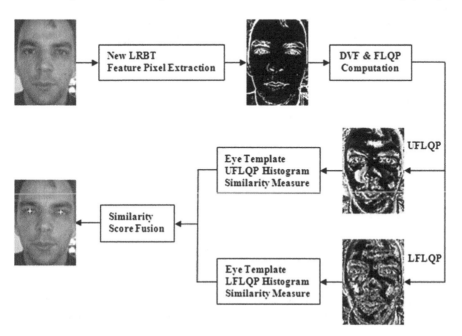

Fig. 7.12   The system architecture of our FLQP-based eye detection method

The LBP representation forms an LBP image, and the LRBT method finally derives the binary LRBT feature image by converting the LBP image to a binary image. After the conversion, the feature pixels in the binary LRBT feature image correspond to the pixels in the LBP image whose LBP code is greater than 0, and the background pixels correspond to the pixels in the LBP image whose LBP code is 0.

In the second step, the FLQP representation of the face image is formed based on the gray-scale image and a distance vector field or DVF, which is obtained by computing the distance vector between each pixel and its nearest feature pixel defined in the binary image. The FLQP code is then split to two binary codes, from which two images, UFLQP and LFLQP images, are formed in this step.

In the final step, each eye candidate is compared with the eye template based on the UFLQP and LFLQP histograms and similarity measures. An eye template is constructed from a number of training eye samples. Each eye sample is divided into a grid of $u \times v$ cells. The occurrences of the UFLQP codes in a cell are collected into a UFLQP histogram. The occurrences of the LFLQP codes in a cell are collected into a LFLQP histogram. The eye template is thus defined by uv UFLQP mean histograms and uv LFLQP mean histograms of the training eye samples. The similarity measure to compare the UFLQP and LFLQP histograms of an eye template T and an eye candidate C is defined as follows:

$$M(C,T) = -\sum_{i=1}^{g} \sum_{j=1}^{b} \frac{(C_{i,j} - T_{i,j})^2}{C_{i,j} + T_{i,j}} \tag{7.18}$$

where $C_{i,j}$ represents the jth bin of the histogram of the ith cell of the eye candidate window, $T_{i,j}$ represents the jth bin of the histogram of the ith cell of the eye template, $g = uv$ is the total number of cells of the u $\times$ v grid, and b is the number of bins of a histogram. The final similarity measure is the sum of similarity values of the UFLQP and LFLQP histograms. We have developed a fast algorithm in histogram and similarity measure computation. The idea of the fast algorithm is to update only two columns or two rows corresponding to the two consecutive eye candidate windows for the histogram and similarity computation instead of repeating the computation for the whole new window. As a result, the fast algorithm significantly improves the computational efficiency of the eye detection method.

7.7   Experiments

We assess our FLQP-based eye detection method using the public BioID database (www.bioid.com), which contains 1,521 gray-scale frontal face images with spatial resolution of 384 $\times$ 286. The images in the BioID database pose challenges to eye detection, due to illumination variations, eye glasses, closed eyes, etc. Prior to applying our proposed method to detect eyes, a face is detected in an image using, for example, the Bayesian discriminating feature (BDF) method [48]. A detected

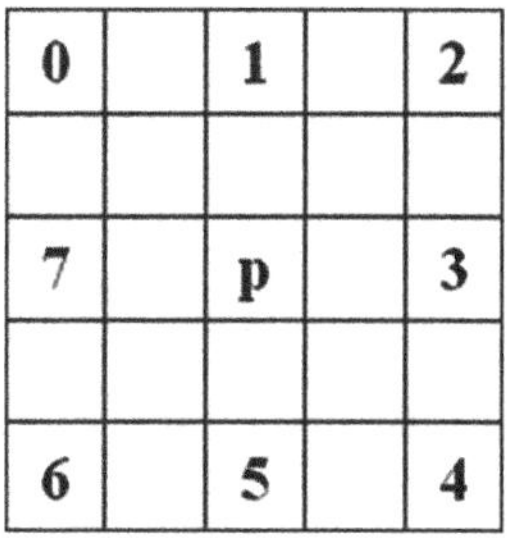

Fig. 7.13 The 5 × 5 neighborhood of the center pixel and the label of its neighbors

0		1		2
7		p		3
6		5		4

Fig. 7.14 The 3 × 4 grid of an eye window

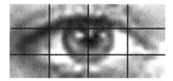

face is then cropped and normalized to the size of 132 × 178. Figure 7.8a shows an example of the cropped and normalized face images from the BioID database. To construct the eye template, we collect 70 pairs of eye samples that are not from the BioID database. As only the right eye template is constructed due to the symmetry between the right and left eyes, the 70 left eyes are flipped horizontally to double the number of the right eye samples. To detect the left eye, we first flip the face image horizontally and then detect eye in the flipped image by comparing it with the right eye template. All eye samples are aligned by the eye center and cropped to the size of 37 × 17.

Eye detection performance is determined by a relative distance error that is defined as follows:

$$\gamma = \frac{d_1}{d_2} \tag{7.19}$$

where d_1 is the Euclidean distance between the detected eye center and the ground truth eye center and d_2 is the interocular distance – the distance between the two ground truth eye centers. The detected eye center is considered inside the eye region, inside the iris, and inside the pupil, when $\gamma \leq 0.25, 0.1$, and 0.05, respectively. We will use the success rate for $\gamma \leq 0.25, 0.1$, and 0.05 and the average γ to assess the performance of our FLQP-based eye detection method.

Our experiments in eye detection using FLBP-based method show that 5 × 5 neighborhood size shown in Fig. 7.13 is better than 3 × 3 neighborhood size, and 3 × 4 grid of an eye window shown in Fig. 7.14 yields the best overall results among 3 × 3, 3 × 4, and 4 × 4 grid size. We therefore apply the 5 × 5 neighborhood size and the 3 × 4 grid in evaluating our FLQP-based eye detection method. The features for our FLQP-based eye detection are derived using the LRBT method with $\beta = 0.2$. The parameters α_v and α_t are set to 0.25 and 0, respectively. The

Table 7.1 The eye detection success rate and average γ of the FLQP-based and LQP-based eye detection methods

Method		$\gamma \leq 0.25$	$\gamma \leq 0.1$	$\gamma \leq 0.05$	Average γ	Rank average γ
FLQP	$\tau = 0.17$	98.59	96.09	89.74	0.0363	2
$r = \tau g_c$	$\tau = 0.18$	98.75	96.19	89.71	0.0360	1
	$\tau = 0.19$	98.75	96.12	89.38	0.0363	2
FLQP	$c = 7$	98.59	94.81	88.59	0.0376	4
$r = c$	$c = 8$	98.59	94.71	88.61	0.0377	5
	$c = 9$	98.62	94.94	88.42	0.0379	6
LQP	$\tau = 0.06$	98.13	95.36	88.95	0.0394	12
$r = \tau g_c$	$\tau = 0.07$	98.39	95.63	89.38	0.0382	8
	$\tau = 0.08$	98.19	94.43	89.48	0.0391	10
LQP	$c = 6$	98.39	95.36	88.72	0.0385	9
$r = c$	$c = 7$	98.55	95.40	88.10	0.0381	7
	$c = 8$	98.32	95.46	88.56	0.0391	10

The parameters β, α_v, and α_t for the FLQP methods are set to 0.2, 0.25, and 0, respectively

feature LTP, or FLTP, is implemented as well for comparison. The feature pixels for the FLTP-based eye detection are obtained using the LRBT method with $\beta = 0.2$, and the parameters α_v and α_t are the same as those used in the FLQP-based eye detection. The parameter r of the threshold function in the experiments is either a constant value ($r = c$) or a relative value ($r = \tau g_c$).

Table 7.1 shows the results of the eye detection success rate and the average γ of the FLQP-based eye detection methods and the LQP-based eye detection methods. The parameters β, α_v, and α_t for the FLQP method are set to 0.2, 0.25, and 0, respectively. The results show that all the FLQP-based eye detection methods have lower average γ than any LQP-based eye detection method. For the FLQP-based eye detection methods, a relative r achieves better eye detection performance than a constant r. For the LQP-based eye detection methods, a relative r have higher success rate for $\gamma \leq 0.05$ than a constant r. A relative r and a constant r have the similar average γ and success rate for $\gamma \leq 0.25$ and 0.1.

Table 7.2 shows the eye detection success rate and the average γ of the FLTP-based and the LTP-based eye detection methods. For fair comparisons, the parameters β, α_v, and α_t for the FLTP method are also set to 0.2, 0.25, and 0, respectively. The results show that all the FLTP-based eye detection methods except when $r = 0.04g_c$ have lower average γ than any LQP-based eye detection method. For both the FLTP-based and LTP-based eye detection methods a constant r achieves lower average γ than a relative r.

Tables 7.3, 7.4, 7.5, and 7.6 compare the performance of the FLQP-based, the LQP-based, the FLTP-based, the LTP-based, the FLBP-based, and the LBP-based eye detection methods. The best experiments are selected for each method to make the comparison. Tables 7.3, 7.4, and 7.5 show the eye detection success rate and the rank when $\gamma \leq 0.25$, 0.1, and 0.05, respectively. Table 7.6 shows the average γ

Table 7.2 The eye detection success rate and average γ of the FLTP-based and LTP-based eye detection methods

Method		$\gamma \leq 0.25$	$\gamma \leq 0.1$	$\gamma \leq 0.05$	Average γ	Rank average γ
FLTP	$\tau = 0.02$	98.46	94.81	88.63	0.0395	5
$r = \tau g_c$	$\tau = 0.03$	98.32	95.00	89.02	0.0388	2
	$\tau = 0.04$	98.06	95.00	89.02	0.0396	7
FLTP	$c = 2$	98.52	95.04	88.46	0.0389	3
$r = c$	$c = 3$	98.29	95.17	89.12	0.0387	1
	$c = 4$	98.16	95.17	88.89	0.0390	4
LTP	$\tau = 0.02$	97.53	94.87	87.34	0.0438	11
$r = \tau g_c$	$\tau = 0.03$	97.44	94.74	87.87	0.0438	11
	$\tau = 0.04$	97.30	94.48	87.84	0.0436	10
LTP	$c = 3$	97.63	95.07	87.67	0.0429	9
$r = c$	$c = 4$	98.03	95.50	88.95	0.0395	5
	$c = 5$	97.80	95.07	88.46	0.0401	8

The parameters β, α_v, and α_t for the FLTP method are set to 0.2, 0.25, and 0, respectively

Table 7.3 The eye detection success rate and rank (when $\gamma \leq 0.25$) of eye detection results using the FLQP-based, the LQP-based, the FLTP-based, the LTP-based, the FLBP-based, and the LBP-based eye detection methods

Method	$\gamma \leq 0.25$	Rank
FLQP, $\beta = 0.2$, $\alpha_v = 0.25$, $\alpha_t = 0$, $r = 0.18g_c$	98.75	1
LQP, $r = 7$	98.55	3
FLTP, $\beta = 0.2$, $\alpha_v = 0.25$, $\alpha_t = 0$, $r = 2$	98.52	4
LTP, $r = 4$	98.03	5
FLBP, $\beta = 0.2$, $\alpha_v = 0.25$, $\alpha_t = 0$	98.65	2
LBP	92.34	6

Table 7.4 The eye detection success rate and rank (when $\gamma \leq 0.1$) of eye detection results using the FLQP-based, the LQP-based, the FLTP-based, the LTP-based, the FLBP-based, and the LBP-based eye detection methods

Method	$\gamma \leq 0.1$	Rank
FLQP, $\beta = 0.2$, $\alpha_v = 0.25$, $\alpha_t = 0$, $r = 0.18g_c$	96.19	1
LQP, $r = 7$	95.63	2
FLTP, $\beta = 0.2$, $\alpha_v = 0.25$, $\alpha_t = 0$, $r = 3$	95.17	5
LTP, $r = 4$	95.50	3
FLBP, $\beta = 0.2$, $\alpha_v = 0.25$, $\alpha_t = 0$	95.23	4
LBP	90.34	6

and the rank of the average γ. The experimental results listed in Tables 7.3, 7.4, 7.5, and 7.6 lead to the following findings.

- LQP performs better than LTP and LBP for eye detection. FLQP performs better than FLTP and FLBP for eye detection. Furthermore, except FLBP archives higher success rate than LQP when $\gamma \leq 0.25$, all the FLQP-based and the LQP-

Table 7.5 The eye detection success rate and rank (when $\gamma \leq 0.05$) of eye detection results using the FLQP-based, the LQP-based, the FLTP-based, the LTP-based, the FLBP-based, and the LBP-based eye detection methods

Method	$\gamma \leq 0.05$	Rank
FLQP, $\beta = 0.2$, $\alpha_v = 0.25$, $\alpha_t = 0$, $r = 0.17g_c$	89.74	1
LQP, $r = 0.08g_c$	89.48	2
FLTP, $\beta = 0.2$, $\alpha_v = 0.25$, $\alpha_t = 0$, $r = 3$	89.12	3
LTP, $r = 4$	88.85	4
FLBP, $\beta = 0.2$, $\alpha_v = 0.25$, $\alpha_t = 0$	87.84	5
LBP	83.14	6

Table 7.6 The average γ and rank of the average γ using the FLQP-based, the LQP-based, the FLTP-based, the LTP-based, the FLBP-based, and the LBP-based eye detection methods

Method	Average γ	Rank
FLQP, $\beta = 0.2$, $\alpha_v = 0.25$, $\alpha_t = 0$, $r = 0.18g_c$	0.0360	1
LQP, $r = 7$	0.0381	2
FLTP, $\beta = 0.2$, $\alpha_v = 0.25$, $\alpha_t = 0$, $r = 3$	0.0387	4
LTP, $r = 4$	0.0395	5
FLBP, $\beta = 0.2$, $\alpha_v = 0.25$, $\alpha_t = 0$	0.0385	3
LBP	0.0812	6

based eye detection methods have better eye detection performance than any other competing method in terms of the eye detection success rate and the average γ. These results demonstrate that the proposed LQP and FLQP, which encode four relationships of local texture, are more effective than the LTP, FLTP, LBP, and FLBP for texture description and pattern recognition, such as eye detection.

- FLQP achieves the best eye detection performance. Specifically, Tables 7.3, 7.4, and 7.5 show that the FLQP-based eye detection method obtains the highest eye detection success rates when $\gamma \leq 0.25$, 0.1, and 0.05, respectively. Table 7.6 shows that the FLQP-based eye detection method has the smallest average γ. The average γ of the LQP-, FLTP-, LTP-, FLBP-, and LBP-based eye detection methods are 5.8%, 7.5%, 9.7%, 6.9%, and 125.6% higher than the average γ of the FLQP-based eye detection method. The results indicate that FLQP improves upon FLTP, LTP, FLBP, and LBP for eye detection.
- FLQP and FLBP perform better than LQP and LBP methods, respectively, in terms of the eye detection success rate when $\gamma \leq 0.25$, 0.1, and 0.05 and the average γ. FLTP methods archive better results than LTP methods except LTP obtains higher success rate than FLTP when $\gamma \leq 0.1$. The results illustrate that the feature local methods (FLQP, FLTP, and FLBP), which encode both local and feature information, perform better than the local methods (LQP, LTP, and LBP) that do not encode feature information.
- Our experiments show that LTP methods improve upon the LBP methods. However, the FLBP methods archive better results than FLTP except FLTP is

better for success rates when $\gamma \leq 0.05$. The FLTP method does not outperform the FLBP method. Our results are consistent with the experimental results reported in [6, 7] which showed that LTP and LBP achieved similar results for face and facial expression recognition, although LTP has a higher computational cost than LBP.

7.8 Conclusions

We present in this paper local quaternary patterns (LQP) and feature local quaternary patterns (FLQP) and assess their performance on an eye detection problem. The LQP, which encodes four relationships of the local texture, includes more information of the local texture than the local binary patterns or LBP and the local ternary patterns or LTP. The FLQP, which encodes both local and feature information, is expected to perform better than the LQP for texture description and pattern recognition. To reduce the feature dimension of LQP and FLQP, a new coding scheme is proposed to split the LQP into two binary codes: the upper LQP (ULQP) and the lower LQP (LLQP), and the FLQP into two binary codes: the upper FLQP (UFLQP) and the lower FLQP (LFLQP). Experimental results using the BioID database show that (1) LQP and FLQP perform better than LTP, FLTP, LBP, and FLBP for eye detection. (2) FLQP achieves the best eye detection performance. (3) FLQP, FLTP, and FLBP perform better than LQP, LTP, and LBP.

Acknowledgments The authors would like to thank the anonymous reviewers for their constructive comments and suggestions, which help improve the quality of the chapter.

References

1. Wang L, He DC (1990) Texture classification using texture spectrum. Pattern Recogn 23:905–910
2. Ojala T, Pietikainen MD, Harwood D (1994) Performance evaluation of texture measures with classification based on kullback discrimination of distributions. In: Proceedings of the 12th IAPR international conference on pattern recognition, Jerusalem, Israel, pp 582–585
3. Ojala T, Pietikainen M, Harwood D (1996) A comparative study of texture measures with classification based on feature distributions. Pattern Recogn 29:51–59
4. Ojala T, Pietikainen M, Maenpaa T (2002) Multiresolution gray-scale and rotation invariant texture classification with local binary patterns. IEEE Trans Pattern Anal Mach Intell 24:971–987
5. Gong P, Marceau DJ, Howarth PJ (1992) A comparison of spatial feature extraction algorithms for land-use classification with SPOT HRV data. Remote Sens Environ 40:137–151
6. Tan X, Triggs B (2010) Enhanced local texture feature sets for face recognition under difficult lighting conditions. IEEE Trans Image Process 19:1635–1650
7. Gritti T, Shan C, Jeanne V, Braspenning R (2008) Local features based facial expression recognition with face registration errors. In: Proceedings of IEEE international conference automatic face and gesture recognition (FG), Amsterdam, Netherlands

8. Gu J, Liu C (2012) Feature local binary patterns. In: Liu C, Mago V (eds) Cross disciplinary biometric systems. Springer, Berlin, NY
9. Liu C, Mago V (2012) Cross disciplinary biometric systems. Springer, Berlin, NY
10. Ahonen T, Hadid A, Pietikainen M (2006) Face description with local binary patterns: application to face recognition. IEEE Trans Pattern Anal Mach Intell 28:2037–2041
11. Liu Z, Liu C (2010) Fusion of color, local spatial and global frequency information for face recognition. Pattern Recogn 43:2882–2890
12. Chan C, Kittler J, Messer K (2007) Multi-scale local binary pattern histograms for face recognition. In: Proceedings of 2nd international conference biometrics (ICB), Seoul, Korea, pp 809–818
13. Hadid A, Pietikäinen M, Ahonen T (2004) A discriminative feature space for detecting and recognizing faces. In: Proceedings of international conference computer vision and pattern recognition (CVPR), Washington, DC, USA, pp 797–804
14. Zhang H, Zhao D (2004) Spatial histogram features for face detection in color images. In: Proceedings of advances in multimedia information processing: 5th pacific rim conference on multimedial, Tokyo, Japan, pp 377–384
15. Shan C, Gong S, McOwan PJ (2009) Facial expression recognition based on local binary patterns: a comprehensive study. Image Vision Comput 27:803–816
16. Feng X, Hadid A, Pietikainen M (2004) A coarse-to-fine classification scheme for facial expression recognition. In: Proceedings of international conference image analysis and recognition (ICIAR), Porto, Portugal, pp 668–675
17. Liao S, Fan W, Chung ACS, Yeung DY (2006) Facial expression recognition using advanced local binary patterns, tsallis entropies and global appearance features. In: Proceedings of IEEE international conference image processing (ICIP), Atlanta, Georgia, USA, pp 665–668
18. Zhao G, Pietikainen M (2007) Experiments with facial expression recognition using spatio-temporal local binary patterns. In: Proceedings of the international conference on multimedia and expo (ICME), pp 1091–1094
19. Moore S, Bowden R (2011) Local binary patterns for multi-view facial expression recognition. Comput Vision Image Understand 115:541–558
20. Jin H, Liu Q, Lu H, Tong X (2006) Face detection using improved LBP under Bayesian framework. In: Proceedings of third international conference on image and graphics, Nanjing, China, pp 306–309
21. Huang X, Li S, Wang Y (2006) Shape localization based on statistical method using extended local binary pattern. In: Proceedings of third international conference on image and graphics, Nanjing, China, pp 184–187
22. Pham-Ngoc PT, Jo KH (2006) Multi-face detection system in video sequence. In: Proceedings of international forum on strategic technology (IFOST), Ulsan, Korea, pp 146–150
23. Liao S, Li SZ (2007) Learning multi-scale block local binary patterns for face recognition. In: Proceedings of international conference on biometrics (ICB), Seoul, Korea, pp 828–837
24. Zhang L, Chu R, Xiang S, Li SZ (2007) Face detection based on multi-block LBP representation. In: Proceedings of international conference on biometrics (ICB), Seoul, Korea, pp 11–18
25. Liao S, Chung ACS (2007) Face recognition by using elongated local binary patterns with average maximum distance gradient magnitude. In: Proceedings of Asian conference computer vision (ACCV), Tokyo, Japan, pp 672–679
26. Fu X, Wei W (2008) Centralized binary patterns embedded with image Euclidean distance for facial expression recognition. In: Proceedings of international conference neural computation (ICNC), pp 115–119
27. Akhloufi M, Bendada A (2010) A new fusion framework for multispectral face recognition in the texture space. In: 10th international conference on quantitative infrared thermograph, Quebec, Canada
28. Liao S, Zhao G, Kellokumpu V et al. (2010) Modeling pixel process with scale invariant local patterns for background subtraction in complex scenes. In: Proceedings of IEEE conference on computer vision and pattern recognition (CVPR), San Francisco, CA, USA, pp 1301–1306

29. Yuille A, Hallinan P, Cohen D (1992) Feature extraction from faces using deformable templates. Int J Comput Vision 8:99–111
30. Xie X, Sudhakar R, Zhuang H (1994) On improving eye feature extraction using deformable templates. Pattern Recogn 27:791–799
31. Lam KM, Yan H (1996) Locating and extracting the eye in human face images. Pattern Recogn 29:771–779
32. Feng GC, Yuen PC (1998) Variance projection function and its application to eye detection for human face recognition. Pattern Recogn Lett 19:899–906
33. Feng GC, Yuen PC (2001) Multi-cues eye detection on gray intensity image. Pattern Recogn 34:1033–1046
34. Zhou ZH, Geng X (2004) Projection functions for eye detection. Pattern Recogn 37:1049–1056
35. Kawato S, Tetsutani N (2002) Real-time detection of between-the-eyes with a circle frequency filter. In: Proceedings of ACCV 2002, Melbourne, Australia, vol I, pp 442–447
36. Sirohey S, Rosenfeld A (2001) Eye detection in a face image using linear and nonlinear filters. Pattern Recogn 34:1367–1391
37. Kawaguchi T, Rizon M (2003) Iris detection using intensity and edge information. Pattern Recogn 36:549–562
38. Wu J, Zhou ZH (2003) Efficient face candidates selector for face detection. Pattern Recogn 36:1175–1186
39. Pentland A, Moghaddam B, Starner T (1994) View-based and modular eigenspaces for face recognition. In: Proceedings of IEEE conference on computer vision and pattern recognition, Seattle, WA, USA, pp 84–91
40. Ryu Y, Oh S (2001) Automatic extraction of eye and mouth fields from a face image using eigenfeatures and multilayer perceptrons. Pattern Recogn 34:2459–2466
41. Asteriadis S, Nikolaidis N, Pitas I (2009) Facial feature detection using distance vector fields. Pattern Recogn 42:1388–1398
42. Danielson P (1980) Euclidean distance mapping. Comput Graph Image Process 14:227–248
43. Liu C, Yang J (2009) ICA color space for pattern recognition. IEEE Trans Neural Netw 20:248–257
44. Liu C (2008) Learning the uncorrelated, independent, and discriminating color spaces for face recognition. IEEE Trans Inf Forensics Secur 3:213–222
45. Liu C (2007) The Bayes decision rule induced similarity measures. IEEE Trans Pattern Anal Mach Intell 29:1086–1090
46. Liu C (2006) Capitalize on dimensionality increasing techniques for improving face recognition grand challenge performance. IEEE Trans Pattern Anal Mach Intell 28:725–737
47. Liu C (2004) Enhanced independent component analysis and its application to content based face image retrieval. IEEE Trans Syst Man Cybern B Cybern 34:1117–1127
48. Liu C (2003) A Bayesian discriminating features method for face detection. IEEE Trans Pattern Anal Mach Intell 25:725–740

Chapter 8
Chaotic Neural Network and Multidimensional Data Analysis in Biometric Applications

Kushan Ahmadian and Marina Gavrilova

Abstract In this book chapter, a novel biometric system from the normalisation level up to the verification level is developed, tested and verified against other multimodal and unimodal systems. The main advantage of a new architecture is in flexibility of combining various features from multimodal biometrics in a new way, suitable for neural-network learner. The system utilises associative memories and pattern matchers as learners of biometric data, but the main advantage of a new architecture is increased resistance to noise and ability of system to compensate for an absence of some biometric traits. Detailed experimental analysis of pros and cons of such system is also provided.

8.1 Introduction

Through the history, humans have used body characteristics such as face, voice and signature to identify and authenticate each other. Biometrics as a science emerged from extensive use in law enforcement to identify criminals, to ensure border protection, to secure financial transactions and so on. Nowadays, biometrics are used in a variety of civilian applications, to gain access to a place of work, for credit card authentication, amusement park entrance, etc. In a practical biometric system (i.e. a system that employs biometrics for personal recognition), there are a number of important issues that should be considered, including *performance* (achievable recognition accuracy and speed) and *circumvention* (system resistance to noise and to being fooled by fraudulent methods). In order for biometric system to meet the high demands on performance and circumvention, more than one type of biometric

K. Ahmadian (✉) • M. Gavrilova
University of Calgary, Calgary, Canada
e-mail: kahmadia@ucalgary.ca; marina@cpsc.ucalgary.ca

K. Saeed and T. Nagashima (eds.), *Biometrics and Kansei Engineering*,
DOI 10.1007/978-1-4614-5608-7_8, © Springer Science+Business Media New York 2012

is often required. Hence, the need arises for the use of multimodal biometrics, which is a combination of different biometric recognition technologies, varying from physical biometrics (such as face, iris and fingerprint recognition) to behavioural characteristics (i.e. signature, voice and gate).

At the same time, paying off the error in a biometric system is too costly in many cases. A simple neglect in the design of the system may result a serious threat to a system or even to the society. Error in biometric systems could be categorised under two main types of problems [1]. First, there is always a small chance of an imposter being accepted as a true identity, and the performance of the biometric system does not satisfy the needed security level [1]. Opposed to the acceptance of imposter, another undesired phenomenon is when the genuine user is being rejected [1].

While many multimodal systems focus on improving algorithms for single biometric recognition or on providing better decision-making and fusion approaches, our focus in this chapter is to establish the way of how system can be more resistant to errors and what to do in case of a single biometric or a biometric feature being compromised or absent.

8.2 Preliminaries

Biometrics are generally used in two major ways: for identification and for verification purposes [1]. *Identification* is a process of determining who a person is. *Verification* is determining if a person is who they say they are. It involves taking the measured characteristic and comparing it to the previously recorded data for that person. In this work, we aim to target the verification problem since the methods used to compare the proposed system are based on the verification process of multimodal biometric features. Another reason to choose the verification process is closeness criterion (especially in neural networks) in verification process, which indicates the accuracy of the proposed method.

A multi-biometric system uses multiple sensors for data acquisition [2]. This allows capturing multiple samples of a single biometric trait (called multi-sample biometrics) and/or samples of multiple biometric traits (called multi-source or multimodal biometrics) [2]. Numerous methods have been developed to date; however, even the best biometric traits are facing problems. In particular, biometric authentication systems generally suffer from enrolment problems due to non-universal biometric traits, susceptibility to biometric spoofing or insufficient accuracy caused by noisy data acquisition in certain environments.

One way to overcome these problems is the use of multi-biometrics. This approach also enables a user who does not possess a particular biometric identifier to still enrol and authenticate using other traits, thus eliminating the enrolment problems and making it universal [2]. A unimodal biometric system [3] consists of three major modules: sensor module, feature extraction module and matching module. A key in

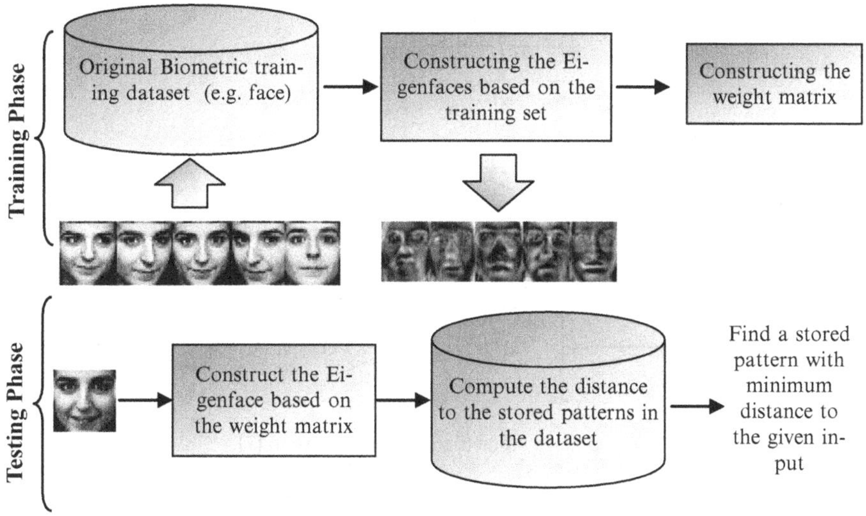

Fig. 8.1 The general training and testing procedure for PCA-based biometric system

multimodal biometric is decision-making module [2], which is based on information fusion approaches and a number of different fusion methods. Some alternative approaches to biometric feature extraction and learning started to appear recently, based on intelligent learning paradigm such as neural network [4, 5]. The main problems faced in biometric system implementation are the biometric system reliability and performance in an operational mode. One of the objectives of this research is to investigate if neural networks combined with dimension analysis provide benefits in improving biometric system performance and circumvention, i.e. resistance to low-quality data or absence of one of biometric traits all together.

First, we aim to find the best subset of biometric features derived from the original dataset. The new subset could be either a portion of the original dataset or a reconstructed set of samples with a reduced dimensionality. As an example, when using the principal component analysis method (PCA), the main goal is to find the principal components of the distribution of features (such as faces, ears and other biometrics utilised in the system), which are eigenvectors of the covariance matrix of the set of biometric images [6]. These eigenvectors can be considered as a set of features which together characterise the variation between biometric samples. A simplified step by step procedure is shown in Fig. 8.1.

The new system architecture that we proposed in [7] with original neural-network representation is shown in Fig. 8.2. The system relies on subspace clustering to identify key features and then trains chaotic neural-network learner to recognise biometric patterns.

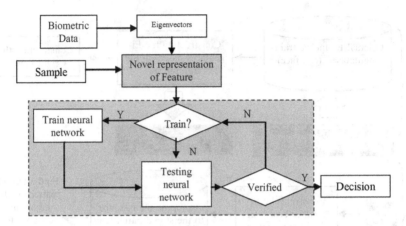

Fig. 8.2 Neural-network-based multi-biometric recognition system [7]

8.3 Multimodal Biometric System: Possible Threats

In the previous section, we reviewed the use of chaotic neural network and subspace clustering as a substitution for conventional dimensionality methods in order to overcome some traditional problems of dimensionality reduction methods, like curse of dimensionality [8, 9]. Since introduced system performs the fusion on the feature level, we need to compare the system to other systems which perform the comparison on the match score level. Note that multimodal biometric system includes not only various biometrics but also various features of the same biometrics, traditionally processed by different algorithms (appearance, geometric, texture, signals, patterns, etc.). Again, the performance of the proposed system in terms of recognition rate outperformed the comparing systems [7]. In terms of the operation speed, the system is still justifiable. However, the system did not undergo vulnerability checks which we aim to perform in this section. We test the vulnerability of the system in the absence of some of the features and also in the presence to huge number of features. In the proposed system, the fusion happens in the feature level. The simplified training structure of the system is shown in Fig. 8.3.

As shown above, the vectors of different biometric systems (here, ear and face) are combined and fed in to the dimensionality reduction phase after conventional normalisations process (correcting illumination, removing noise and adjusting rotations). Afterwards, the chaotic neural model based on Hopfield network is used to learn the obtained pattern [10]. The input vector to the subspace clustering method is defined as $x = (x_1, \ldots, x_d)^T$. In the case of multimodal biometric system, the vector is a combination of all the features from different biometrics. By other means,

$$X = (x_1, ..., x_d, u_1, ..., u_m, v_1, ..., v_n)^T \tag{8.1}$$

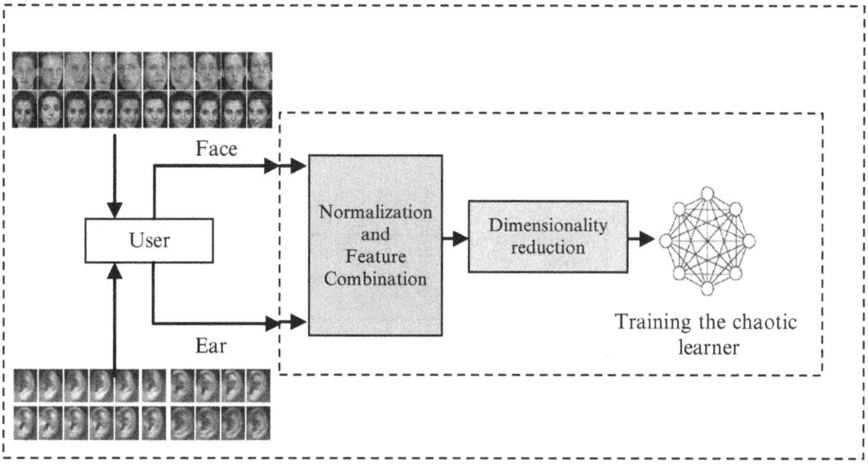

Fig. 8.3 The training phase of the neural-network-based system

where X, U and V are different input biometrics and d, m and n are their dimensions, respectively. The new subspace is labelled as follows:

$$x' = \left(x'_1, ..., x'_{d'}\right)^{\mathrm{T}} \tag{8.2}$$

where $d' \ll d + m + n$. The chaotic neural network is trained by the whole of the new feature subspace.

After training the neural network, test patterns are fed into the system. The testing phase is illustrated in Fig. 8.4. First, the input pattern is introduced to the system. Different biometric features are collected from the user and analysed through the system. If the learner converged the input pattern into a stored pattern within a reasonable threshold, then person is verified and access is granted to enter into the system. Otherwise the person would be rejected.

Multi-biometric systems are not guaranteed to perform a full data gathering for any person at any time. In some cases, the user is not able to provide one or more features due to health, privacy or personal issues. For example, a bonded head would not let the system to collect the ear images for further analysis. Normally, multi-biometric systems are required to handle such situations while minimalising the risk of fraud and imposters.

In the proposed of system, the chaotic neural network is trained using the whole feature set from all the biometric data from training database. By other means, regardless of the type of features of the testing phase, they will be compared against the complete dataset. We analyse this situation below:

In Fig. 8.5, the missing path is depicted by dashed line. While the normalisation is mostly independent for each biometric, the neural-network testing phase needs a complete set of biometric data to verify the user.

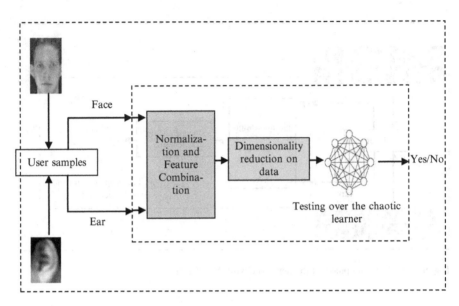

Fig. 8.4 The combined multimodal architecture

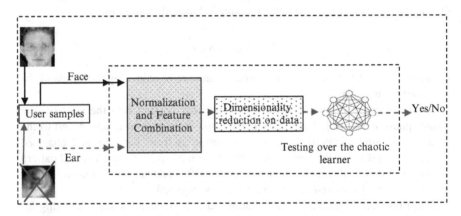

Fig. 8.5 Absence of one of the biometric features

8.3.1 FAR, FRR and GAR Rates

As well known in literature, the outcome of validation in a multimodal biometric system is either considered as a 'genuine individual' or an 'imposter'. In each case, there are two possible situations that may arise during the test phase. The user may be rejected or accepted into the system. Hence, there are four possible cases that may arise: (1) a genuine user is rejected falsely; (2) an imposter is rejected correctly; (3) a genuine user is accepted correctly, and (4) an imposter is accepted falsely.

Two types of errors are used to characterise the genuine and imposter distributions. These errors are described below:

1. False acceptance rate (FAR) [1]: FAR is the chance of an imposter or invalid pattern to be accepted as genuine. FAR is measured to be the portion of imposter score exceeding the predefined threshold.
2. False rejection rate (FRR) [1]: FRR is the probability of a genuine or valid pattern to be rejected as imposter. FRR is measured to be the portion of genuine score below the predefined threshold.

Balancing the FAR and FRR rates are important challenges of every biometric system. In most of the cases, adjusting the threshold to decrease one rate results in a dramatic increase in the other. When the value of FAR is zero, it means that system accepts no risk of imposters regardless of the fact that FRR may grow dramatically.

In addition to the above terms, sometimes another term is used to measure the accuracy of a biometric system which is called genuine acceptance rate (GAR) and is defined as follows:

$$GAR = 1 - FRR \qquad (8.3)$$

which is the measured as the portion of genuine score exceeding the predefined threshold.

8.3.2 Analysis of the Proposed System

Adjusting different values for convergence of the chaotic neural network results in different FAR and FRR values. Figure 8.6 illustrates the FAR-FRR graph of the original system for face and ear biometrics.

The system has been tested on separate ear and face biometrics and their combinations. As it can be seen in Fig. 8.6, for a FAR rate of 1.5%, the usage of ear biometric solely results in 5.4% false rejection rate error, while this rate reduces to 2.3% for face database. When the biometrics are combined together, the resulting system benefits from only a 1.7% rejection rate which is a significant improvement. Remember that for the ear trend, the learner is trained by only the ear samples, which is why the FRR and FAR rates are so low.

Since the neural network is trained by the ear and face samples concurrently, we expect a significant drop in recognition rate, when only one of the patterns are presented to the neural network. If the idea is supported by experiments, then we could emphasise the main drawback of the proposed system and a way to deal with it.

In experimentation on original system architecture, we noted that by removing the ear features the FRR rate for the same FAR value increases to 22.3%. For FAR rate of 0%, the FRR rate increases to 31%, while by presenting the face features, the value becomes 10%. These results were predictable due to the nature of neural

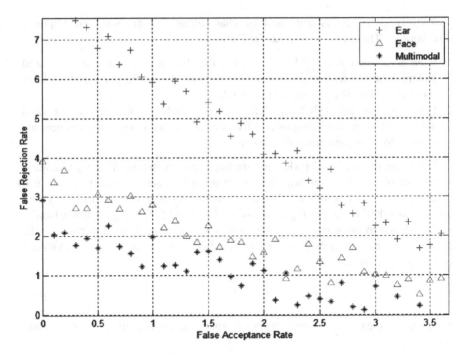

Fig. 8.6 FAR-FRR graphs for original multimodal biometric system

network which used to utilise all the vectors in the training phase. By eliminating any of the feature sets, the network would experience confusion in convergence patterns. In the next section, we will propose a modified system, which tends to overcome the described issue.

8.4 Multimodal Biometric System: A New Architecture

In the original architecture [5, 7], we proposed to create multimodal system in the feature level, meaning that the features from different biometrics are combined in the feature level, and after data analysis, the new subspace of feature set is fed into the learner which in this case is a chaotic neural network. As described in the previous section, one important drawback of such a system is the significant reduction in the accuracy of the system, in the absence of one or more of the input biometrics, while this situation is rare in practice, there should be a way to address it.

While we can maintain the subspace clustering analysis and the proposed chaotic neural network, in this section we will describe a system in which the fusion is moved to the rank level. We will illustrate benefits of such a modification to

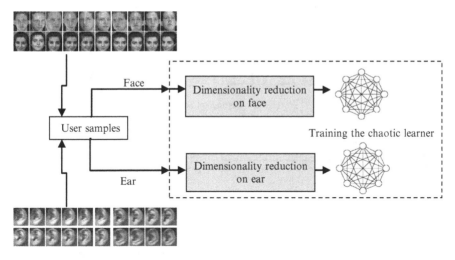

Fig. 8.7 Training phase of the new architecture

increase the reliability of the system in the absence of any of the biometrics. The architecture of the new system is shown in Fig. 8.7.

According to the new architecture, the feature vectors of different biometrics are treated separately. Instead of one large vector which contains the features of all the biometrics, we have several vectors, as:

$$X = (x_1, ..., x_d)^T$$

$$u = (u_1, ..., u_m)^T$$

$$v = (v_1, ..., v_n)^T$$

and for each vector, a separate neural network is trained. By other means, instead of single classifier, we have k classifiers where k is the number of biometrics. Within the testing phase and when a new pattern is introduced into the system, once the normalisation phase is passed, each pattern is fed into its corresponding learner system as shown in Fig. 8.8.

In case of verification, each neural network returns the closest distance between the new pattern and one of the stored pattern in the database. If the distance is greater than the FAR-FRR ratio threshold, then the pattern is simply classified as imposter. Once the system obtains the yes/no results from all its neural subsystems, it performs a simple majority voting mechanism to verify/reject the user.

The main advantage of the new architecture is to avoid system crashes during the absence of some of the input biometrics. Meanwhile, we sacrifice the correlation between many of the features from different biometrics. For example, the skin tone is highly correlated in the ear and face areas, while they are treated separately in the

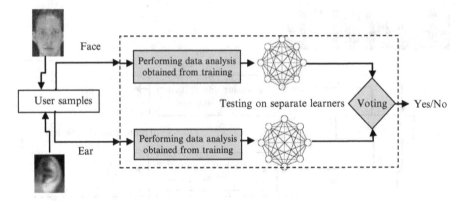

Fig. 8.8 The testing phase of the new architecture

new architecture. In order to evaluate the new architecture, first we compare a similar set of face and ear samples and their corresponding FAR-FRR graph. The system 1 architecture has slightly better performance compared to the new one, where approximately 2% more accuracy is visible in the graph. Moreover, by increasing the FAR threshold close to 2.5%, the false rejection rate drops to 0%, while the minimum FAR rate for the new architecture is 4.35% in order to gain the FRR rate of 0%.

While making the separate feature sets and training separate classifiers based on each set results in a slightly less accurate system, it is advantageous if one biometric is missing. The old architecture is very sensitive to the absence of any of the input biometrics. Hereby, we examine the effect of removing the ear biometric on both of the systems. The results are shown for the multimodal systems in Fig. 8.9.

The red graph represents the new experimented system which allows one biometric trait to be missing altogether, and the black graph represents the original system. While in the presence of all biometric data the original system performs slightly better, when we eliminate one of the resources, the original system performance is worse than that of a new system. According to the graph, the new architectures is affected by approximately a 2× FRR rate (e.g. for FAR of 2%, and the FRR rate is increased from 3.5% to 6%). The original architecture (the black graph) is affected to a much bigger degree. Hereby, we justify the low rate of accuracy reduction in the new system according the new architecture. Figure 8.10 shows the behaviour of the new system in the absence of one of the resources.

As it can be seen in the above figure, the overall effect of eliminating one of the feature sets impacts the precision of the final decision. Despite of this, it does not interfere with the process of verification on the other learners (e.g. face neural network in this case). The dashed path shows the parts of the system, which are affected by the absence of the data. While the neural network associated with the ear patterns is completely out of track, the face learner works flawlessly. Finally, the voting system ignores the ear learner, since there is no output, and the whole system reduces to a single biometric system based on the face biometric.

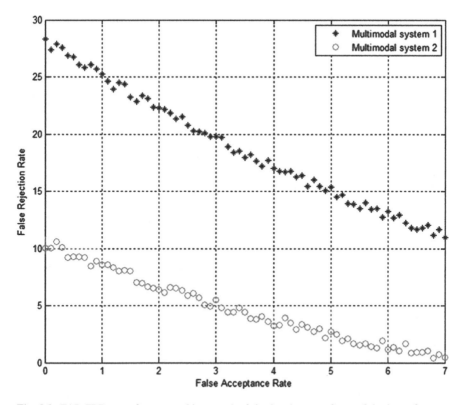

Fig. 8.9 FAR-FRR rates for new architecture (*red*) in the absence of one of the input features versus original architecture (*black*)

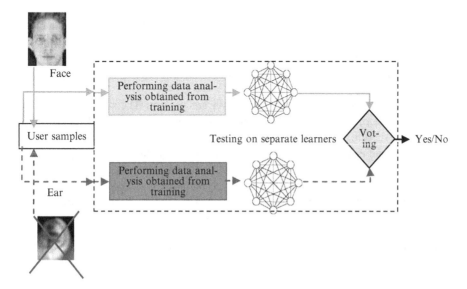

Fig. 8.10 The effect of eliminating one of the biometrics on the new architecture

8.5 Multimodal Biometric System: Effect of Using Chaotic Neural Network

Up to this point, we have compared the system with different architectures, different fusion levels and different types of data. However, the effect of using neural network is not investigated in detail. We aim to discuss the neural-network pros and cons in this section and provide a general overview on the effect of using neural networks in the proposed system.

According to the literature, most of the current researches on multimodal biometric systems on feature level focus on the effect of utilising a better data mining approach and optimising the general architecture. Meanwhile, the learners are chosen to be as simple as possible. The main reason is that most of the biometric systems work in real time; thus, computation efficiency is very demanding in such systems.

After processing the data, normally a significantly smaller subset is obtained, which is used for recognition/verification purposes. A very effective and simple solution for comparing the incoming pattern with the stored ones would be computing the Euclidean distance of the obtained subspace with stored patterns. The closer distance means the higher probability of being a member of the candidate class. Suppose an imaginary system provides a vector, $\Omega^T = [\omega_1, \ldots, \omega_M]$, as the candidate vectors for the input patterns. The candidate of the newly introduced pattern Ω_k is computed, and the closest pattern is found by minimising the following equation:

$$\varepsilon_k = \left\| \Omega - \Omega_k \right\|^2 \tag{8.4}$$

The input face is considered to belong to a class if ε_k if it is below an established threshold $\theta\varepsilon$. By changing this threshold, we can obtain different FAR and FRR rates. We have replaced the chaotic neural network with a conventional distance approach to compare the effect of using the same data mining approach but without the chaotic neural network. The new system architecture in the training phase is shown in Fig. 8.11.

We assume that all of the biometric data are present. The discussion on the absence of one of the biometrics is exactly the same as we provided for the new architecture section, and the similar results are expected. Here we target the original architecture and exclude the discussion of feature elimination.

Both systems (with and without neural-network learner) are trained and experimented with the same set of data. The systems are also inspected with single biometrics (ear and face) and their combination. The FRR-FAR rates are calculated for both of the systems. In the original system, the threshold is set based on the number of neuron values change, while in the Euclidean system, the neighbourhood distance is used as the a measure of threshold. The results of both of the systems are shown in Fig. 8.12a, b.

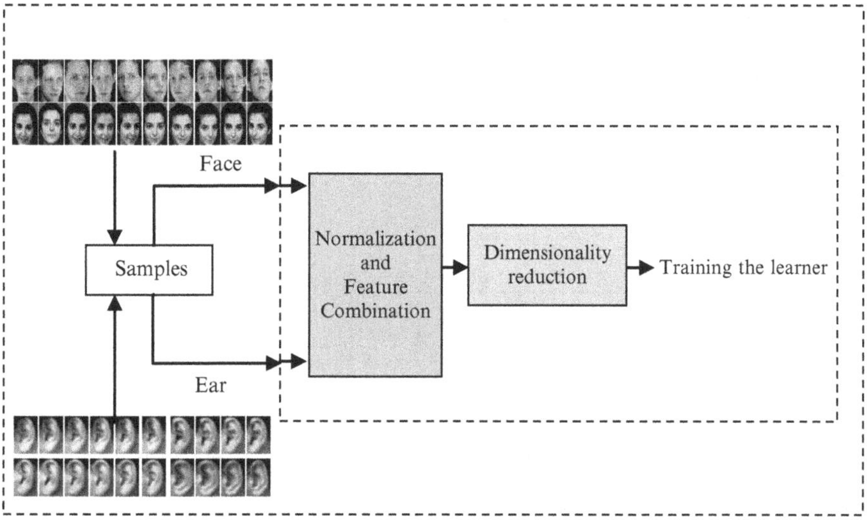

Fig. 8.11 The structure of the system without chaotic neural network

As shown in Fig. 8.12, the system experiences a doubled error rate when using Euclidean learner instead of chaotic neural network. The accuracy rate is high enough to call the original system a dominant winner. Where using the Euclidean learner is not advisable, yet it is the most commonly used method up to date.

Many real-world applications of biometrics include hundreds of thousands of patterns stored in the system. One significant limitation of chaotic neural networks (and neural networks in general) is their need for large amount of memory to store large patterns. For a network of size n, a Hopfield neural network is proven to be limited to store approximately n/7 classes of patterns. This value for chaotic neural network exceeds to n/2.5 which is a significant improvement but still limiting.

The training phase could accept as many patterns as introduced. However, the limitation could be translated as a troublesome accuracy decrementing in the test phase. To illustrate the problem, we ran some experiments on the boundary condition of neural learner which is depicted below.

In our first experiment, we examine a network with huge number of neurons (10 K); each corresponding to a single feature in the obtained subspace. For a database size of 117 patterns, we expect the network to have a minimum size of approximately 200 neurons to be completely functional. In our experiments, the network size is 10 K which is way above the expected value, and hence the performance should not be affected. The test was repeated for datasets of size 312, 465 and 512 patterns. For the given range, the minimum required network size is around 1 K which is still below the size of the actual network.

In this experiment, the GAR-FAR rate graphs are shown in Fig. 8.13 to compare the fallibility of the network. The GAR/FAR rate is very small, and hence the log values of the x vector (FAR) are shown.

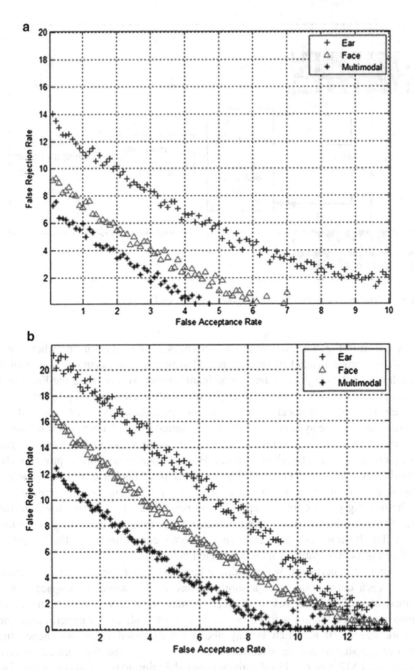

Fig. 8.12 The FRR-FAR rates for the original system (**a**) with neural learner (**b**) with Euclidean learner

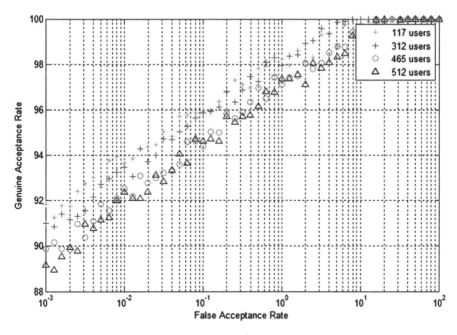

Fig. 8.13 The GAR-FAR graph for different number of users with sufficient number of neurons

The results show that for a sufficient number of neurons, the system is complex enough to store the given patterns. In the previous experiment, we utilised sufficient number neurons to support all input patterns. In the next experiment (Fig. 8.14), we will confine the number of neurons to 250 neurons which is sufficient to support the 117 users experiment case. As seen from Fig. 8.14, the GAR rate is decreased for a given FAR where the number of neurons are reduced. As we limit the number of users to a reasonable number below 1,000, the system works well. However, for greater number of users in real-world application, the network size should grow as well. The main challenge of designing such networks is the amount of memory needed to build the network. While virtual memory can always overcome such problems, the usage of slower memory devices will affect the computation speed of the system.

8.6 Conclusion

In this work, we described an alternative architecture for multimodal biometric system which was critically examined from the different perspectives. In order to build a more robust system, a new architecture is proposed, where a system is

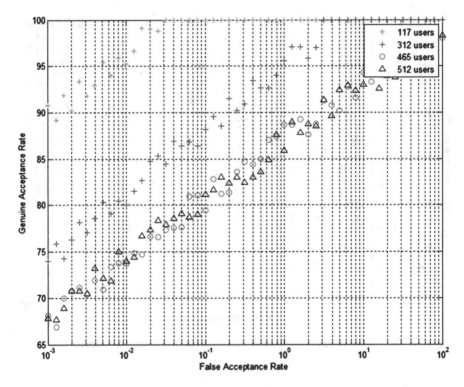

Fig. 8.14 The GAR-FAR graph for different number of users with confined number of neurons

resistant to absence of some features. Extensive experimentation was performed. Finally, the limitations and advantages of the systems which utilise chaotic neural network were discussed.

Acknowledgements Authors acknowledge invaluable help and advice for Prof Khalid Saeed while working on this chapter. This research was partially supported by NSERC.

References

1. Jain AK, Ross A, Prabhakar A (2004) An introduction to biometric recognition. IEEE Trans Circ Syst Video Technol Spec Iss ImageVideo-Based Biometrics 14(1):4–20
2. Ross A, Jain A (2004) Multimodal biometrics: an overview. In: Proceedings of 12th European signal processing conference (EUSIPCO), Vienna, Austria, pp 1221–1224
3. Tolba AS, Rezq AA (2000) Combined classifier for invariant face recognition. Pattern Anal Appl 4:289–302
4. Rowley HA, Baluja S, Kanade T (1998) Neural network-based face detection. IEEE Trans Pattern Anal Mach Intell 20(1):23–38
5. Ahmadian K, Gavrilova M (2011) A novel multi-modal biometric architecture for high-dimensional features. In: Cyberworlds, Banff, Canada, IEEE proceedings, pp 9–16

6. Yambor W (2000) Analysis of PCA-based and fisher discriminant-based image recognition. Technical report. Computer Science Department, Colorado State University
7. Gavrilova M, Ahmadian K (2011) Dealing with biometric multi-dimensionality through novel chaotic neural network methodology in issue on advances and trends in biometrics. Int J Inf Technol Manage 11(1/2):18–34
8. Belkin M, Niyogi P (2003) Laplacian eigenmaps for dimensionality reduction and data representation. Neural Comput 15(6):1373–1396
9. Tenenbaum JB, de Silva V, Langford JC (2000) A global geometric framework for nonlinear dimensionality reduction. Science 290:2319–2323
10. Hopfield JJ (1990) The effectiveness of analogue 'neural network' hardware. Netw Comput Neural Syst 1(1):27–40

Part II
Kansei Engineering

Chapter 9
Introduction to Kansei Engineering

Tomomasa Nagashima

Abstract Aiming at improving the quality of life (QOL) of people in everyday living, Kansei Engineering (KE) has been proposed. Since then, while industrial sectors in Japan have applied KE, its methodology has not made much marked progress. The fact that the foundation of KE differs from any of modern technologies seems to bring some difficulties to its application. In order to reduce such difficulties, we begin with the fundamental definition of Kansei and a brief introduction to the characteristic elements of technologies in KE.

9.1 Needs for New Engineering

In recent decades, markets of industrial products have been significantly globalized [1]. This trend has resulted in general reduction of time to develop new products, whose life cycle is not necessarily long, along with harsh competition among manufacturers. All these trends force the manufacturers to adapt methods that enable rapid development and production (see Chap. 10).

Meanwhile, consumers' demands have also risen due to improved cognitive ergonomics and education/knowledge of advanced consumer products. In other words, consumers' sense of value is changing, and therefore, consumer products are required to have high performance, better function, and high quality.

It is worth mentioning here that the concept of "quality of products" has been evolved as industries have been developed. According to traditional manufacturing, the quality of products means a functional property of products which is controlled and measured merely by the standard in production processes. Therefore, quality is determined only by the manufacturing side.

T. Nagashima (✉)
Graduate School of Engineering, Muroran Institute of Technology, 27-1, Mizumoto,
Muroran, Hokkaido 050-8585, Japan
e-mail: nagasima@csse.muroran-it.ac.jp

K. Saeed and T. Nagashima (eds.), *Biometrics and Kansei Engineering*,
DOI 10.1007/978-1-4614-5608-7_9, © Springer Science+Business Media New York 2012

However, it is crucial for *Kansei* engineering to understand that the quality of products is not determined solely by the functional aspect of products but also on the user's keen demands and their subtle evaluations. That is, impressions and feelings evoked by products have a prominent role in making their purchase decisions. Therefore, designing products attractive to customers requires knowledge of consumers' feelings and impressions.

Thus, manufacturers can no longer ignore the critical change of a user's mind to softer issues determined by interactions between products and the human mind, in particular human sensations and emotions.

9.2 Proposal of *KANSI* Engineering

The ultimate goal of KE is to construct novel engineering systems which support improvement of consumers' daily quality of life (QOL). In order to achieve the central purpose of KE, it is essential to put the production systems in the perspectives of users. The general production processes in KE will be summarized in the following scheme:

Designers(in Makers) = >Products in Markets{Cars, Housing, Dresses, or Food}
= >Users = >(feedback to) = >Designers(in Makers)

The most important characteristic of KE stems from the fact that the final evaluation of products is made by user's mind, not by specifications made by the makers' side [2]. In this respect, KE seems to have something in common with ergonomics and biometrics. However, there is a slight difference between them. While ergonomics and biometrics have a tendency to attach weight to physiological or behavioral aspects of humans, respectively, KE has a tendency to attach weight to psychological aspect including emotions.

KE today highlights the role of users' favorable impression or positive emotions provoked by products or services. For instance, a sense of "comfortable" or "pleasurable" has now become an interesting new target in engineering industrial goods.

When a product evokes positive emotions or pleasant feelings in users by looking at or touching the product, a kind of value called "*Kansei* value" is generated. The logic behind it is shown as follows: if a user is strongly moved by or attached to a product, the product will be worth the price for the user, which could be more than the price evaluated in a regular market.

In order to realize the new concept "*Kansei* value," KE focuses on the cooperation between designers on the maker's side and users in the process of manufacturing. That is, designers propose new ideas for products to users, and users give them feedback back and forth in an interactive environment. The interactive production style mentioned above is called "co-creation" [3], where a common *Kansei* value between designers and users is brought up through mutual communications via dialogue. It should be emphasized from a KE point of view that in this communication process, the essential issue is to establish a mutual understanding accompanied by empathy between designers and users.

9.3 The Term *"Kansei"*

While it has been clarified that the most important characteristic of KE arises from the interactions between products/services and the human (user's) mind including sensations, feelings, and emotions, the definition of *Kansei* itself has not been well established yet.

In the following section, we will discuss the basic meanings of *Kansei*. It is a Japanese noun typically referring to sensitivity of human mind to stimuli. For instance, we say things like "she has a fine sensitivity (*Kansei*) to colors." It would be agreeable to state that the meaning of this sentence is more or less equivalent to "she has a fine sense of color." Thus, the term *Kansei* in Japanese has been used in reference to the notion of aesthetics such as expression of aesthetic features of an individual's impression by a variety of visual stimuli. Indeed, the meanings of *Kansei* which can be found in the major Japanese dictionaries have been selected basically from the texts of modern European philosophy. In particular, it is suggested that the term *Kansei* corresponds to the term "aesthetisch" employed by German philosophers Alexander Gottlieb Baumgarten and Immanuel Kant in the middle of the eighteenth century. It is worth mentioning that Baumgarten was a founder of the study of aesthetics which deals with the theory of beauty in arts and Kant was a philosopher whose ideas still have strong influence on the foundation of people's thoughts for over 250 years.

There seem to be several reasons that make it difficult to define the term *"Kansei."* The first problem is concerned with the extent to which the term "aesthetic" can be applied with a question if the term "aesthetic" includes sentiments or not. The second problem is concerned with the passivity involved in the term "sensitivity." This question reveals serious shortage in the original definition given by philosophers like Kant, especially examining *Kansei* from a point of view in engineering. This is because if we apply *Kansei* to engineering problems, it is absolutely necessary for *Kansei* to take part in active information processing in the brain including passive aspect of it. In other words, *Kansei* is expected to play an active role in expressing or representing something, for instance, aesthetics in the production process (see Chap. 11), and this active aspect or the expressive ability of *Kansei* will be essential for designing. This is because designers must develop novel products or services which meet users' demands. This active aspect of *Kansei*'s expressive ability can be shown by examples such as an audience moved by the performance of professional athletes as well as people touched by artistic works by artists with excellent techniques.

9.4   Several Characteristic Elements of *Kansei* Engineering: The Status Quo

Splendid works by excellent artists attract and fascinate people. This seems to be an indisputable fact, caused by the interactions between art works and the human mind. The interactions must strongly influence a person's mind, but this aspect has not yet received sufficient scientific consideration.

In a similar manner, people are attracted to excellent manufactured products such as luxury cars. This provides strong support for the materialization of KE. In other words, the central issue in KE becomes the interactions between products and the human mind which evoke positive emotions such as attractive or pleasant feelings.

Let us revisit the proposal of KE and the previously mentioned two characteristic notions in KE: *Kansei* value and co-creation. Because empathy [4] lies in a deep part both in *Kansei* value and co-creation, it is believed that empathy can be the key issue of KE. Hence, it is not unnatural to adopt empathy as a possible working definition of *Kansei* for KE. Note that the notion of empathy is independent from the issue of the shortage of passivity in the original definition of *Kansei*, and it is believed to have a connection to the functions of mirror neurons recently found in the brain of monkeys [5].

Another characteristic element is concerned with the problem of how to acquire information of *Kansei*, and there are basically two kinds of methods, verbal and nonverbal. In the nonverbal method, it pays attention to the recognition of face, voices, and gestures. In particular, a change of facial color and shape is supposed to be revealed when one gets some emotions responding to stimuli (see Chap. 12). As for the verbal method, it is common to make appropriate questionnaires, in which users' personal preference and demands are reflected. Ordinarily, the results are analyzed by means of statistical methods.

At this point, it should be remarked that there are strong demands on further development of information technology which is able to grasp and cope with individual's *Kansei* (see Chap. 13), particularly applicable to nursing service robots (see Chap. 14).

References

1. Shinohara A, Shimizu Y, Sakamoto H (1996) Invitation to *Kansei* engineering, Morikita, Japan (in Japanese)
2. Nagashima T, Tanaka H, Uozumi T (2008) An overview of Kansei engineering: a proposal of *Kansei* informatics toward realizing safety and pleasantness of individuals in information network society. Int J Biometrics 1(1):3–19
3. Ministry of Economy, Trade and Industry in Japan (2009) *Kansei* initiative. http://www.meti. go.jp/english/policy/mon_info_service/mono/kansei2009/inind.html
4. Smith A (1759) The theory of moral aentiments. Edinburgh, London
5. Gallese V, Goldman A (1998) Mirror neurons and the simulation theory of mind reading. Trends Cogn Sci 12:494–501

Chapter 10
Human Being and Kansei Engineering

Yoshio Shimizu

Abstract This chapter explains human being and Kansei engineering which is the basis of postmodern technology. Modern technology has taken an important role after the industrial revolution. The society has been developed according to the modern technology, but it comes to a deadlock now. Therefore, our main concern is how to evade the deadlock. We proposed postmodern technology named Kansei engineering which was based on Kansei. Kansei is an integrated human ability which includes emotion, feeling, recognition, modeling, and expression. The new technology is characterized by an interactive method and a network structure. The beauty of modern technology as a single logic method of deduction exists in simplicity and power of exploitation, while the beauty of Kansei technology exists in complexity and tolerance in heterogeneity. We apply Kansei technology to industry, and then we can escape from various kinds of crises.

10.1 Introduction

Here, we will discuss features of modern technology. Modern science and technology have developed tools and methods that help to improve people's lives and society, but nowadays, it cannot sufficiently perform its mission. The beauty of modern science and technology exists in the simple form of deductive method. However, this method alone will not be able to solve the complex problems of modern society. We live in a very complicated society where we have to accept various kinds of principles and we have to continuously remake our society. We need new science and technology in order to solve modern problems such as explosion of population, energy crisis, and broken economic system. Kansei engineering is one of the new adjustable science and technologies that are able to realize a symbiotic relationship in the society [1].

Y. Shimizu (✉)
Shinshu University, Nagano, Japan
e-mail: y.shimizu@shinshu-u.ac.jp

K. Saeed and T. Nagashima (eds.), *Biometrics and Kansei Engineering*,
DOI 10.1007/978-1-4614-5608-7_10, © Springer Science+Business Media New York 2012

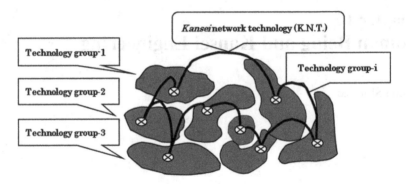

Fig. 10.1 The *Kansei* network technology makes good relations of people and makes a good solution

Figure 10.1 shows a conceptual picture of Kansei network technology (KNT). KNT is one of Kansei engineering technologies, and it can solve problems and make design products by collaborating with different technologies. Groups of different fields are combined by KNT system. People participating in the network system from different groups offer information about ideas, designs, opinions, tools, methods, and so on. They are the designers, coordinators, producers, retailers, and end-consumers, and they make in real time some plans, models, processing methods, and other things by using the brainstorming method. KNT is characterized by making a better structure of human relation. The structure includes different kinds of peoples, that is, from designers to end-consumers. How to coordinate these peoples is the key technology of KNT. Modern technology which has a sharp edge of special field makes solutions by making new technology; meanwhile, Kansei engineering as a postmodern technology makes solutions by making a good human relation. Good human relation makes good ideas by seeing and thinking from various directions.

10.2 Particle's Kansei and Kansei

10.2.1 Definition of Kansei

If there is only one particle in the world, then there is no world because one particle cannot make space and world (Fig. 10.2a). If there are two particles and they have some interaction force, then a world of space will be yielded (Fig. 10.2b). We defined this interaction force as particle's Kansei. When we exchange a particle for a human being, we change the name of "particle's Kansei" into Kansei.

Kansei of human being is more complicated since there are many relations between two persons (Fig. 10.2c).

Fig. 10.2 Particle's *Kansei*
will be made by more than
two particles (**a**), (**b**). Kansei
is shown in (**c**). (**a**) One
particle cannot produce
space; (**b**) two particles
produce interaction called
particle's *Kansei*; (**c**) *Kansei*
with N relations

a

One particle cannot produce space.

b

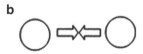

Two particles produce interaction called particle's *Kansei*.

c

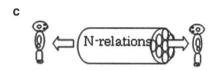

Kansei with N- relations

10.2.2   An Aggregated Structure by Particle's Kansei

Particle's Kansei (an interactive force between particles) which is defined as
potential energy (PE) is made by the feature of two-particle relation. Particle's
Kansei is given as a differential function of PE. The aggregated structure is made by
particle's Kansei. A general function of PE is shown in Fig. 10.3a. This function has
repulsion force and attraction force, and this was first proposed in 1924 by
J. Lennard-Jones [2]. According to this function, particles keep constant distance
and aggregate, as shown in Fig. 10.3b.

There are many kinds of particle's Kansei according to a different combination of
particles or changes with circumstances. Therefore, various aggregation structures
will be expected. Figure 10.4a shows PE of particle's Kansei with repulsion force.
In this case, each particle cannot come closer more than certain distance and
particles gather at random, as shown in Fig. 10.4b.

As stated above, particles have their form according to their particle's Kansei.
Next, we would like to discuss the aggregation form of human beings and Kansei
(instead of particle's Kansei).

10.3   From a Particle to a Person

Instead of an aggregation structure of particles, next we will consider about a cohered
structure of persons. If only we exchange a particle for a person, can we calculate feature
of a human society? It is easy to estimate the feature of the structure of particles, but in

Fig. 10.3 Potential energy
(PE) of particle's *Kansei*
and the aggregated structure:
(a) potential energy (PE)
of particle's *Kansei*;
(b) a structure of by
particle's *Kansei* of (a)

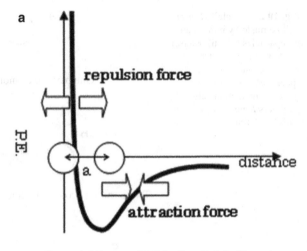

Potential Energy (P.E.) of particle's *Kansei*

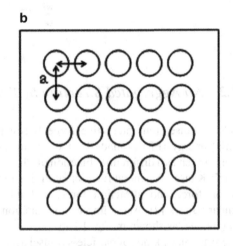

A structure of by particle's *Kansei* of (a)

the case of a human being, it is more difficult to calculate the feature of society as an aggregation of persons. Because human being has complicated relations with each other, then we have to assume various kinds of mutual interactions (Fig. 10.2c).

10.3.1 Cohered People

There are repulsive or attractive forces among people: people who feel a sense of closeness gather, and those who hate each other go away. By this human feature, we make a community.

Fig. 10.4 Potential energy (PE) of particle's *Kansei* has only repulsion force and the aggregated structure: (**a**) PE of particle's *Kansei* with repulsion force; (**b**) a random particle structure with only repulsion force

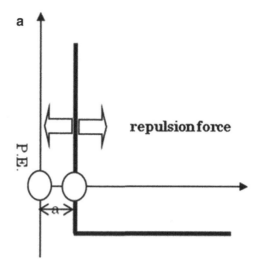

P.E. of particle's *Kansei* with repulsion force

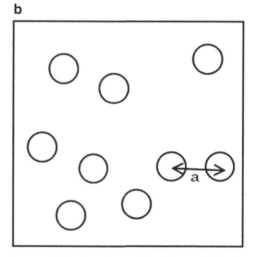

A random particles structure with only repulsion force

We try to make an aggregated structure of people by the relation of potential energy. The curve of a PE function is assumed, as shown in Fig. 10.5a. Region (a) is influenced by an attractive force, and region (b) is influenced by repulsive force. Owing to these two regions, many cohesion structures (colonies) are made (Fig. 10.5b).

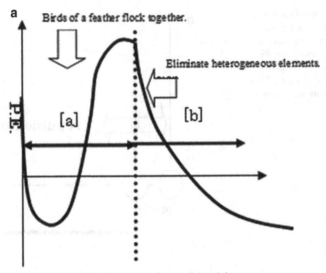

P.E. for aggregation and repulsion

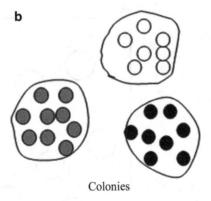

Colonies

Fig. 10.5 A potential energy for colonies: (**a**) PE for aggregation and repulsion; (**b**) colonies

10.3.2 Kansei of Hierarchy

A human being has greed of lots of kinds. Some needs originate from greed of instinct, and some wants come from the desire for more great positions. The bigger structure of society gives us the more safety and security. As described in Erich Fromm's theory "Escape from freedom (1941)," therefore, people want to belong to a big organization and want to get a great position. The curve of potential energy for human relations which make a hierarchical structure is given, as shown in Fig. 10.6a. This curve has many peaks and valleys, and it has an upward slant. The hierarchy structure has a strong stability, and it is the basis form of a country,

Fig. 10.6 A potential energy
of hierarchy, the structure of
hierarchy, and a collision of
hierarchy

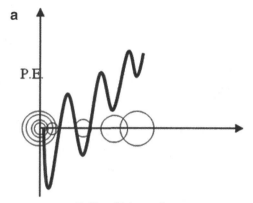

P.E. of hierarchy

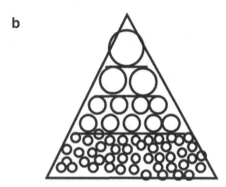

The structure of hierarchy

A collision of hierarchy

a company, and other organization (Fig. 10.6b). The structure sometimes merges others or vanishes into others by means of wars or fights (Fig. 10.6c).

Today, we live in various kinds of structure, namely, a hierarchy structure, a plain structure, and a network structure. The network structure becomes friendlier to us – it gives us more freedom and a richer life in culture – while the hierarchy structure becomes weak.

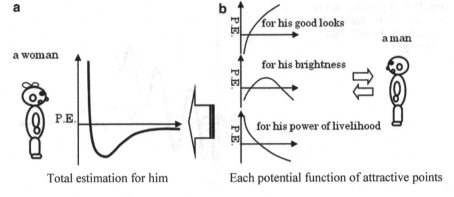

Fig. 10.7 A woman's estimation for a man: (**a**) total estimation for him; (**b**) each potential function of attractive points

10.3.3 Try to Estimate a Person's Kansei

It is difficult to estimate a certain person's Kansei. Our action or reaction, our behavior of our feeling or emotion, and another activity of our mind seem to usually have a certain pattern, but sometimes, these patterns are different from usual. Because of these spiritual activities are controlled by Kansei, we have flexible mind and consonance in Kansei in uncertain. We nevertheless want to estimate human Kansei by an artificial method. A simple sample is shown in Fig. 10.7. When a certain woman will estimate a certain man who is a friend of her, many kinds of items for attractive points will be used for estimation. These are consideration, power of livelihood, brightness, and handsomeness. In her case, she abstracts good looking, brightness, and power of livelihood as attractive points, and each of their potential function is decided, as shown in Fig. 10.7b. She likes his good looking but dislikes his poor power of livelihoods and has complication for his brightness. The total potential function is then shown in Fig. 10.7a. Finally we can imagine that she will keep a certain distance from him, but continues her friendship.

10.4 Kansei Originates New Values

10.4.1 Kansei Circulates Through People

When the world continues in a peace, rich, and stable condition, we can live in the affluent society of Kansei. The affluent society of Kansei can allow many kinds of values and accept a different type of religion.

Till now, we use a hard technology, and we live toward the rich of materials. From now, we use Kansei technology, and we make new value of Kansei.

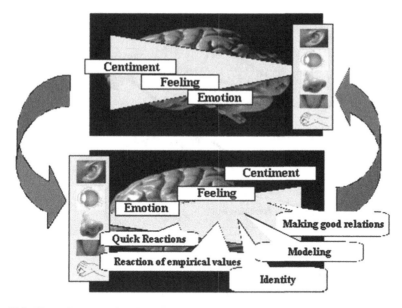

Fig. 10.8 *Kansei* has many functions and circulates through people

Kansei is concerned with sophisticated human abilities such as sensibility, recognition, identification, relationship making, and originating action. A short-time reaction of Kansei is a an emotion such as smile or amazement, a middle-time reaction is a feeling such as a sense of music or a picture, and a long-time reaction is a sentiment such as identification or modeling, as shown in Fig. 10.8.

10.4.2   The Modern Technology and the Postmodern Technology of Kansei Engineering

Kansei is the human power for exchange, so it necessarily includes all actions of values. When a person exchanges their opinion through interactive action, in their mind, this person has recognition for values from outer world and reconstructs their values in an originated model. When we do something according to Kansei, our method varies from the traditional modern science and technology.

Traditional one is a simple logic and a deductive method. It has beauty in simple and in strong power for exploitation. We have got into ecstasy in solving a problem with a single stroke of it. The design method is simple, but many projects will be unsuccessful for a long span of time. This simple method brought us many problems such as the pollution of the environment.

On the other hand, Kansei science and technology is a diverse and an interactive form. We have to spend much time to discuss each other and spend much energy to comprehend different kinds of cultures and values. This method brings us to

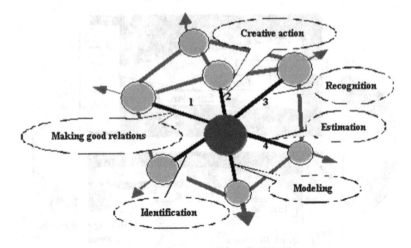

1) Relativity / Interaction
2) Multi-dimensional
3) Diversification (of values, religious style, logics, etc.)
4) Symbiosis
5) Sustainable, Recycling , etc.

Fig. 10.9 *Kansei* makes N-dimensional network world

wonderful world where we can say many thanks to each and feel sympathy for each other according to the recognition for variety of cultures and tasting a lot of experiences. The beauty of Kansei is an interactive form and a symbiosis form of networks (Fig. 10.9). From a long time ago, such beauty has been handed down from generation to generation. It commonly exists everywhere, both in the East and West, but we cannot see it in modern industry stream; thus, interactive industry is inferior to modern industry in number.

It is our responsibility to realize the importance of Kansei technology in the industry and thereby change our economics and culture gradually. For example, the interactive method will be introduced to industry, and the interactive production system replaces a good technology instead of mass-production system. This replacement may bring us to postindustrial age.

10.5 Industrial Capitalism and Postindustrial Capitalism

Our present society is based on capitalist economy dominated by mass-production systems. But it is found to be lacking in meeting the demands placed on it by our modern society. Therefore, we will propose a new production system with the ability to meet the demands of our society to replace the current system. We call this interactive production system.

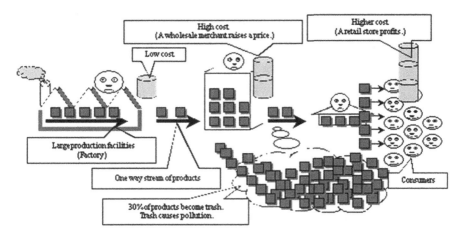

Fig. 10.10   A mass-production and mass-consumption systems with distribution of one way

10.5.1   The Distribution-Based Economy Supporting Industrial Capitalism

In our industrial capitalistic economy, we aim for full production and consumption within the system to maximize its effectiveness. To this end, products are standardized, so they can be more easily processed and produced. The resulting industrial product is lacking in individuality. It is one more "thing," one of many as a result of trying to maximize capital or labor resources. In this economic model, the most efficient way to exploit the "thing" is to circulate it through a market, with essentially a one-way flow. It is argued that this one-way flow results in the "thing" being pushed from the business into the consumers. For this reason, the industrial capitalist economy is maintained by this mass-production/mass-consumption economy, as illustrated in Fig. 10.10. This is also known as the physical distribution economy. The core of this approach relies on standardized products, manufactured at cheap price through economies of scale, and shipped off to consumers through a maze of intermediate layers such as wholesalers, retailers, and a number of transportation handlers. The cost to the consumer is not so cheap because along the way, each intermediate party is required to secure an appropriate profit for handling the product. Because the "thing" is produced in large quantities, they often remain unsold. This surplus supply to the actual demand results in dead stock. Not only does this dead stock produce inefficiencies in the system by gathering dust, but it can also lead to a further burden on the environment by first consuming valuable resources in its production only to be returned in the form of pollution or part of the ever-growing waste dumps, which blight our communities. Another result of this system is the overproduction of certain products, causing excessive supply and prices to plummet in order to stimulate demand. As businesses are forced to cut costs to win competition, they remain on an endless cycle of diminishing profits. It is often difficult for entrepreneurs to escape this make-to-stock production because of the lack of a viable alternative.

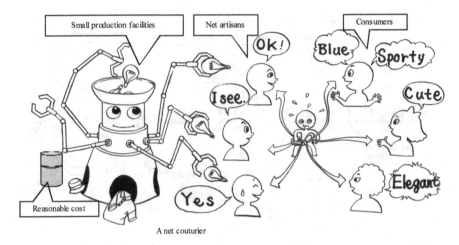

Fig. 10.11 An example of interactive production system of apparel industry

10.5.2 Kansei Distribution Supporting Postindustrial Capitalism

We think that few would object to a new improved system of capitalism, which accents the positive aspects of the current system while minimizes the negative aspects. In our modern-age society dominated by modern science and technology, we argue for a postindustrial form of capitalism, which offers stability and wealth for the many, not just for the few. We think that such a system should have collaboration between the producer and the consumer. In a physical distribution economy, the focus is often on the planning, design, manufacture, distribution, and marketing with little direct contact between the consumer and those beyond the retail level. We believe that workers involved in the manufacturing process require an active meaning to their labor, which does not currently exist. Instead, the workers are marginalized as small cog in the greater economic machine. We would argue that if producers and consumers could collaborate on the design and production of a product, the mutual opinion would produce a more creative and superior product. We call this end result an interactive product in recognition of the collaboration that takes place from the two-way flow of information. We broaden the perspective of the product to include the interaction itself as part of the product, not simply a by-product. The resulting distribution economy can be called Kansei distribution, meaning the joint design production system between producer and consumer. More precisely, we have decided to call this system "the interactive production system." For a concrete example of how this theory can be expressed in practical terms, we will explain in more detail the interactive production system apparel, as shown in Fig. 10.11.

10.6   Conclusion

In this chapter, Kansei engineering is introduced as a postmodern technology different from modern technology of hard and strong material's technology. Postmodern technology is prepared for solving the modern problems and crisis. The features of Kansei engineering are explained as making good human relations among people, while modern technology solves the problem by simple logic and a deductive method. Good human relation makes good idea by seeing and thinking from various directions.

The basic feature of Kansei is defined as adjustable functions and ability of improving relationships among things.

For the coming postmodern industry society, Kansei engineering is establishing an interactive industry in order to change and save the chaotic modern industry world.

An interactive industry system will be anticipated to advance people's Kansei – workers, retailers, consumers, etc. who can live in an affluent society.

References

1. Shimizu Y, Shinohara K, Aoki H, Katou S, Kamijo M, Shimizu H, Takeda T (2005) The role of Kansei engineering in modern society. Reports by Kansei Engineering Technical Committee of Liaison Committee on Human Research and Engineering in Science Council of Japan
2. Lennard-Jones JE (1924) On the determination of molecular fields. Proc R Soc Lond A 106 (738):463–477

Chapter 11
Concepts of *Kansei* and Aesthetic Thoughts

Tomomasa Nagashima, Yoshifumi Okada, and Yuzuko Nagashima

Abstract *Kansei* engineering has proposed a novel system of production and services which evokes the user's mind/sense of value as embedded in the products or services. In this system, interactions between the products and the human mind are the core issue in developing the products. While its applications in industries have been stimulated, methodological development has not been marked yet. Aiming at promoting the method capable of developing basic ideas of *Kansei* engineering, we discuss the two fundamental topics in it. The first topic is concerned with the notion of *Kansei* and its varieties. We examine *Kansei* in relation to philosophy centered on aesthetics established in the eighteenth century. The second issue is concerned with a possible relation of *Kansei* to thinking within the human mind, that is, the problem of how it forms connection into thoughts. We present two kinds of aesthetic thoughts as concrete examples. Finally, we discuss the problem of quality evaluation of products, that is, how to evaluate products from *Kansei* point of view.

T. Nagashima (✉)
Graduate School of Engineering, Muroran Institute of Technology, 27-1, Mizumoto,
Hokkaido, Muroran 050-8585, Japan
e-mail: nagasima@csse.muroran-it.ac.jp

Y. Okada
Muroran Institute of Technology, Muroran, Japan

Y. Nagashima
University of Hawaii at Manoa, Honolulu, HI, USA

K. Saeed and T. Nagashima (eds.), *Biometrics and Kansei Engineering*,   191
DOI 10.1007/978-1-4614-5608-7_11, © Springer Science+Business Media New York 2012

11.1 Proposal of *Kansei* Engineering

11.1.1 The Background and the Aim of Kansei Engineering

One of the most challenging issues for the current engineering will be to develop a novel method in which to overcome various tasks of social influence such as environmental pollution brought by the mass production-consumption regime. In order to tackle these problems, *Kansei* engineering (KE) has been proposed [1]. It could be said the ultimate goal of KE is to construct various systems which help to improve the quality of life (QOL) of people in their everyday living. For that purpose, it is essential for KE to develop the manufacturing systems to be focused on the perspective of the users. The general production processes proposed by KE will be summarized by the following scheme:

Designers(in Makers) = >Products in Markets{Cars, Housing, Clothes, Food, , }
= >Users = >(feedback to) = >Designers(in Makers) = >...

What is important in this scheme is the cycle of information flow from designers toward users, where there is continuous interaction between the makers' side and the users' side.

11.1.2 Novel Concepts in the Proposal of Kansei Engineering

The summary of important characteristics in the production process flow chart above has two points. The first characteristic is concerned with a concept of a new sense of value called "*Kansei* value." It refers to users' mind/feeling as a sense of attachment, or caring to details of products, which represents an individual's value latent in the users' mind. However, this value could be one of economic priority, especially for a group of multiple users who love the same products [2].

The second characteristic is concerned with the production process through which the product with *Kansei* value is developed. In this process, the interactive cooperation between designers on the maker's side and users has become indispensable in order to share and establish a common sense of value surrounding the products. Such a production process is referred to as a "co-creation" between them (Fig. 11.1).

It is interesting to consider what the origin of the human mind which enables us to "co-create" is. One of the theories for this question is empathy. In order to substantiate and establish the concept of "co-creation" within the production process of *Kansei* products, it is necessary to reestablish the wide range of knowledge systems and not focus solely on the systems of engineering. In particular, one of the most important issues here is to develop new methods of engineering, where products are created by exchanging their aesthetic feelings as well as their demands between designers and users.

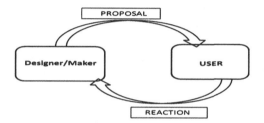

Fig. 11.1 Concept of co-creation between a designer and a user. The user participates in production processes in cooperation with the designer, sharing a common *Kansei* value for the product concerned

11.1.3 Method of Kansei Engineering: The Status Quo

In order to develop a variety of products in our daily lives by following KE, it is necessary to start cross-sectional studies which would extend into quite different fields such as art and bioscience. This means that we have to construct a methodology which enables us to integrate the results of different research fields such as design engineering, system engineering, material science, and sensory engineering, although the most difficult task would be to establish such a cross-sectional method.

In order to achieve this goal, it will be reasonable to start our discussion with the following two fundamental topics. The first topic is concerned with the notions of *Kansei*. While there seems to be a variety of approaches to it, we will adopt the approach introduced by modern western philosophy in the eighteenth century. While this approach seems to be unique compared to a conventional Japanese point of view, we claim that it fosters mutual understanding among different countries with different cultural backgrounds. In order to develop the methods for KE, it is necessary to create a new framework of ideas which is quite different from conventional epistemology in science and logic. Therefore, we will discuss a new framework of ideas to utilize *Kansei*. For this purpose, we are going to discuss two types of ideas. The first one is about aesthetic judgment by Immanuel Kant, and the second one is empathetic understanding introduced by Adam Smith.

11.2 Concept of Kansei and Its Diversity

11.2.1 Kansei and Modernization of the West

It seems plausible for many people that the notion of *Kansei* is specific in Japan because of Japanese words such as the *wabi* and *sabi*. There is a wide range of arguments about what exactly *Kansei* is [3, 4], but in this chapter, we would like to examine the emergence of it in the west in relation to the modern western philosophy.

In the middle of the eighteenth century, Western Europe was moving toward full-scale capitalistic economies and democratic societies which were about to emerge. It is often said that around this time, there lay a fundamental skepticism about what was right, what they knew, and what they did not know because of the setback of medieval authority. Cartesianism represented by Rene Descartes' famous remark "I think, therefore I am" was coined to answer such questions [5].

In short, his remark "I think therefore I am" shows his belief that even with the new found knowledge that created uncertainty in the era in which he lived, the fact that "I exist" itself is certain and this is not going to change. Descartes, based on his own beliefs, achieved magnificent results through modern methods of natural science in order to elucidate materials in the natural world. Nonetheless, his belief of existence was to a certain extent flawed. According to his logic, "I" can still think without a physical body, that is, one can purely know the self as "I, who think" regardless of their physical form. Thus, it means that "I" can recognize the self directly without external and physical stimuli, which "I" is a spiritual subject independent from the material body. This is the origin where his so-called dualism comes from.

At the same time, a wide-scaled enlightenment movement was gaining popularity in the Western Europe. It is important to understand that modern Western Europe was born after the enlightenment movement and the history that was directly connected to the modern society opened by the French Revolution and Industrial Revolution. It is particularly important to note this because it became the prototype for Japan at the time when the Meiji Restoration started after the end of the national seclusion period during Edo era. What was it about the enlightenment movement which influenced the initial formation of modern Europe? The fundamental idea in it, the "human image" which explained what humans are, was so thought-provoking that, in a sense, it should regain our attention today. Here, we are going to examine what *Kansei* is by focusing on the enlightenment movement, particularly its idea of the "human image."

11.2.2 The Foundation of Aesthetics as a Study of Kansei

11.2.2.1 Western Modernization and a Study of Kansei = Aesthetics

Originally from Japan, KE is considered a new field of engineering in terms of the conception of introducing human *Kansei* into technologies. It is also commonly believed that Japanese culture has historically nurtured its own unique *Kansei*. However, it should be noted that it was in the modern West where *Kansei*, as a clear form, emerged into the history. That is to say, it emerged as a form of aesthetics in the middle of the eighteenth century.

In other words, *Kansei* in the West was used as a yardstick to measure the value of creativity in their new culture. There lies a branching point where the Western Europe nurtured a different kind of *Kansei* from the one in Japan. They invented a concept of *Kansei* as a scale in order to measure the creativity of artistic works and the artists who created them. It could also be thought that attractiveness of humans was the scale used to determine a human's overall ability or values. Alexander G. Baumgarten authored "Aesthetics" [6] during this era. It is often said that aesthetics as the objective of *Kansei* became the center of the art since this book was published.

11.2.2.2 What Is the Value of Kansei?

On one hand, the new area of science was thought to play a decisive role in developing the modern world as Isaac Newton became famous. On the other hand, art was considered to bear a supporting role for reasoning in the modern world. *Kansei* was expected to measure and evaluate quality or value, thus the creativity of new works in the field of art. In a new realm of study, aesthetics was considered as an important topic in figuring out what the value of art and beauty was. Although it is difficult to conjecture this since it is not a common subject of argument anymore today, what sort of values did art and beauty have back then?

According to specialists in aesthetics, the following was the primary point in axiology in those days [7]. In the eighteenth century, there was a sense of conflict among people because there were those who were seeking gain for their own benefit. On the other hand, in the fictional world of art, people empathized with faithful people who were facing difficulties. Thus, it can be said that a concept of art creating a fictional world plays a role of education in showing the composition of society. Also, enjoying the beauty of an object is fundamentally different from the desire to own the object, and thus, it has a social meaning, so does the concept of art as a fictional world. It is a concept of pricelessness in art where people appreciate the object and measure the value based on a scale of pleasure regardless of the existing rational concepts of advantages and disadvantages.

Therefore, these were the two values, the concept of art as a fictional world and the concept of indifference in art which gave the reasons of existence of art and beauty, and social value in those days. However, such argument eventually disappeared as the social status of art formed and recognized [7].

11.2.2.3 The Study of Kansei Was Aesthetics: What Is Aesthetics

In the time of Greek, Aristotle employed the term aesthetics. Baumgarten took it as a part of his framework of metaphysics and defined aesthetics as follows:

> Aesthetics is the study of aesthetic recognition and its presentation (as a study of subordinate recognition, as a study of art, as a technology of beautiful thoughts, and as a technology that bears resemblance to reasoning).

Except for the proviso in the parentheses, it seems that aesthetics is a study of recognition and presentation, that is, expression. It can be assumed that this definition implies a system of study which includes "*the method of recognition and expression from the standpoint of creative poems*"; his major research concern was poetry. Hence, this leads to another question of what aesthetic recognition means according to his definition. In the explanation in the parentheses, it can be suggested that he was aiming at constructing a study of poems as a part of metaphysics and at envisioning a new area of study centered on it.

It is well-known that the representation of sound of ocean waves exemplifies the nature of Baumgarten's idea in aesthetics [6]. When one hears the sound of the waves, one interprets it as an impression of the collective sound. However, this implies that one cannot separately recognize the sound of each rippling wave, infinitesimal representation, which composes the waves as a whole. This is considered the realm of *Kansei* where each of the infinitesimal waves is in an intermingled state. The ability to do so is called the subordinate recognition ability by Baumgarten. His aesthetics were focused on its unique way of seizing these waves. On the other hand, the objective of logic as a basis of reason is to clearly identify each individual infinitesimal wave, and this is where aesthetics parts from logic.

Baumgarten claimed that "denotatively perspicuous representation" refers to the uniqueness of representation by having a variety of infinitesimals. He divided perspicuity into two: the state where one can recognize each separate infinitesimal is called "connotative perspicuity" and the state where one cannot is called "denotative perspicuity." Denotative perspicuity is characterized by the strength that the representation has. According to Baumgarten, what one find attractive comes from the way it exists in a physical way and its brilliance, and it corresponds to the denotative perspicuity characterized by the strength. The more variety of infinitesimals it contains, the more individuality it has. Also each infinitesimal that forms each separate entity also includes a connectivity to other entities. What one finds attractive is considered "the representation with implication" which includes a variety of connectivities like this. This is the primary concern of aesthetics by Baumgarten.

However, his work did not cover the question of "how one's opinion that something is beautiful occurs and how it is possible" which eventually became the primary concern in aesthetics later. This is not so well-known, but Immanuel Kant tried to answer this question in his book "Critique of Judgment" which is separate from another work of his "Critique of Pure Reason." Here, let us briefly discuss the nuance of beauty, particularly the nuance that is relevant in certain Japanese words.

11.2.2.4   The Endless Argument of Beauty: "Beautiful" and "Beauty"

First of all, let us discuss the difference between a Japanese word "utsukushii" meaning beautiful and "utsukushisa" meaning "beauty." "Beautiful" is an adjective and "beauty" is a noun. This is obvious, but when comparing "beauty" with "beautiful" as an adjective, one can find "beauty" a concept with generality following a certain standard. On the other hand, "beautiful" does not have such a connection with generality, but it has the ability to create separate and individual

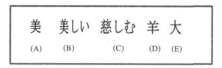

美　美しい　慈しむ　羊　大
(A)　(B)　　(C)　　(D)　(E)

Fig. 11.2 Japanese Kanji characters representing beauty (**A**), beautiful (**B**), affectionate to (**C**), constituent parts of the character representing beauty (**D**) and (**E**)

epithets or attributes. Here, we are going to examine "beautiful." "Beautiful" as an adjective makes sense in Japanese. Although people commonly say "a pretty person," they do not say "a beautiful person" so much because in Japanese, it seems to carry a connotation of distance. Where does this distance come from? According to some specialists, they explain that although a character for beautiful [Character{A}] originally comes from Chinese, its pronunciation "utsukushii" [Character{B}] is a derivative of a verb "itsukushimu" [Character{C}] meaning "affectionate to/love," which is Yamato kotoba, Japanese words having their origins in the time before the introduction of Chinese. Thus, an adjective "beautiful" originally in Japan refers to something that one feels affectionate to. On the other hand, as a Chinese character for "beautiful" [Character {A}] consists of two separate characters [Character{D}] and [Character{E}] each meaning sheep and big, it implies something large and magnificent, which obviously holds different meaning from the original Yamato kotoba (Fig. 11.2).

If you look up a word "beautiful" in New Oxford American Dictionary, it says

A combination of qualities, such as shape, color or form, that pleases the aesthetic senses, esp., the sight; ex. (a) I was struck by her beauty, (b) an area of outstanding natural beauty.

It seems that its definition in English corresponds to the Chinese character. The problem here is that an adjective "beautiful" in Yamato kotoba describes something different from the one in Chinese and English. In other words, it seems that the word "beautiful" in Japanese has not been integrated well in their daily life. Since this word "beautiful" plays a central part in aesthetics, it is natural to assume that their understanding of the word also influences their *Kansei* as well. The difference of the word between the *Yamato kotoba* and the Chinese character could be subtle, but this would be the only possible manner for a person's heart to open up their channel for *Kansei* and communicate together after understanding such a subtle difference.

11.2.3 Epistemology and Kansei

11.2.3.1 Kant and His Epistemology

The aim of this section is to examine aesthetics by Immanuel Kant [8]. In order to do so, it is necessary to summarize first his work "Critique of Pure Reason" where the concept of aesthetics appears, and then move on to the argument of aesthetics.

First of all, in the second half of the eighteenth century, Kant systematized the epistemology of subject itself rather than the object that is recognized in order to answer the question of "what can humans know? And what can humans not know?" His epistemology, considered one of the most influential thoughts even today, was developed through his three major works, "Critique of Pure Reason," "Critique of Practical Reason," and "Critique of Judgment."

Here, let us take a look at "Critique of Pure Reason" where the word "aesthetics" appears in order to investigate how he grasped it. For understanding the purpose of the book, it is important to know the background of his era where there was a transition from the world controlled by God to the modern world due to the scientific revolution started by Isaac Newton. Newton scientifically explained the natural system of the world, particularly the motion of our planets, but it was more important for Kant to understand how and why humans can systematize such movement of our planets, and this was where he started questioning the system of human recognition. Thus, Newton, on one hand, figured out the law of the movement of the celestial bodies, and Kant, on the other hand, considered what conditions are required of human subjects (subjects of recognition) and how it is possible to correctly understand notions such as motion.

Kant thought that human recognition exists in a system consisting of aesthetics/sensitivity, intelligence, and reason. Reason is ranked as the highest, and "intelligence" integrates experiences that are accessed by intuitive sensitivity and judges them. Reason makes a higher-ordered judgment based on the primitive judgment formed by intelligence. On one hand, intelligence applies categories (genera) to the subject matters called intuitive objects and judges what the objects are by employing concepts. On the other hand, reason is used to integrate various judgments of objects created by intelligence through deduction and extracts some sort of principles of generality. For example, if one says "there is an apple," the recognition of the existence of the apple is by intelligence. Reason, on the other hand, develops and generalizes individual matter into more universal objects, in this case, such as "it is food" or "it is a sweet fruit."

Let us go back to the issue of epistemology by Kant about the matter of celestial bodies, that is, movement of stars. His conclusion for this was, in short, that the movement that humans experience by observation is actually happening in the framework of time and space, but this framework transcends the ability that humans were born with, not something that they can gain through daily experiences. So, one of his conclusions was that if humans could not have this framework, it should be impossible for them to correctly recognize what is happening in the natural world such as the movement above.

Thus, Kant's epistemology is different from Descartes'. On one hand, Descartes thought the human spirit is independent from their physical body. On the other hand, Kant thought that human cognition is possible on two levels: giving content through intuitive aesthetics/sensitivity and then thinking conceptually. Roughly speaking, while the former corresponds to *Kansei*, the latter corresponds to intelligence.

Let us further explore the relationship between aesthetics/sensitivity and intelligence which frames Kant's epistemology. In his epistemology, thinking begins with experiences, stating that "human cognition of matters starts with experiences." This is the most important point in order to examine his epistemology. However, one cannot know everything only from experiences. This is because one has to depend on the framework of time and space as an ability to intuitively cognize the object before experiencing it. One has the ability to directly sense external objects, and Kant calls this ability to accept them aesthetics/sensitivity (*Kansei*). The key point is that the framework of time and space is neither something one can obtain through experiences nor objectively recognizes as an external factor, and it rather should be considered as a transcendental form of intuition that one was born with as a condition to cognize subjectively. However, in terms of matter as objects which gives acceptance to aesthetic representation, what one can cognize is considered incomplete "phenomenon" different from the matter itself. According to him, only God knows matter itself, and humans cannot even see or know it.

Intelligence plays an important role in Kant's epistemology to accept a direct impression from aesthetics/sensitivity, to arrange the variety of phenomena, and to conceptually judge it. As well as aesthetics/sensitivity, intelligence has a framework as a transcendental form and can be summarized in four elements; category, transcendental apperception, schema, and principle. Category is the framework used to arrange intuition based on various sensations and to conceptually judge them as objects, and it is composed of quantity, quality, relations, and form. Second, apperception refers to human's sense of self. When "I recognize the object as X," it is always accompanied by self-identification that "I think the object is X." The third element, schema exists between aesthetics/sensitivity and intelligence and is considered the compositional ability (imaginative power). Principle at last is referred when categories are applied to intuitions.

It should be noted anything that one can experience is a phenomena, but what is required for the phenomena to be liberated from subjectivity and to become objective? In order for "my representation" to become an object, the representation has to be prescribed according to the universal principles. The phenomena here become separated from simple aesthetics/sensitivity represented by individual sensation/perception and become directly related to the concept of the object. In order for this to be achieved, intelligence should be related to, not removed from, aesthetics/sensitivity. This way, Kant claimed that the objectivity of human recognition is guaranteed by the function of intelligence that limits the intuition brought on by aesthetics/sensitivity (*Kansei*) to the phenomena related to the objects.

11.2.3.2   Aesthetics in Critique of Pure Reason by Kant

What is unique about Kant's epistemology is that aesthetics/sensitivity, intelligence, and reason each has its own distinctive material and form and that material is formed through experiences, but form is not, and it is rather intuitively formed transcendentally, that is, prior to experiences. When matter is formed, it becomes the subject's object because the object touches the subject's soul by some methods. What Kant calls *Kansei* (sensitivity) in the transcendental aesthetics is this passive ability to perceive the representation of the object through the contact denotation by the object. This is how the subject is forming the object by the mediation of sensitivity, which creates intuition toward the object.

As is mentioned above, Kant paid attention to the fact that whatever humans experience occurs in the framework of time and space, assuming that every object that humans experience is phenomenon and thus, the subject cannot reach the realm of the matter itself. Here, let me explain the purpose of the dichotomy between material and form. When the object faces the subject "I," the subject is sensing something, such as sensations of colors and sounds. This sensation corresponds to the material of phenomenon given through experiences. On the other hand, the form of aesthetics/sensitivity has to be a form within the framework of time and space. That is, if there is an apple in front of us, the only way that the subject can cognize the object (an apple) is to cognize the relationship between certain time and space, that is, the framework of time (an apple being here right now) and space (the size of the apple). Furthermore, the material of the object (an apple) provides information of intuitive image about what color the apple is and how it looks. In *Kansei* engineering, this information of intuitive image is called *Kansei* information.

Incidentally, before Kant, aesthetics/sensitivity (*Kansei*) had been considered an unwelcoming and disturbing entity for objective thought which cannot be mistaken for intelligence because it could obscure and endanger the objectivity. However, in "Critique of Pure Reason," sensitivity (*Kansei*) became essential for human cognition, at least theoretically. However, aesthetics/sensitivity in his theory was different from the other variety of sensitivity (aesthetics/*Kansei*) that is required for the creativity in the field of art. Indeed, it seems that aesthetics (sensitivity/*Kansei*) in his theory could not define the purpose of *Kansei* itself. Basically Kant's aesthetics/ sensitivity is the ability to intuitively cognize an object and is accompanied by a sensuous image of the object as a representation. Despite this, it is often thought that it is not clear what this representation itself indicates; we argue here that it indicates fundamental information acquired by human cognition and cannot be disregarded as something meaningless. Because this information could potentially comprise important information about *Kansei* being related to what has not been discussed enough yet, such as a sixth sense.

Kant himself considered beauty as a problem of subjective emotions called aesthetic/emotional judgment in his later work "Critique of Judgment." This is discussed further in the following section, but in brief, *Kansei* in "Critique of Pure Reason" should be independent from aesthetic/emotions as a separate category that is discussed in "Critique of Judgment."

Figure 11.3 represents the conceptual map of the process of human cognition [9]. This map contains the elements related to cognition suggested by Kant's work developed in "Critique of Pure Reason." In this figure, the function of aesthetics/ sensitivity according to him responds to Sensor that gives sensation, and the function of intelligence according to him corresponds to intelligence on the right

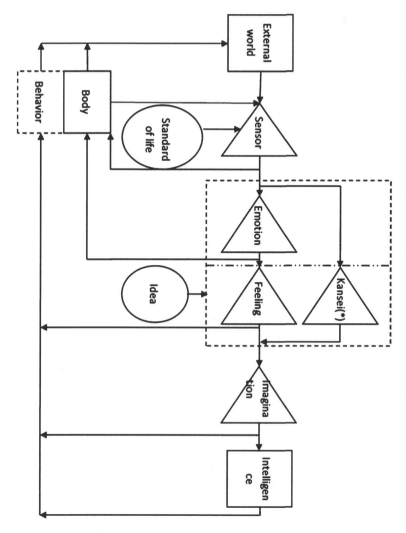

Fig. 11.3 Schematic diagram for human recognition

side of the figure. However, "Critique of Pure Reason" does not consider the elements that corresponds to emotion, Feeling, and *Kansei* (*) inside of the dashed line in the middle. The *Kansei* (*) inside of the dashed line is different from aesthetics/sensitivity as sensation as put forth by Kant. This seems confusing, but in brief, *Kansei* (*) is a sensation that the subject senses as a part of their spirit, which is independent from their emotions. In the next section, the term "aesthetic" refers to emotions in a wider definition as a part of *Kansei*. In Fig. 11.3, the right part of the box made of dashed lines represents a group of *Kansei* consisting of Feeling and *Kansei* (*), where Feeling represents a class having sensitivity to mild awakened emotions, and *Kansei* (*) represents a class separate from emotions.

11.3 Aesthetic Thoughts

11.3.1 Aesthetics and Thoughts

Our daily life has a lot to do with aesthetics (*Kansei*). However, since there still are individual technologies for developing products and services which meet uses' requirement, it is necessary to develop cross-sectional methods that traverse various related technologies beyond individual ones. As the first step toward this direction, let us explore the various forms of thought for these methods we should develop. It is important to make sure that our original starting point is to "feel/sense." By taking "feel/sense" as our starting point to develop new areas of manufacturing and service, it is necessary to examine new thoughts and paths starting from those that intersect with imagination and creativity.

We are going to examine aesthetic thoughts revolving around *Kansei* as one of the methods. Aesthetic thoughts here mean thoughts which position the ability to have feelings or sensations that is located at the most upstream of recognition in humans at the core and is connected to creativity. It can be said that conventional scientific thoughts are based on intellectualism where objectivity is supported by intellect, being located at the downstream in the cognition process, is considered the most important. On the other hand, we consider here the ability to have feelings/sensation as the basic sense of value of human beings. Hence, we are going to trace back to the most upstream part of human cognition where feelings/sensations occur. In the following, we will particularly focus our discussion on judgment, the smallest unit of thought.

11.3.2 Aesthetic/Emotional Judgment by Immanuel Kant: Subjective Universal Validity

Immanuel Kant wrote "Critique of Judgment" as his third "Critique" book following "Critique of Pure Reason" and "Critique of Practical Reason" [10]. This book is not as well-known as his two other books, but in which he argues his ideas about aesthetics which became the classical work for aesthetics later. However, he not only covers aesthetics but also passion and sentiments such as being sublime and being pleasant in general, which could be confusing. Furthermore, there are some parts in this book where he seems to ignore its order in his description and put forth inconsistent arguments. Thus, many specialists and scholars of Kant have had struggled with these difficulties, and there have been a variety of commentaries on this book [11]. Based on the commentaries, let us make clear what his thoughts on aesthetics and emotions were.

11.3.2.1 Judgment on Beauty (Aesthetic Judgment)

"Critique of Judgment" is composed of two sections and titled "Critique of Aesthetic/Emotional Judgment" for the first part and "Critique of Teleological Judgment" for the second part. That is, in the first part, he discusses aesthetic judgment and other sorts of emotional judgment. "Aesthetic judgment" in its title comes from a German term "aesthetisch." We are going to mainly focus "a sense of beauty" here among other emotions and discuss the issue of how humans can correctly judge the sense of beauty.

Judgment refers to the function to express "P is Q" as a proposition. Thus, the issue in aesthetic/emotional judgment is to examine if a proposition holds for "__ is aesthetic." The judgment in this book, however, is different from logical or intelligent judgment which involves the concept of objects, and we have to make sure that it is the judgment involving subject's aesthetics/emotions such as sensation, feelings, or *Kansei*. Being aesthetic/emotional in this sense means that representation is connected with emotion (pleasure or displeasure) of the subject, and the subject is in a condition where they are aware of the representation that they created and is shaken by their own emotions. In this situation, the representation is aesthetic, and the judgment based on it, including judgment on emotions such as sublimity and beauty, is called aesthetic/emotional judgment. As is mentioned above, being aesthetic means something different from the process where the representation is related to understanding and creates objective cognition. Rather it means it is involved with the subject's emotions such as pleasure and displeasure.

What are the conditions when the subject makes aesthetic/emotional judgments? In order to analyze beauty, Kant distinguishes the characteristics of beauty based on its properties, quantity, quality, relations, and modality. To be concise, his argument is as follows:

When the subject "I" feels and judges an object as something beautiful,

1. The object provides the subject with pleasure (Wohlgefallen) regardless of the subject's interests.
2. Our soul is in a condition of "free play of compositional ability and intelligence," and there is no certain cognition. Thus, the object is lack of concept.
3. The subject perceives beauty when the subject feels that it contains the form of finality.
4. Something aesthetic inevitably brings every human pleasure regardless of the fact that it lacks concepts. This is because all the humans have *Gemeinsinn*, that is, mutual emotions.

Thus, although the judgment on the object as something beautiful depends on the subject, every human should have mutual agreement on it with inevitability and universality. What does "free play of compositional ability and understanding" refer to? First of all, let us explain the definitions of the terms. Compositional ability more or less refers to imagination. It is thought that when Kant considered the aesthetic/emotional judgment, he assumed that beauty (aesthetics) has its existence within a form.

This idea is reflected in a metaphor of beauty (aesthetics) that he employed in his book. This metaphor plays an important role in understanding his argument on aesthetic judgment, so let us quote this metaphor. For example, on a peaceful spring day, the scene of the ocean infinitely expanding toward the horizon where ripples come and go is beautiful. Also on an autumn day, a gently sloping ridgeline of high mountains reflecting sunlight is beautiful. Based on these two typical beautiful sceneries, the implication concerning the terms "the play of compositional ability and intelligence" can be explained as follows:

When a subject seeks for the form of the beautiful object, the compositional ability would never be betrayed. When a subject follows the gently sloping ridgeline, their compositional ability holds the image of the gentle slope line that gives the subject pleasure in the present and predicts the following line of the series of slopes. The compositional ability aligns with *what is fixed and determined in a form* and, at the same time, is playing within *the form without a random unpredictable surprise* in its aesthetic judgment. The underlined parts refer to the function of intelligence, and this would be the summary of the content of his argument of "free play of compositional ability and intelligence."

As another example of aesthetic/emotional judgment, let us talk about judgment "this rose is beautiful." This judgment has nothing to do with certain conditions such that the subject likes roses nor that the flower belongs to a species called rose. Such judgment excludes knowledge or concepts judged by the subject and is made only based on an emotion of "pleasure" simply given to the subject in a state of indifference.

As stated above, "aesthetic judgment" can be summarized as follows:

Judgment is made based on emotions either of "pleasure" or of "displeasure" which is (1) neither defined by objectivity, (2) nor dependant on personal interests or preference, but (3) subjective and (4) indifferent. Sometimes, these conditions are called aesthetic conditions as a standard to make a judgment on aesthetics.

There is disagreement on his theory of aesthetic/emotional judgment, so let us explain some of the disagreement here. The problem with his argument is that the conditions of aesthetic judgment are given solely within the subject, or at least it seems that way. In short, that means that whatever the object is, the subject makes an aesthetic judgment independently without a concept of beauty. In reality, from the point of view of *Kansei* engineering, this explanation is not enough. This is because the subjective aesthetic/emotional judgment cannot have a connection to the fundamental creativity which is required to produce new products. Let us give some supplemental explanation about this. At that time, nature and the natural world, rather than artistic works, were the subjects of Kant's research in order to argue the problem with beauty. Since nature cannot be the creation of humans, humans consider it as something that they can only observe and enjoy. That is, "aesthetic/emotional judgment," whether the object is beautiful or not was the only issue that time. However, when it comes to artistic works as objects, there is another issue about how the subject can create such an artistic piece. In this sense, it is necessary to grasp aesthetics as a process for creativity which Kant neither considered nor came to a conclusion about in his works.

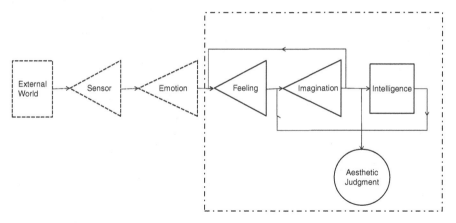

Fig. 11.4 Schematic diagram of aesthetic judgment. Judgment is made by the processes drawn within the large broken rectangle

From this perspective, Kant's aesthetic judgment is not necessarily perfect, but there is a point in his argument that we still should consider as important today. He pointed out that the function of aesthetics or emotions and its judgment comes prior to rational judgment. For example, he stated that there is something in the judgment on nature that grabs the subject's attention about the finality in difference to humans' intelligence. Besides, aesthetic judgment follows the subject's emotions of "pleasure" as an origin of judgment prior to any sort of cognition. He claimed that, however, it is also true that such judgment on pleasure is so prevalent in our daily life that the subject possibly gets used to it and takes it for granted. This argument above is the foundation of modern aesthetics as fundamental principles of aesthetic/emotional judgment.

Anyway, he claims that whatever is beautiful attracts humans and provides them with a sense of positive pleasure. Figure 11.4 above shows the conceptual diagram of aesthetic judgment (aesthetic/emotional judgment without concepts). In this diagram, the polygons made of a solid line denote the elements related to aesthetic/emotional judgment, and the polygons made of a broken line refer to the other elements of human cognition which appeared in Fig. 11.3.

11.3.3 Empathetic Understanding and Its Application

Humans become emotionally involved when faced with certain objects. This is one of the most basic and significant abilities that humans have, but in a conventional scientific world, depending only on reasoning, and therefore often underestimates such an important ability of humans. In short, being emotionally involved means "to move someone's heart." The basic theory of empathy is that humans become interested in others and touched by events that occur to others. It is not possible to

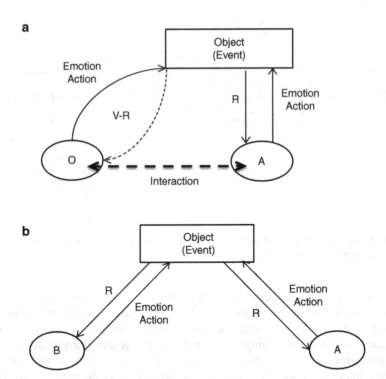

Fig. 11.5 Mechanism of empathy (**a**) and "passion/being touched" (**b**). In empathy, participant (*A*) involved in an event has a relation (*R*) to an object which evokes him an emotion and action. Observer (*O*) only has a virtual relation (*V–R*) to the object, which would evoke some emotion to the observer

go over the entire history of empathy because of the limitation of space, but we would like to point out that Adam Smith, the author of "The Wealth of Nations," and Jean-Jacques Rousseau, the author of "The Social Contract," considered empathy as a foundation of human societies [12–14]. Let us discuss first the structure of phenomenon of empathy and the implications of empathy.

11.3.3.1   The Structure of Empathy and the Formation of Human "Bonds" via Communication of Passion

First of all, let us start with the basics of how empathy occurs as a structure. As Fig. 11.5 below shows, empathy means that a subject as a participant is actually experiencing an event, but this is possible only when there is another subject as an observer with the subject. In general, of course the observer cannot get detailed information about the subject, so all he/she can do as an observer is to imagine how the subject feels. Thus, the observer imagines the subject as if he/she were the participant. By doing so, if the observer can imagine how the subject as a

Fig. 11.6 Empathy in case of one involved participant and many observers (**a**), and passion in case of many observers (**b**)

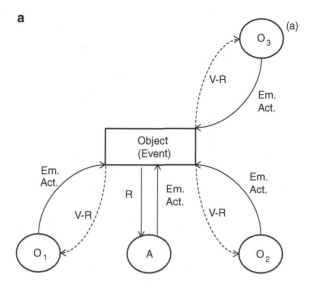

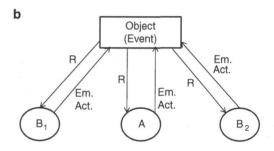

participant feels like and acts like, and if he/she feels the same say, it means that the observer empathizes with the participant. At this time, the observer accepts how the subject feels and gains an access to how the subject is feeling through empathy. As a result, there is a human bond between them. Also the feeling of the subject as an actual participant becomes strengthened by the fact that the observer empathizes with them. On the other hand, if the observer cannot accept how the subject feels or their actions, there becomes an antipathy, that is, negative feelings between them.

By the way, what is the difference between "empathy," where there is a subject and an observer, and "becoming emotionally involved" where there are two participants experiencing the same event? In this case, even if there are two subjects who are experiencing the same event, a special relationship will not be formed if the subjects do not care about and ignore the existence of each other.

Similar analysis of "becoming emotionally involved" is possible even when there are more than two participants. Let us explain this with some examples. In the case of one participant and more than two observers shown in Fig. 11.6, if they all approve how the subject as a participant feels, deep emotions spread among them and there becomes a bond between the subject and observers. Further, if the observers can see each other, they have secondary empathy among them, and as a result, they form a network among themselves by connecting with each other directly. This means that being able to "see" each other functions as essentially connecting them to create a bond among them. This can be found in various situations. For example, due to some weighty events such as serious incidents, the participants form a bond among them, speculators at a theater form a bond with actors on the stage, or audience at a sport stadium empathizes with actual players.

Therefore, empathy has a function leading humans to form a natural connection based on emotions or sentiments that they mutually have. Conversely, you could also say that bonds due to empathy lie behind the elements of certain groups or societies. Further, as Rousseau claimed, you can also say that the language used functions as a tool to boost a sense of belonging as a group.

11.3.3.2 Co-creation Between Designers and Users

As is mentioned at the beginning, *Kansei* engineering has proposed the idea of co-creation between designers and users as a method to produce products and service which create *Kansei* value. In the following, we discuss the mechanism of co-creation. Our understanding of co-creation is based on an idea of empathy toward producers by observers through their products, which originally comes from an idea that the speculators empathize with artists through the artists' works.

Let us think about the image of a product with designers as actively involved participants. Designers as participants have a relationship with the object to create the image of the product, and by doing so, they care about the "object" which is the product itself, or image of it, and thus have emotions such as pride. If the subject is an observer, they make a judgment if their image or emotions match the participant's idea and intention by experiencing the characteristics of the product such as form, color, and texture. If it matches, they approve (empathize with) the product; if not, they disapprove.

It is important to pay special attention to the scheme of empathy regarding products. Users in this case as observers are in a state where they can directly see the product made by the producer, but in general, users have to imagine designer's intention to produce the product and the background of it without seeing the designer. That is, there would be a problem that this situation is quite different from a situation where an observer can directly see the participants.

Interest in empathy has become a lot more popular since the discovery of the "mirror neuron" [15]. It is brain nerve cells discovered by experiments with monkeys which respond to activities that he/she sees others do as if he/she were the one doing the activities. It is predicted that these neurons have a deep relationship with a sense of empathy that we have considered here. It has already been discussed in the relationship with philosophy such as intersubjectivism. In reality, it seems possible that empathy can occur even when conditions stated above are not applied, such as an occasion where observers cannot see the participants but only words. For example, as a part of a research in empathetic understanding, there has been a research of understanding novels. However, there are still issues in order to prove in what situation empathy occurs or to clarify the "conditions" where empathy is formed between users and designers.

11.3.3.3 Aesthetic (Kansei) Quality Evaluation Method

We have pointed out that co-creation can be considered as empathy between designers and users that gives the disciplines. In a case of artistic works, the primary value of it corresponds to the impression evoked by the works to the observers. More generally, the quality of the products also depends on the designers' *Kansei*. What are the methods to evaluate the aesthetic quality of products? As Miyahara also points out, to establish such methods is still a primary issue in *Kansei* engineering. Indeed, Miyahara has developed high-quality speaker system. In order to evaluate its aesthetic quality, he conducted a questionnaire and collected an interesting group of adjectives expressing the participants' impression [16].

Here, we would like to propose an evaluation method of aesthetic quality based on empathy. That is, when there is a certain number of audience members (observant = the subject) responsive to a producer of a product, you can consider the ratio of the audience who approves and empathizes with the product by the producer as the index of evaluation of the product. It is possible that the results of the evaluation would be different depending on if the audience is experts or amateurs in the area of the product. However, this difference of results revels the difference of the extent "how easy it is to empathize with," because the ability of empathy is different from the amount of knowledge or sharpness of sensory organs. This index can be interpreted as cultural standard depending on groups or areas. This is expected to be an effective standard regarding regional characteristics of *Kansei*.

11.4 Conclusion

Based on the viewpoint that the primary point of the proposal of *Kansei* engineering exists within the framework of new point of view, (1) *Kansei* value and (2) co-creation of designers and users. This chapter has discussed fundamental ways of thought which will be useful for developing this new concept. The summary of this chapter is as follows:

1. We have proposed a basic mechanism of co-creation based on the concept of empathy between designer and users, as a foundation of *Kansei* engineering.
2. We have claimed that aesthetic judgment and empathy introduced, respectively, by Kant and Smith are the models of aesthetic thoughts because such judgments are involved with individual's emotions. Since a judgment composed of an aesthetic judgment and empathy is also an aesthetic judgment, this chapter has

shown that this can be a model for aesthetic evaluation of objects. Although it is hard to examine to what extent what Kant called subjective universal legitimacy in "Critique of Judgment" is universal practically, this chapter has shown that if an object is judged as something aesthetic, we can make aesthetic evaluation as a specific standard by combining a sense of empathy of several observers and calculate the ratio of them feeling empathetic with the object.

3. Another variety of aesthetics by Kant that was discussed in "Critique of Pure Reason" have not been given originally an active meaning in itself, but we have suggested that it can be a base of aesthetics that is not accompanied by emotions.

Among many problems left to be solved, including the problem of defining Kansei properly, it is particularly necessary to substantiate these aesthetic thoughts further.

With that being said, it is significant to tackle issues such as thoughts by *Kansei* and analogies or expansion of meanings in daily life by metaphors.

References

1. Shinohara A, Shimizu Y, Sakamoto H (1996) Invitation to *Kansei* engineering. Morikita, Japan
2. Ministry of Economy, Trade and Industry in Japan (2009) Kansei initiative. http://www.meti. go.jp/english/policy/mono_info_service/mono/kansei2009/inind.html
3. Sasaki K (2010) Japanese Kansei, Chuko Shinsho, Japan (in Japanese)
4. Kuwako T (2001) Philosophy of Kansei. NHK Books, Japan (in Japanese)
5. Descarte Rene (1637) Discourse on method; Japanese translation by Noda M (2001) Chuo-koron, Japan
6. Ohkuma H (2011) Metaphysics by Baumgarten. In: Kumano S (ed) Excellent books in modern philosophy. Chuko-Shinsho, Japan, pp 214–223
7. Sasaki K (2009) Invitation to aesthetics, Chuko Shinsho, Japan (in Japanese)
8. Kant I (2005) Kritik der reinen Vernuft; Japanese translation by Hara H (2005), Heibonsha, Japan
9. Nagashima T, Sawai M, Nagashima Y (2010) Conceptual cognitive scheme of Kansei on referring to the usage of human language. In: International conference on biometrics and Kansei engineering (ICBAKE) 2010, D-15, Kagawa
10. Kant I (1790) Kritik der Urteilskraft; Japanese translation by Utsunomiya Y (1994), Ibunsha, Japan
11. Watanabe J (1998) Philosophy of art, Chikuma Shobou, Japan (in Japanese)
12. Smith A (1759) The theory of moral sentiments; Japanese translation by Mizuta H (2003), Iwanami Shoten, Japan
13. Doume T (2008) Adam Smith, Chuko Shinsho, Japan (in Japanese)
14. Rousseau JJ (1781) Essay on the origin of language; Japanese translation by Kobayashi Y (1970), Gendaisichosha, Japan
15. Gallese V, Goldman A (1988) A mirror neurons and the simulation theory of mind reading. Trends Cogn Sci 12:494–501
16. Ishikawa T, Miyahara M (2006) A proposal of psycho-physiological evaluation based on bodily sensation important for VR. ITE J 60(3):446–44

Chapter 12
Kansei Measurement in Cooperative Development Techniques

Masayoshi Kamijo and Yoshio Shimizu

Abstract This chapter concentrates on topics of *"Kansei"* measurement to create the new criterion through measuring human's action and psychological and physiological responses. *"Kansei"* is the ability to receive the variety of information coming from another party, understand, and then apply this information to one's own thoughts. *Kansei* is absolutely indispensable to interactive dialogue. For interactive co-creation, consumers and manufacturers creating products through mutual and consensual dialogue and discussion are completely necessary. Nevertheless, it is extremely difficult for us humans to communicate our thoughts and consider others' desires. We must create a new criterion for understanding each other via physiological response. The availability of diverse methods of interaction promotes interpersonal communication and deepens mutual understanding.

12.1 Introduction

We use our physical sensations to get a feeling of our surroundings, gain a sense of satisfaction and contentment according to our *"Kansei"* (emotional state or response), and therefore take away a fulfilling experience. Up until now, this has been how we assess the physical results of manufacturing processes. In May 2007, The Japanese Ministry of Education, Trade and Industry (METI) announced to the nation the creation of a *"Kansei* initiative" [1]. According to this announcement, *"Kansei* value" is a special type of value that is actualized when a product or service appeals to the *"Kansei"* of ordinary citizens and arouses their emotions and

M. Kamijo (✉)
Interdisciplinary Graduate School of Science and Technology, Shinshu University,
3-15-1, Tokida, Ueda, Nagano, 386-8578, Japan
e-mail: kamijo@shinshu-u.ac.jp

Y. Shimizu
Shinshu University, Ueda, Nagano, Japan

K. Saeed and T. Nagashima (eds.), *Biometrics and Kansei Engineering*,
DOI 10.1007/978-1-4614-5608-7_12, © Springer Science+Business Media New York 2012

empathy. In addition to the preexisting criteria for evaluating products (functionality, construction quality, and price), a fourth criteria of "*Kansei*" will now be included. This will be an assessment of sensitivity and the emotional response created in the user. This will have the effect of bringing "*Kansei* engineering" to the attention of not just Japan but the entire world. In addition, a recognition of the need to leverage sensitivity in industrial manufacturing systems will be widely promoted, and awareness of the formal scientific techniques of "*Kansei* engineering" will be brought to the attention of a wide range of industries.

In order to facilitate the co-creation of standards of sensitivity, some key points must be identified. Techniques must be backed up by dialogue in order to promote the mutual understanding necessary to co-creation. Recognition of the fundamental importance of the communication process will enable the involved parties to effectively co-create. One key point is that, for the sake of the connection between consumer and manufacturer, the manufacturer must fully understand the consumer's exact needs and the consumer, through dialogue, must show the reasons behind those needs. In other words, communication, circulation, and connection techniques must be constructed in accordance with dialogue, and we must act in order to improve the connections between ourselves, others, society, and our environment. "*Kansei* engineering" is, essentially, the structuring and crafting of techniques to support the formation of relationships as well as aiding individuals in maintaining effective awareness and harmonious interaction with their environment and the objects therein.

12.2 Creating *Kansei* Value Through Co-creation

12.2.1 Cooperative Creation of Value Assessment Methods

In order to allow the implementation of manufacturing processes leading to products and consumer goods with high "*Kansei*," proactive cooperation between consumers and manufacturers in planning the manufacturing processes of these products and goods should be considered. Consumers and manufacturers, by forming creative communities which allow them to share their personal experiences, feelings, and impressions of the manufacturing process, will be able to gain a sense of achievement, understanding, and personal accomplishment. Students from Shinshu University Department's *Kansei* Engineering Group have formed a picture-book design cooperative. They are working with groups of students and locals in putting together a group for those hoping to create picture books and then working together toward the creation of the books themselves [2]. The students and local consumers will be experiencing this process from the point of view of the manufacturers, and from this, they are able to examine each individual's impressions of "*Kansei*" as it pertains to this work. Throughout their time with the picture-book group, the students acting as manufacturers were assessed using the POMS (profile of mood state) scale [3], which assesses mood states. From these changes, a feeling of fatigue combined with a feeling of vigor can be shown. Consumers were asked "If a book you had made were lost, how much monetary compensation would you need?" in order to assess their personal feeling of value. The answers ranged from 0 yen to 100 million yen, with a median value of 10,000 yen. This figure was four times the value of the 2,500 yen fee required to join the picture-book cooperative. Furthermore, the answers of "0 yen" indicated a feeling that the experience of creating the picture book in cooperation with staff and other participants was essentially priceless. These results showed that *Kansei* value resulting from co-creation can potentially produce economic value.

12.2.2 Industrial Development

Clothing can be taken as a representative luxury goods from the textile and apparel industries. These would have originally been manufactured by family members or professional tailors to match the body shape of the individual user. Nowadays, clothes are mass-produced consumer goods, made to fit an average, standardized body shape based on the estimates of the industry. From 1992 to 1994, a company called Research Institute of Human Engineering for Quality Life (HQL) took measurements from 34,000 men and women between 7 and 90 years of age. This data became the foundation for a revision in the standardized human body sizing system in Japan.

In creating well-fitting products, the textile and apparel industry must now (1) promote designs and fashions influenced by the preferences of individuals and (2) promote structures that will improve the health and emotional state of the user. The implementation of this system of clothing manufacture should not be based on preexisting systems of family-made or family-tailored clothing but rather on the practical usage of modern scientific techniques and dialogue-supported cooperative systems – *Kansei* Engineering.

In Fig. 12.1, those desiring to purchase clothing (consumers), communicating with manufacturers through a network, show their ideal design setting for clothing. Consumers and manufacturers form a manufacturing community together and communicate their ideas to each other through mutual dialogue, and by cooperating and understanding each other, they do not merely create a physical product but rather a process that provides *Kansei* value or worth to the participants. The finished product, despite having a physical basis, will also, through this process, form an emotional attachment leading to self-actualization.

The prevailing wisdom regarding clothing is that it is difficult for consumers and manufacturers to find common ground and understand where the other party is coming from. It is necessary to construct a system for effective dialogue, and Fig. 12.1 describes a proposed dialogue-supported system. Consumers and manufacturers, in simple terms, find it difficult to understand and empathize with each other. Because of this, each system put forth in Fig. 12.1 is required as techniques which foster dialogue.

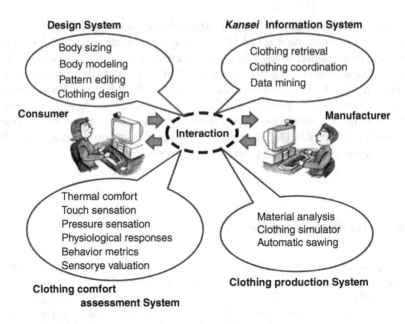

Fig. 12.1 An interactive and cooperative creation clothing system

Specific examples of systems for cooperatively designing clothes are detailed here. For example, when a consumer says, "I want a suit that flatters me and makes me feel good," the manufacturer's designers end up with an abstract image. The manufacturer, for their part, is essentially guessing at the consumer's idea. To make this "guess" more accurate, a system is used which takes the customer's words, matches them with specific real pieces of clothing, and shows them to the consumer and mines this data. It uses written questions such as "Is this the kind of clothing you want?" and makes use of an editing system to support decision-making. The design system assists communication by including material and pattern as design factors. After obtaining the basic design specifications, the individual's measurements are procured, allowing the computer to generate a CGI design concept and simulate the appearance and movements of the user to allow the user to be sure of their choices. In the actual manufacturing process, the clothing design system can create patterns and templates from the customer's physical measurements, instruct automatic sewing machines as they cut, and then manufacture the piece of clothing required, using direct applications of artificial intelligence techniques.

The consumer's physical measurements and condition are essential to the inter-active and personalized manufacture of clothing. The National Institute of Advanced Industrial Science and Technology and The Research Institute of Human Engineering for Quality Life (HQL) are developing equipment to speedily take the measurements of users. To generate a design from the consumer's physical information, the consumer will, in a store, have their measurements taken, their gross physical movements and skin deformation recorded along with their specific

Fig. 12.2 Illustration of human clothing measurement system. Case of wearable human-form measuring system

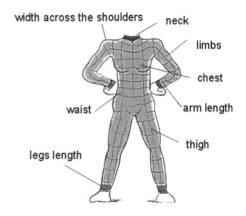

width across the shoulders   neck

limbs

chest

waist

arm length

thigh

legs length

sizing preferences, and the design must allow extra material for slack. The specific characteristics of a fabric and its effects on movement must be taken into account. The design must allow for free movement of the limbs. The physiological toll of the design on the muscular system can be measured, evaluated, and tested [4, 5]. To this end, development of the human clothing measurement system (see Fig. 12.2), which assesses variations in movement of the physique, is needed.

One reason for having one's own clothes is maintaining one's health. Designed clothes must care for the body and ideally contain features to actively promote health. The clothing comfort is the relation between clothing and people, which informs sizing and worth, and also gives rise to indicators of the dialogue between humans and their clothing.

The primary factors deciding the clothing comfort for the wearer are (1) clothing climate, which is what we can call the internal climate, humidity, and temperature of the clothing; (2) clothing pressure, which is what we can call the specific pressures that the clothing exerts on the skin; and (3) the feeling of the texture and material on the skin. From the simple stimulus according to these three factors, mental responses, physiological responses, and bodily movement are measured respectively. By considering those results in conjunction with medical expertise, comfort levels can be assessed. When considering the forces behind these three comfort-related factors, temperature, friction, pressure, pain, and the circulation of air must be recognized as stressors. The physical stimulus of these stressors in mental responses, physiological responses, and bodily movement and their relationship has become an ongoing research project in assessing stress levels and comfort.

The stresses resulting from one's clothing unconsciously accumulate, soon leading to poor health or illness, and the process of perceiving stress is in itself a cause of stress. Waist belts, girdles, and so on exert direct pressure on the body to control body shape, immediately leading to a feeling of psychological oppression and discomfort. The wearer, however, almost immediately acclimates and becomes unconscious of these feelings. Nevertheless, physiologically speaking, it is known that reduced circulation, reduced salivation, slowed digestion, and reduction of brain-wave activity [6], along with other events, are then exhibited.

By measurement of these physiological signs, we can understand the stress responses being undergone by the body. They are physiological indicators of mind-body interaction.

As the mental and physical responses to stress vary depending on the particular stressor, our understanding and evaluation must also be aided by other indicators. In cold environments, brain function is inhibited, causing the sympathetic nervous system to dominate [7]. Pressure stimulus, which is particularly registered by the sympathetic nervous system, epidermal discomfort, and pain stimulus lead to event-related potential [8], perspiration, and increase in other secretions such as amylase. In order to measure and evaluate these simple physiological signs, the establishment of stress indices for clothing is needed. Also, the development of a wearable sensor system for easy measuring of physiological responses will be a research project from this point on.

The feeling of material and its makeup on the skin can be called "fabric hand." Textiles, whether natural or synthetic, possess a wide variety of differing physical characteristics arising from raw materials, thread composition and patterning, variations in weaving- and surface manufacture. The communication of fabric hand, due to its physical basis, requires a variety of unique, specialized language, such as "*KOSHI* (resemblance to springiness)," "*NUMERI* (resemblance to sliminess)," and "*SHARI* (crisp)" in Japan. People usually assess fabric hand by feeling the material with their fingers, but very few people can accurately assess fabric hand in this way, as different people move their fingers differently. To understand the mechanisms of finger movement being used to perceive fabric hand and to formalize the abstract experience of fabric hand into a scale usable by measuring devices, we hope to study the interaction between the human hand and a robot hand. In conjunction with research showing that people with high levels of physical discernment actually move their fingers in a simple repetitive way [9], study into the interaction between fingers, fingertips, skeletal structure, and muscular motion may allow new and fresh study into the detailed and precise analysis of human movement.

12.3 Role of Kansei Measurement

Easy and effective interaction is the key to cooperative creation. For interactive co-creation, consumers and manufacturers creating products through mutual and consensual dialogue and discussion are completely necessary. Nevertheless, we know that it is extremely difficult for humans to communicate our thoughts and consider others' desires. *Kansei* is the ability to receive the variety of information coming from another party, understand, and then apply this information to one's own thoughts. *Kansei* is absolutely indispensable to interactive dialogue. People who possess the ability to understand others and express their own reception can be said to be truly abundance of *Kansei* beings. One way to obtain excellent *Kansei* is to have many experiences, which we feel informs one's ability to interact in many diverse ways.

The communication of infants are unable to communicate via speech. In order to understand the emotional state or health of other people, a nonverbal mode of expression is needed. It is difficult to construct a model of communication based solely on verbal utterances, so therefore a variety of communicative methods must be utilized. There have always been numerous situations where we cannot express our own state of health or understand that of others. To measure *Kansei*, new methods of interaction and new ways to express our emotional state or health must be investigated. The availability of diverse methods of interaction promotes interpersonal communication. When considering purely the manufacturing process, the connections between consumer and product become in other words user-friendliness, mood, comfort, usability, stress, etc. Taking clothing products as an example, shedding light on the connections between the clothing and the person allows us to better evaluate the clothing comfort of the wearer. One reason for clothing oneself is physical protection. Well-designed clothes maintain the health of the wearer and may even, ideally, be able to promote health. As for the pleasantness of one's clothes (or comfort), clarifying the connections between humans and clothing will allow us to create systems and indices to assess and measure the interaction between humans and clothing. Clothing-related stress accumulates in the body at an unconscious level and eventually leads to poor health or illness and the conscious perception of stress.

Various physiological and psychological stimuli received from clothing can be measured, and the development of techniques for assessing their mutual relations is a landmark in *Kansei* measurement. Of course, a variety of stimuli arise from clothing, but we find ourselves struggling to understand the degree of each stimulus and which stimulus leads to which experience. We do not always find ourselves able to judge which stimulus is good for the health and which bad. We can take clothing as an example, but all manufactured goods are essentially the same in this respect. There are many unexplained ways in which clothing somehow creates a feeling of comfort. The purpose of *Kansei* measurement is to classify and specify this by means of an inclusive and interactive methodology. Here we wish to introduce some ways that we can increase our understanding of health by physio-logical measurement of the nervous system, brain activity, and so on. Much of this can be assessed through the use of devices for the measurement and analysis of physiological responses, but there are also some situations where our specialist knowledge is difficult to apply. People can, using a variety of information, to some extent, assess stress and other stimuli without using any specialist equipment.

For a great deal of time, humans have mostly been farmers, needing to be sensitive to changes in their natural physical environment. If we are unable to assess changes in humans and our environment, we cannot survive. So humans must have possessed great powers of *Kansei* for a very long span of time. Modern people, in order to nourish our faculties for evaluating physical objects rather than let it degrade, require "*Kansei* engineering." I believe that the development of techniques for measuring emotions, in order to promote the development of human sensitivity, is an essential field.

Some general research topics for *Kansei* measurement are outlined below.

12.4   Techniques for Assessing Mental and Physical States from Facial Expression

Facial expression is an excellent indicator of pleasant/unpleasant stimulus. Nonverbal communication plays a large role in interaction. We assess the state of another person through the geometrical shape of their facial expression. Facial expression is the main indicator we use for assessing the mental and physical state of people. Whether the other person is sleepy, happy, or unwell, we are able to assess their condition by looking at their face. When people experience a pleasant stimulus, they smile. When people receive an unpleasant stimulus, they grimace. When assessing emotional state, there is a lot of autonomic activity that can be measured; however, measuring negative emotion is easier than measuring positive emotion. With facial expression, however, both positive and negative emotional states can be more easily observed. Some of the underlying assumptions in research on assessing physical and mental state through facial expression will be introduced below.

12.4.1   Recognizing a Nice Smile and Its Development

Smiles are attractive for the observer and are the symbol of happiness and calm. The smiles of the Mona Lisa or a happy child are of course very different, but both attractive. In a smile, the most attractive and aesthetically pleasing aspects are the sense of happiness, health, and fun it conveys. The smile can be an indicator of positive emotional states.

We say that one of the most attractive parts of a smile is the eyes. Groundbreaking work by Yarbus [10] in tracking eye movements shows that the gaze, when directed at a smiling young woman, is concentrated on the eyes, mouth, and facial shape. We surveyed 50 university students with the question, "which part of the smile do you find the most attractive?" After the most popular feature, the mouth, the next was the corners of the mouth and eyes, showing that the eyes as well as the mouth are a significant part of what makes a smile attractive. It can be thought that the key points of a smile are the mouth and the eyes [13].

Each individual's face differs greatly. Eye shape and color, skin color, eyebrow width, and the contours of the face are never the same between two people. Nevertheless, we are able to understand the feelings by seeing the facial expressions of any kinds of people of any race or culture. Ekman [11] famously carried out a great deal of research into facial recognition. The commonality of understanding between different cultures can be shown by the identical style of simple drawings of faces, expressions, and body language across cultures. In short, we can say that faces can convey a great deal of information despite great differences. If we theorize that large changes in parts of the face are greatly significant to facial recognition of emotion, the role of the eyes and mouth in making an attractive smile can be understood [12].

In human facial recognition, despite the importance of extremely subtle changes in the eyes and mouth, the parts must be thought about as a whole. As shown in

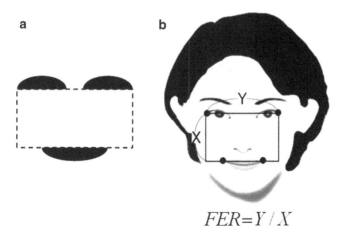

$$FER = Y\ /\ X$$

Fig. 12.3 Geometrical feature of attractive smile: (**a**) visual illusion in facial expression, (**b**) aspect ratio of facial expression rectangle (FER)

Fig. 12.3, we can draw a rectangle by drawing a line between the corners of the eyes, drawing another line between the corners of the mouth, and then connecting these two lines. This rectangle is defined as the facial expression rectangle [13]. As it is impractical to remember the shape or features of the smile, the human faculty for facial recognition is based on a characteristically human act. From physically distinct planes, contours are perceived, causing particular shapes to appear, as shown by Kanisza in his report on illusory contours [14].

In determining the details of the facial rectangle, the rectangle's height and width (aspect ratio) must be found. Twenty university students (10 male and 10 female), when discerning between expressionless faces and those with attractive smiles, showed that the aspect ratio of expressionless faces had a mean of 1.40 ± 0.07, compared to a mean aspect ratio of 1.63 ± 0.04 for smiling faces. This showed that smiling faces had a mean aspect ratio close to the golden ratio of 1.618 (see Fig. 12.4). The aspect ratio of expressionless faces and smiling faces was observed to be significant difference with significance level of 1%. In the recognition of the human smile, the symbol of classical beauty, the golden rectangle, can be clearly found. Few people, on seeing said smile, would be aware of the reason or the reference, but nevertheless, the reasons for this particular impression are clearly shown in these results.

12.4.2 Sensing the Early Stages of Drowsiness

One of the causes of deaths in road traffic accidents is drowsiness leading to poor driving. The automobile industry is searching for methods of detecting drowsiness in drivers in order to prevent road traffic accidents. Until now, brain wave, heart

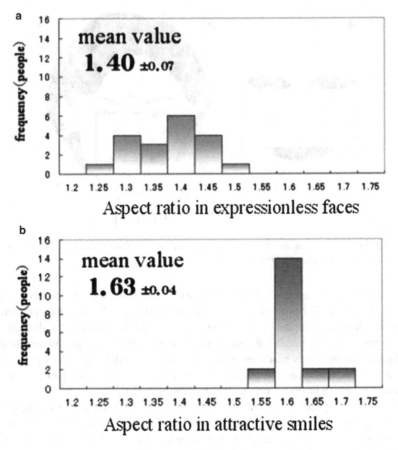

Fig. 12.4 Histogram that shows frequency of FER: (**a**) aspect ratio in expressionless faces, (**b**) aspect ratio in attractive smiles

rate, pulse wave, heart rate variability, etc., have been used as indicators of driving performance in a variety of research into how to detect sleepy drivers [15]. In recent years, research into Facial Recognition Consultation (FRC) has been increasing. FRC is when an image of the driver's face is shown to a third party to assess their level of drowsiness. Training is necessary for this consultation, which uses a video recording of the driver's face, but it does have the merit of being a consensual nonbinding way of assessing drowsiness levels. However, the process is time-consuming and hard on the consultant and is reliant on the judgment, sense, and individual skill of the consultant. Due to these problems, the development of a real-time automated consultation system is greatly desired.

The effectiveness of techniques for assessing indicators of reduced alertness levels is being compared through experimentation on the following: facial expression during tracking and choice making during tasks, tracking error, time taken for choice making, brain-wave activity, and electrocardiogram (ECG) readings

Fig. 12.5 Frontalis muscle

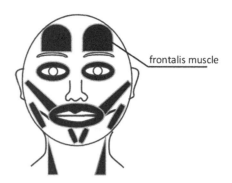

frontalis muscle

accompanying reduced alertness levels in five test subjects. Electrodes for measuring brain-wave activity were attached according to the international 10–20 system at Pz and the standard electrode attached to each earlobe. Facial expression of drowsiness levels was assessed by taking the average rating of seven FRC consultants.

A strong correlation between FRC facial assessment levels and alpha wave activity was indicated. The correlation coefficient of this relationship in each individual was higher than that of tracking error, eye closure, and choice-selection time, and the scattering between individuals was extremely small. Furthermore, the relation between FRC level and sudden deterioration of performance had a nonlinear relation, whereas changes in facial expression and decreased cortical function had a linear relationship. This relationship is considered to have a higher degree of coincidence than that with performance or eye closure. Facial expression is therefore thought to be a faster method of assessing reduced alertness levels than task performance.

In addition, seven facial consultants were used to assess the drowsiness levels of nine recordings of subjects engaged in a simulation of high-speed highway driving. When consultants were asked which parts of the face they looked at to assess the drowsiness levels of the subjects, from 60 different factors, the following 4 factors were found to be significant difference with significance level of 5%: eyebrow raising, slackening of face or mouth, movement of the mouth, and drooping of the head.

In general research into techniques for automatic assessment of emotional state from facial expression, Ekman and Friesen's [11] proposed Facial Action Coding System (FACS) has many practical applications. FACS produces a clearly defined map of facial movement relating to distinct features and the interaction between these. The facial changes when drowsy of 17 subjects were measured by electromyogram (EMG) and then analyzed [16]. In 16 out of the 17 subjects (94.1%), contraction of the frontalis muscle (see Fig. 12.5) was shown to be a distinctive sign of drowsiness (see Fig. 12.6). Upon the onset of actual sleep, however, the frontalis muscle was seen to relax.

When the eyelids become shut, contraction of the frontalis muscle is caused along with raising of the eyebrows. When under tasking tasks while instructed to

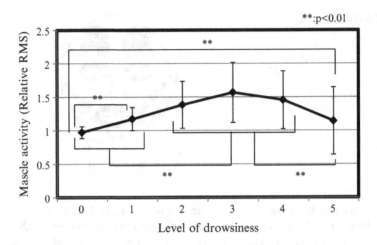

Fig. 12.6 Relationship between frontalis muscle activity and the level of drowsiness

stay awake, this leads to a necessary focus of the field of vision to the front. It is thought that contracting the frontalis muscle and lowering the eyelids cause an action that lifts the eyebrows. We guess that this action is the first step indicator in falling asleep while driving. If this facial expression can be detected, the stress levels of the driver can perhaps be reduced.

12.5 Techniques for Assessing Clothing Comfort by Measurement of Physiological Responses

As mentioned before, the physical roles clothing plays in emotional well-being are (1) internal temperature, humidity, and airflow, (2) pressure and force exerted on the skin, and (3) the feeling of the texture of the material on the skin. These three simple physical factors have on mental state, physiological state, and bodily movement can be measured, considered, and collated to allow assessment of the well-being of the wearer. The underlying factors affecting physical well-being are heat, touch, pressure, pain, and stuffiness, which can be thought of as stressors. By measuring psychological response, physiological responses, and body movements through developing techniques, the connection and interaction between humans and their clothing can be improved. Measuring the psychological and physiological changes that objects create in humans and studying the interactions are thought to be the base of emotional measuring technology. Below, some research topics on touch sensation are introduced in order to deepen our understanding of the relation between physiological and psychological responses and the assessment of well-being.

12.5.1 Assessing Touch Sensation

The contact of material and textiles on the skin is called texture. Textiles, whether natural or synthetic, possess a wide variety of differing physical characteristics arising from raw materials, thread composition and patterning, variations in weaving, and surface manufacture. The communication of "texture," due to its physical basis, requires a variety of unique, specialized language, such as *"KOSHI," "NUMERI,"* and *"SHARI."* The feel of material on the skin along with the internal heat, humidity, airflow, and pressure is the primary factor relating to the well-being of the wearer. Touch is the way that people actively move their fingers and fingertips against the material when assessing it. Feel is a passive sensation of the material interacting with the skin. A great deal of research has been carried out into "feel" and the act of emotional assessment of the physical properties of the material. With the Kawabata Evaluation System (KES) [17], a method of physical assessment, feel can be assessed using the special characteristics of the surfaces of the material, its flexibility, its elasticity, its strength, its compressibility, and according to the JIS system, its absorbency and permeability. Research into texture has been going on for a few decades, and the contribution of Kawabata, mapping adjectives with physical characteristics and allowing the manufacture of testing tools and measurement systems, has been huge. As the assessment of fabric hand is subjective, psychological methods of assessment have been the norm. People use not just words such as soft, hard, thick, thin but also *KOSHI, NUMERI, SHARI, HARI* (resemblance to stiff), scratchy, slimy, dry, grainy, moist, damp, silky, fluffy, and more in their assessments. There has been much research into these sense-words, which combine multiple physical characteristics into each word. Recently, research into sense and sensitivity has made use of measurement of brain activity and ECG to form a distinct area of research focused on objective physiological responses and stimuli, differing in experimental methodology from research into psychological responses.

Dawes and Owen reported on the use of the thumb and other digits in assessing flexibility, contact, and smoothness in the subjective assessment of qualify of fabric [18]. Nishimatsu, in their studies, shows the importance of firm pressure and steady movement of the fingertips on the surface of the material in the active assessment of coarseness in textiles and fabric [19]. As a voice from sales and manufacture, a new methodology for assessment is needed because the classification of sense adjectives remains incomplete and indistinct.

Until now, methods of assessing material have been focused on the mechanical interaction with a single piece of material and the evaluation of sensory impressions. Humans, however, assess material through a wide variety of movements of the fingertips and the collation of the sense impressions they receive. Research into the human assessment of feel requires greater knowledge of finger movement. Humans can sense physical sensations such as coarseness, softness, flexibility, and more through their fingertips, allowing them to discern different materials from one another, we know. In this research, robotic hands are being developed, allowing further analysis of mechanical movement of the fingertips [20] and, through use of motion-capture systems, quantitative analysis of the movements of the finger joints [21]. Accelerometers attached to the five digits and measurement of the load on the fingertips allow for the collection of data while touching coarse, thick, rough, etc. material, allowing for detailed analysis [9].

12.5.2 Measuring Finger Movement in Palpation

Humans assess fabric by actively touching it and feeling it. However, few people understand the way in which they move their fingers and the way that they can discern different materials – there are many ways that humans interact with fabrics. It is possible to classify the movements of the fingertips, but in everyday life, people move their fingertips in many different ways and people who understand which movements allow them to assess which characteristics (softness, coarseness, thickness, etc.) are perhaps very rare.

It is hoped that the development of robot hands and the study of their interaction with a human hand will afford more abstract information on fabric hand, allowing for the formation of linear scale of fabric hand assessment and measuring devices. Research has shown that people with his abilities to assess fabric move their fingers in simple, monotonous ways [9]. Analysis of the way in which skin, fingertips, sense organs, the skeletal system, and the musculature interact in fabric assessment may be fruitful. Here we will introduce research using accelerometers and pressure sensors attached to the fingers.

By preliminary tests of assessing roughness of fabric, six subjects who demonstrated high ability in assessing fabric were selected, along with another six subjects who demonstrated poor ability in this area. The finger pressure of these subjects while assessing the elasticity, flexibility, softness, and smoothness of nonwoven fabrics such as felt was measured. The cloth was suspended from a hanger, and the finger movements of the thumb, index finger, and middle finger were measured with a three-dimensional accelerometer (MA3 Series by Microstone Ltd, Japan) as they palpated the material. The exact assessments carried out by the subjects were elasticity (the feeling of the fabric pushing back), coarseness (the feeling of bumpiness), bendiness (the ease of bending the material), and softness (the material is easily deformed and easily compressed).

In Fig. 12.7, the XYZ axes are as follows: the Z-axis is pushing against the surface of the cloth, moving the fingers relative to the wrist is the Y-axis, and movement perpendicular to the line formed by the thumb and little finger is the X-axis.

Figure 12.8 shows data collated from the sensors while the subjects tried to assess ease of flexibility. The arrows show the expected direction of finger motion. Figure 12.8a shows the results from subjects with high assessment abilities, and Fig. 12.8b shows the results from those with poor assessment abilities. Comparing the lines of finger movements in these two groups, differences can be clearly observed. It is thought that simple finger movement aids in the assessment of

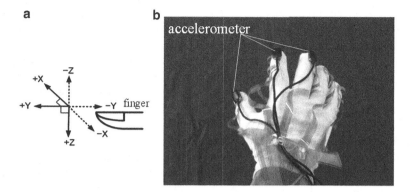

Fig. 12.7 Glove-type measurement system: (**a**) direction of finger motion, (**b**) photo

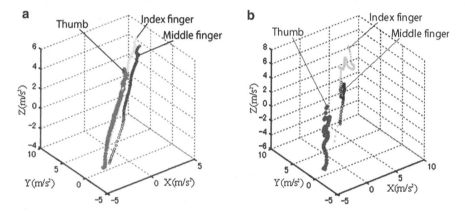

Fig. 12.8 Finger movement while evaluating flexibility: (**a**) high correct answer rate subjects, (**b**) low correct answer rate subjects

texture by touch. It is not clear whether people consciously move in this manner, but it is possible that this faculty may be improved through training. Though not shown here, the range of movement recorded while assessing the various qualities of material listed above is shown to be quite different. Recent advances in the miniaturization of recording devices have allowed us to have next insight into the mechanisms of the human sense of touch.

12.5.3   Brain-Wave Measurement in the Assessment of Touch Sensation

There are several different physiological factors which can be used in the study of material assessment by touch. Hirao et al. reported on the fluctuations in the patterns of electromyograms (EMG) in the assessment of varying kinds of fabric [22]. Shiotani measured the fluctuations in brain waves when subjects had pleasurable or uncomfortable experiences touching materials and showed that those fluctuations were greater when touching "pleasant" fabrics [23]. These are representative samples of research being carried out at that time and are integral to our understanding of touch-based assessment, but differential analysis of the interaction between physiological stimulus and response at the moment of touch is also required. The physiological changes in sense data at the moment of touch can be captured and measured as event-related potential (ERP) [24].

ERP measures the fluctuations in brain response from millisecond to millisecond caused by thoughts and perception and is thought to be of great use in the development of texture assessment. Brain waves produce tiny changes in potential depending on the stimuli experienced by the individual. ERP differs from the more widely known alpha waves in that it shows clear characteristic variations in brain function caused by stimuli and so shows the reasons for change in brain function clearly. Also, millisecond by millisecond changes in data processing by the brain from perceptions and thoughts can be observed. Many different components of ERP have been defined, allowing insight into their psychological interaction. An often-used component is called P300. The P300 has a latency of around 300 milliseconds and a comparatively large amplitude and is used in many experiments due its reproducibility, ubiquity, and shorter latency.

In this section, ERP is used as an objective measure of the response to texture. From the ERP measured when touching a sample of material, the distinct characteristic of coarseness can be used to develop indices for assessment of texture, as detailed in the experimentation introduced below [8].

Three differing samples were used: blanket, cotton cloth, and sandpaper. The contact of these with the inner forearm of the subjects was measured by ERP when introduced. Various large pieces were used at first to record passive ERP measurements. The temperature was 20 °C and the indoor relative humidity below 50%. Six healthy male university students sitting in chairs were used as test subjects. Electrodes were attached according to the international 10–20 system at F3, F4, C3, C4, P3, P4, and the standard electrode attached to each earlobe. ERP was initiated, using an A/D converter and a sampling interval of 1 ms to record the body's amperage to a computer. Samples were touched to the inner left forearm for a period of 3 s, and this was repeated 20 times. The same procedure was performed for each of the three samples, and the mean accompanying ERP assessed.

The results of FRP are shown in Fig. 12.9. The topography of this is shown in Fig. 12.10. The brightness at the center of the figure shows a high ERP. Sandpaper showed the largest ERP. Figure 12.11 shows the results of the assessment of texture by the sensory test. There were five levels: quite rough, slightly rough, neither, slightly smooth, and quite smooth. These correlated with assessments of pleasantness ($P < 0.05$) in 20 subjects, with the blanket being described as pleasant, the sandpaper as unpleasant, and the cotton as neither. ERP allows us to capture the physiological moment behind the feeling of touching something unpleasant.

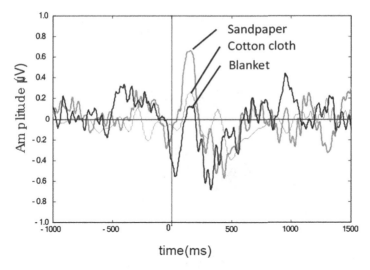

Fig. 12.9 ERP

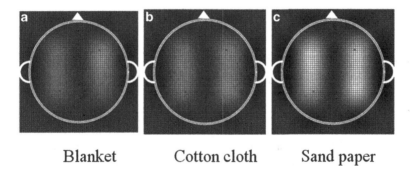

Fig. 12.10 Topograph of ERP: (**a**) blanket, (**b**) cotton cloth, (**c**) sandpaper

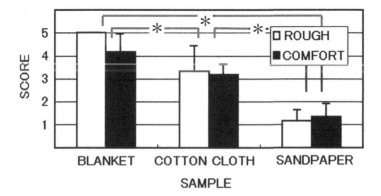

Fig. 12.11 Sensory evaluation results for degree of comfort and sense of roughness

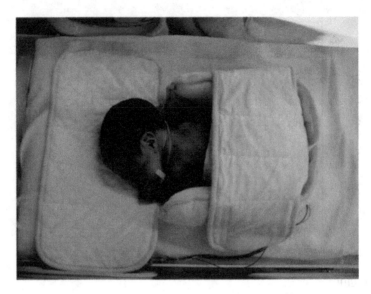

Fig. 12.12 Positioning mat

12.5.4 Assessing the Touch Sensation of Towels Through Measurement of Mind/Body Responses

The level of care provided to newborn infants in Japan is currently one of the highest in the world, and infant mortality remains the lowest in the world. To this end, developments in specialist developmental care for newborn infants in NICUs are being pursued, with the goal of reducing mortality rates in very low birth-weight babies, sometimes called premature babies. One way in which developmental care can reduce the stress on the premature infant is positioning. Figure 12.12 shows the way in which a positioning mat (PM) adjusts the orientation of the infant so that when held by the mother or father, the position of the infant is similar to the way it was positioned while in the womb. The premature infant reduces the stresses of the incubator because it can secure the functional position using the positioning mat. Study of the role of the textural surface of the positioning mat in this was sought. However, the importance of fabric handle (touch sensation on fabric) must not be ignored, and the textural surface may be changed by repeated washing, so this must also be taken into account.

Here research into the physiological effects of the stress caused on the premature infant by the changes in the texture of the PM caused by repeated washing will be introduced [25]. We cannot know the premature infant's sensory evaluation of the texture of the towel as they are unable to speak. Development of new methodology for assessing physiological condition would be very useful in this situation. The PM is constructed with cut-piles, a netlike loop of threads, and after manufactured using

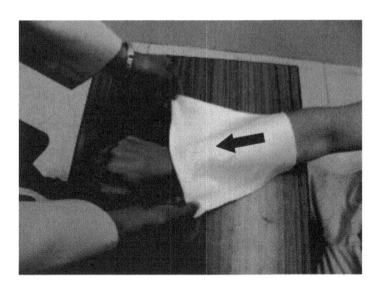

Fig. 12.13 Experiment scene

shirring, cut to a pile of 2 mm. The PM is comprised of 80% cotton and 20% polyester, but the pile is 100% cotton. An experiment where the PM was washed in five different ways was undertaken (these five different ways were to wash the PM 0, 1, 10, 30, and 50 times). In order to assess the impact of fabric conditioner (biological type), it was used, and the washes (0, 1, 10, 30, and 50 times) were performed in identical ways.

Figure 12.13 shows the psychological and physiological responses exhibited when the cloth sample was moved against the left inner forearm of the subject. In order to standardize this contact, the sample formed into an envelope and 230 gf of silicone laminate placed inside. For the physiological response, autonomic nervous system arousal was measured by ECG. Psychological response was measured with the SD system using six terms: fine, soft, pleasant, warm, familiar (to touch), and healing, which were rated in five levels. The test subjects were 13 university students in general good health.

Figure 12.14 shows the calculations of autonomic nervous system activity derived from the results of the ECG. It has been found that, in the autonomic nervous system, the relation between the sympathetic nervous system (SNS) and the parasympathetic nervous system (PSNS) is such that, when excited, the SNS displays activity and when in more controlled situations, the PSNS displays activity. Figure 12.14a shows SNS activity for LF/HF. Figure 12.14b shows PSNS activity for HF/LF + HF. When contact with the toweling sample is comfortable, the SNS is greatly aroused (LF/HF), but when this contact is uncomfortable, the SNS is somewhat aroused, but the PSNS shows a higher level of arousal. The "o" mark in the figure denotes the results for a toweling sample which did not use fabric softener, and the "a" mark denotes the results for a sample which did use fabric softener. These results are relative to the control of a resting state – the

Fig. 12.14 Activity index of autonomic nervous: (**a**) LF/HF, (**b**) HF/(LF + HF)

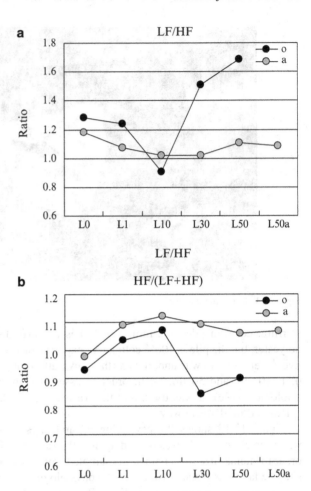

physiological arousal during a resting state was defined as level 1, and the exposure to the toweling sample produced a level of greater than 1. L50a refers to a sample which was washed 50 times after being conditioned twice.

In Fig. 12.14, it is shown that up until 10 washes, the SNS indicator (LF/HF) tended to be low, but the PSNS indicator HF/(LF + HF) tended to increase. This shows that the stress arousal arising from contact with the sample is falling rather than increasing. After 30 washes, the unconditioned sample gave rise to increased SNS activity, demonstrating a stressed condition. This shows that after 30 washes, the toweling sample becomes worn and stiff. This confirms that quantitative analysis of changes in the autonomic nervous system due to stress on the mind or body caused by changes in the fabric hand of material can be measured by ECG.

12.6 Conclusion

Our impressions are dependent on our individual experiences, but by careful testing of the bases of our perceptions, we can create indicators for standardized assessment. We can acquire diverse information from people, and from this data, we can create new interaction-based techniques for understanding how we feel. This may have an invigorating effect on the development of manufacturing processes. New products will convey the wonder of our lives. By relying on reliable phenomena and mathematics, we can ensure harmony and agreement. The practical applications of sensitivity include the design and construction of products and through the open cooperation of people, a unique sense of worth. We must create a new language for understanding each other by further vigorous research into the *Kansei* measurement.

References

1. Ministry of Economy, Trade and Industry in Japan: Kansei initiative (2009) http://www.meti. go.jp/english/policy/mono_info_service/mono/kansei2009/inind.html. Accessed 3 April 2012
2. Kamijo M, Uemae T (2010) Study of emerging of Kansei value on co-creating picture books. J Human Life Eng 11(2):10–15 (in Japanese)
3. McNair DM, Lorr M, Droppleman LF (1992) Profile of mood state. Educational and Industrial Testing Service, San Diego
4. Kanai H, Tsuji H, Kamijo M, Matsumoto Y, Nishimatsu T, Shibata K (2007) Evaluation of kinetic performance for men's suit jacket in exercise of shoulder joint. Sen-i Gakkaishi 63 (6):159–164
5. Kanai H, Tsuji H, Kawasaki J, Nishimatsu T, Okamura M, Shibata K (2007) Evaluation of kinetic performance on men's suit jacket by psycho-physiological measurement. In: Proceedings of the international conference on kansei engineering and emotional research, CDROM, Sapporo
6. Horiba Y, Kamijo M, Sadoyama T, Shimizu Y, Sasaki K, Shimizu H (2001) Effect on brain activity of clothing pressure by waist belts. Kansei Eng Int 2(1):1–8
7. Horiba Y, Kamijo M, Hosoya S, Takatera M, Sadoyama T, Shimizu Y (2000) Availability of evaluating thermal comfortable feeling by using electroencephalogram (EEG). Kansei Eng Int 1(2):9–14
8. Horiba Y, Kamijo M, Hosoya S, Takatera M, Shimizu Y, Sadoyama T (2000) Evaluation of tactile sensation for wearing by using event related potential. Sen-I Gakkaishi 56(1):47–54 (in Japanese)
9. Lee S, Kamijo M, Honywood M, Nishimatsu T, Shimizu Y (2007) Analysis of finger motion in evaluating the hand of a cloth using a glove-type measurement system. Text Res J 77:13–19
10. Yarbus AL (1967) Eye movement and vision. Plenum Press, New York
11. Ekman P, Friesen WV (2003) Unmasking the face. Malor Books, Cambridge, pp 21–33
12. Sugahara T, Yamada N, Sadoyama T, Kamijo M, Iguchi T, Nakamura T (2008) Analysis of the relationship between an attractive smile and eye shape. Kansei Eng Int 7(2):155–161
13. Sugahara T, Sadoyama T, Kamijo M, Hosoya S, Iguchi T (2004) Muscle activity pattern and geometrical features in attractive facial expressions. In: Proceedings (CDROM) of joint 2nd international conference of soft computing and intelligent system and 5th international symposium on advanced intelligent systems, Tokyo

14. Kanizsa G (1976) Subjective contours. Sci Am 234(4):48–52
15. Hachisuka S, Kimura T, Ishida K, Nakatani H, Ozaki N (2010) Drowsiness detection using facial expression features. In: 2010 SAE world congress, Intelligent vehicle initiatives, SP-2264, pp 81–90
16. Ishida K, Ichimura A, Kamijo M (2010) A study of facial muscular activities in drowsy expression. Kansei Eng Int J 9(2):57–66
17. Kawabata S (1980) The standardization and analysis of hand evaluation. The Textile Machinery Society of Japan, Osaka
18. Dawes VH, Owen JD (1971) The assessment of fabric handle part II: smoothness. J Text Inst 62:245–250
19. Nishimatsu T, Sowa K, Sekiguchi S, Toba E, Ono E (1998) Measurement of active tactual motion in judging hand of materials of fabrics. Sen-I Gakkai-shi 54(9):452–458 (in Japanese)
20. Nicholls A, Lee K (1989) A survey of robot tactile sensing technology. Int J Robotic Res 8(3):3–30
21. Braido P, Zhang X (2004) Quantitative analysis of finger motion coordination in hand manipulative and gestic acts. Hum Movement Sci 22:661–678
22. Hirao N, Yagi A (1997) Evaluation of fabric hand by electromyogram in active touch. J Jpn Res Assoc Text End-Uses 38(4):52–57 (in Japanese)
23. Shiotani T (1996) Methods for evaluating and analyzing texture of fabrics. Sen-i Gakkaishi 52(6):247–252 (in Japanese)
24. Steven JL (2005) An introduction to the event-related potential technique. The MIT Press, Cambridge, MA
25. Kwon E, Sugahara T, HoribaY, Shimizu Y, Kamijo M, Kihara H (2007) The study of the physiological and psychological response to the deterioration of the texture of a towel cloth through washing. In: Proceedings of international conference on Kansei engineering and emotion research 2007, CD-ROM, Sapporo

Chapter 13
Information Theoretic Methodology for Kansei Engineering: Kansei Channel and SPRT

Tetsuo Hattori and Hiromichi Kawano

Abstract This chapter provides an application of some notions in information theory to Kansei engineering toward a mathematical methodology for the analysis in Kansei engineering field. First, we propose a new definition of correlation using the mutual information in information theory. Second, we present a relation between Bayes' updating using the notion of binary channel and sequential probability ratio test (SPRT). Third, we illustrate that, for structural change detection of time series data, the SPRT is a very useful method that meets our intuition or Kansei very well. Moreover, we show the effectiveness of SPRT, comparing with Chow test that is well known as a standard method for the change detection.

13.1 Introduction

Generally, in Kansei engineering field, the analysis for the correlation and/or correspondence between some objects and human feeling (or sensory information) becomes an important problem. For this problem, many statistical methods in multivariate analysis have been applied, such as multiple linear regression analysis, principal component analysis, and factor analysis.

However, the notions of them are mainly based on linearity. As the typical example, the normal definition of correlation has meaning of linearity. On the other hand, in the well-known information theory, the relation between discrete input events (or objects) and output ones (or observation values) are represented as communication channel corresponding to a transition matrix, where each component shows a conditional probability [1–3]. And, various quantities based on the

T. Hattori (✉)
Kagawa University, Kagawa, Japan
e-mail: hattori@eng.kagawa-u.ac.jp

H. Kawano
NTT Advanced Technology, Tokyo, Japan

K. Saeed and T. Nagashima (eds.), *Biometrics and Kansei Engineering*,
DOI 10.1007/978-1-4614-5608-7_13, © Springer Science+Business Media New York 2012

probability such as entropy are defined on the notion of "channel." Those notions based on channel seem to be very useful for various analyses and feature extraction in the field of Kansei engineering.

In this chapter, we propose a new definition of correlation using the mutual information in the information theory, by extending the definition of probability to the subjective one as shown in [4]. And, using the notion of binary channel, we present a relation between Bayes' updating [5] and sequential probability ratio test (SPRT) [6–8]. Moreover, we show that the SPRT is very useful for the structural change detection of time series data by various experimental results, comparing with Chow test that is well known as a standard change detection method.

13.2 A New Definition of Correlation

13.2.1 *Definitions*

Let input event X and output event Y be represented as follows, respectively.

$$X = \begin{pmatrix} x_1, x_2, & \cdots, & x_N \\ p(1), p(2), & \cdots, p(N) \end{pmatrix} \tag{13.1}$$

$$0 \le p(i) \le 1, \quad \sum_i p(i) = 1 \quad (i = 1, ..., N)$$

$$Y = \begin{pmatrix} y_1, y_2, & \cdots, & y_M \\ q(1), q(2), & \cdots, q(M) \end{pmatrix} \tag{13.2}$$

$$0 \le q(j) \le 1, \quad \sum_j q(j) = 1 \quad (j = 1, ..., M)$$

Using the probability distribution, the *entropy* $H(X)$, $H(Y)$, *joint entropy* $H(X,Y)$, *conditional entropy* $H(X|Y)$, $H(Y|X)$, and *mutual information* $I(X,Y)$ are defined as nonnegative values, in the information theory.

From the definition of those entropies, the various relational equations between them are obtained as below.

$$I(X, Y) = H(X) - H(X|Y) = H(Y) - H(Y|X) \tag{13.3}$$

$$\begin{aligned} H(X, Y) &= H(X) + H(Y) - I(X, Y) \\ &= H(Y) + H(Y|X) \\ &= H(X) + H(X|Y) \end{aligned} \tag{13.4}$$

Fig. 13.1 Conceptual image of the relationsip between entropy and mutual information

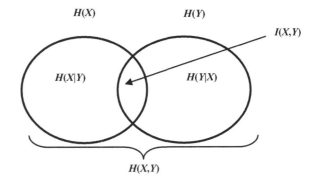

The conceptual image of the relation between those entropies and mutual information is illustrated in Fig. 13.1.

Taking a discrete memoryless channel (DMC) for an example, the *channel capacity* C is defined as follows.

$$C = \max_{p \in X} I(X, Y) \tag{13.5}$$

The input probability distribution that gives the maximum mutual information is called optimal input probability distribution (OIPD).

Based on the notion of channel capacity (maximum mutual information), we propose a new definition of correlation as a rate of channel capacity C and the entropy H(X) at the OIPD. That is, let COR denote the correlation.

$$COR = \frac{C}{H(X)} \tag{13.6}$$

From (13.3), we have the following inequality.

$$I(X, Y) = H(X) - H(X|Y) \le H(X) \tag{13.7}$$

Then, we have (13.8) and (13.9).

$$C = \max I(X, Y) \le H(X) \tag{13.8}$$

$$0 \le COR \le 1 \tag{13.9}$$

13.2.2   Effectiveness

Let X, Y be the input and output event, respectively. And let x and y be random variables in the events X and Y, respectively. Then, we identify as X = x and Y = y.

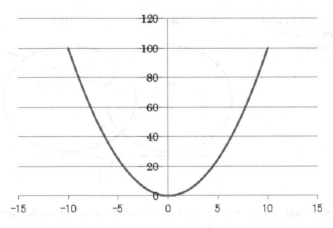

Fig. 13.2 Example of the case where normal correlation $= 0$

Let $\bar{x}$ and $\bar{y}$ be the average of x and y, respectively. Let $E[x]$ denote the expectation of the x, then the normal definition of correlation between X and Y is as follows.

$$E[(x - \bar{x})(y - \bar{y})] \tag{13.10}$$

If we assume that the following functional relation holds as shown in Fig. 13.2,

$$y = x^2 \tag{13.11}$$

we have

$$E[(x - \bar{x})(y - \bar{y})] = 0 \tag{13.12}$$

However, according to the definitions of channel capacity and OIPD, we have

$$COR = 1 \tag{13.13}$$

Since there is a clear functional relation between x and y, the above value of COR is more desirable than the definition of the normal correlation.

13.3 Relation Between SPRT and Bayes' Updating

13.3.1 SPRT

Generally, sequential probability ratio test (SPRT) is used for testing a null hypothesis H_0 (e.g., the quality is under prespecified limit 1 %) against hypothesis H_1 (e.g., the quality is over prespecified limit 1 %). And it is defined as follows.

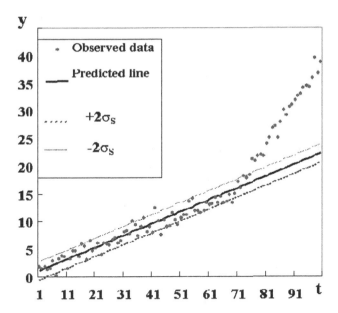

Fig. 13.3 Example of time series data in case where the true change point tc $= 7$

Let $Z_1, Z_2, \ldots, Z_i$ be respectively observed time series data at each stage of successive events, the probability ratio λ_i is computed as follows.

$$\lambda_1 = \frac{P(Z_1|H_1) \cdot P(Z_2|H_1) \cdots P(Z_i|H_1)}{P(Z_1|H_0) \cdot P(Z_2|H_0) \cdots P(Z_i|H_0)} \quad (13.14)$$

where $P(Z | H_0)$ denotes the distribution of Z if H_0 is true, and similarly, $P(Z | H_1)$ denotes the distribution of Z if H_1 is true.

Two positive constants C_1 and C_2 ($C_1 < C_2$) are chosen. If $C_1 < \lambda_i < C_2$, the experiment is continued by taking an additional observation. If $C_2 < \lambda_i$, the process is terminated with the rejection of H_0 (acceptance of H_1). If $\lambda_i < C_1$, then terminate this process with the acceptance of H_0.

$$C_1 = \frac{\beta}{1 - \alpha}, C_2 = \frac{1 - \beta}{\alpha} \quad (13.15)$$

where α means type I error (reject a true null hypothesis), and β means type II error (accept a null hypothesis as true one when it is actually false).

We have proposed to apply this SPRT to a structural change point detection problem of time series data as shown in Fig. 13.3 [6–8].

Fig. 13.4 Binary channel

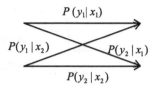

13.3.2 Bayes' Updating Based on Binary Channel

We regard that the observation and SPRT process for the aforementioned structural change point detection of time series data is essentially a kind of Bayes' updating by a binary channel as shown in Fig. 13.4, where input event $X = (x_1, x_2)$ and output event $Y = (y_1, y_2)$.

The transition matrix (or channel matrix) P_B is represented using conditional probability as follows.

$$P_B = \begin{bmatrix} P(y_1|x_1) & P(y_2|x_1) \\ P(y_1|x_2) & P(y_2|x_2) \end{bmatrix} \tag{13.16}$$

Let the prior probability distribution of input event X be $\{P_0(x_1), P_0(x_2)\}$ as initial values. Let the observed output sequence $\{y_{j_1}, y_{j_2}, \ldots, y_{j_n}\}$ ($y_{j_k} = y_1$ or y_2 ($k = 1, 2, \ldots, n$)). Then, by the first observation of output, the posterior probability is given by Bayes' theorem.

$$p(x_1|y_{j_1}) = \frac{P_0(x_1)P(y_{j_1}|x_1)}{P(y_{j_1})}$$

$$p(x_2|y_{j_1}) = \frac{P_0(x_2)P(y_{j_1}|x_2)}{P(y_{j_1})}$$

$$where, P(y_{j_1}) = \sum_i P_0(x_i)P(y_{j_1}|x_i) \tag{13.17}$$

According to the Bayes' updating rule, we have the following updated prior probability $\{P_1(x_1), P_1(x_2)\}$.

$$P_1(x_1) = p(x_1|y_{j_1}) = \frac{P_0(x_1)p(y_{j_1}|x_1)}{P(y_{j_1})}$$

$$P_1(x_2) = p(x_2|y_{j_1}) = \frac{P_0(x_2)p(y_{j_1}|x_2)}{P(y_{j_1})} \tag{13.18}$$

Similarly, by the second observation, we have

$$P_2(x_1) = p\left(x_1|y_{j_2}\right) = \frac{P_1(x_1)p\left(y_{j_2}|x_1\right)}{P\left(y_{j_2}\right)}$$

$$P_2(x_2) = p\left(x_2|y_{j_2}\right) = \frac{P_1(x_2)p\left(y_{j_2}|x_2\right)}{P\left(y_{j_2}\right)}$$

$$where,\ P\left(y_{j_2}\right) = \sum_i P_1(x_i)P\left(y_{j_2}|x_i\right) \tag{13.19}$$

Thus, by the nth observation of output, we have

$$P_n(x_i) = p\left(x_i|y_{j_n}\right) = \frac{P_{n-1}(x_i)P\left(y_{j_n}|x_i\right)}{P\left(y_{j_n}\right)}$$

$$= \frac{P_0(x_i)\prod\limits_{k=1}^{n} P\left(y_{j_k}|x_2\right)}{\prod\limits_{k=1}^{n} P\left(y_{j_k}\right)}\ (i = 1, 2) \tag{13.20}$$

Then the probability ratio λ_n is as follows.

$$\lambda_n = \frac{P_n(x_2)}{P_n(x_1)} = \frac{P_0(x_2)\prod\limits_{k=1}^{n} P\left(y_{j_k}|x_2\right)}{P_0(x_1)\prod\limits_{k=1}^{n} P\left(y_{j_k}|x_1\right)} \tag{13.21}$$

If we assume that

$$P_0(x_1) = P_0(x_2) = \frac{1}{2} \tag{13.22}$$

Then, we obtain the same ratio as that of SPRT. Therefore, we consider that Bayes' updating based on binary channel is a kind of generalization of SPRT.

As for the conditional probability, we can introduce our subjective probability in order to meet our intuition. Then, we can adopt not only the discrete probability but also continuous density function.

13.4   Structural Change Detection

For the early structural change detection problem, we propose an application of sequential probability ratio test (SPRT) that has been mainly used in the field of quality control.

13.4.1 Application of SPRT to Change Detection

For simplicity, we describe our proposed method for structural change detection of
time series by taking an example. We assume that the time series is generated in the
following equation as a function of time t.

$$y_t = \beta_1 \cdot t + \beta_0 + \varepsilon \qquad (13.23)$$

where $\varepsilon \approx N(0,\sigma^2)$, that is, the error ε is a random variable subject to the normal
distribution with the average 0 and the variation σ^2.

Then we also assume that the structural change occurred at the time point tc*
(what we call change point), involving the change of equation coefficients β_1, β_0.
Concretely speaking, such data is generated by the following equations.

$$y_t = \beta_{11} \cdot t + \beta_{10} + \varepsilon \ (t \leq tc^*) \qquad (13.24)$$

$$y_t = \beta_{21} \cdot t + \beta_{20} + \varepsilon \ (tc \leq t^*) \qquad (13.25)$$

where tc* is called a change point in the structural change. In Fig. 13.3, a time series
data based on the above (13.24) and (13.25) is plotted, where $\beta_{11} = 0.2, \beta_{10} = 1.0$,
$\beta_{21} = 0.8$, $\beta_{20} = -41.0$, and tc* = 70, $\varepsilon \approx N(0, 1)$. Moreover, σ_s means the
standard deviation of error between early observed data $\{ y_t | 1 \leq t \leq 40\}$ and the
predicted line obtained from the early data.

The concrete procedure of structural change detection is as follows (see Fig. 13.5):

Step 1: Make a prediction expression and set the tolerance band (*a*) (e.g., $a = 2\sigma_s$)
that means permissible error margin between the predicted data and the
observed one.

Step 2: Set up the null hypothesis H_0 and alternative hypothesis H_1.
H_0: Change has not occurred yet.
H_1: Change has occurred.

Set the values α, β and compute C_1 and C_2 according to (13.15). Initialize i = 0,
$\lambda_0 = 1$.
Remark
The statement of the null hypothesis H_0, "Change has not occurred yet," means
in statistical sense. It means that the generation probability for the data to go out
from the tolerance band is less than (or equal to) θ_0 (for instance, 1 %). Similarly,
the statement of the alternative hypothesis H_1, "Change has occurred," means that
the generation probability for the data to go out from the tolerance band is greater
than (or equal to) θ_1 (for instance, 99 %). Additionally, we suppose that θ_1 is
considerably greater than θ_0.

Step 3: Incrementing i (i = i + 1), observe the following data y_i. Evaluate the error
$|\varepsilon_i|$ between the data y_i and the predicted value from the aforementioned
prediction expression.

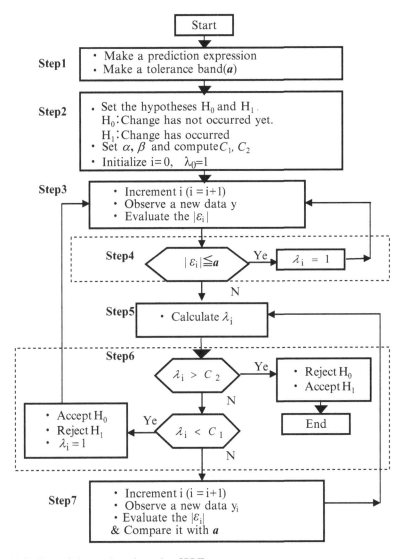

Fig. 13.5 Flow of change detection using SPRT

Step 4: Judge as to whether the data y_i goes in the tolerance band or not, that is, the ε_i is less than (or equal to) the permissible error margin or not. If it is yes, then set $\lambda_i = 1$ and return to Step 3. Otherwise, advance to Step 5.

Step 5: Calculate the probability ratio λ_i using the following (13.26) that is equivalent to (13.14).

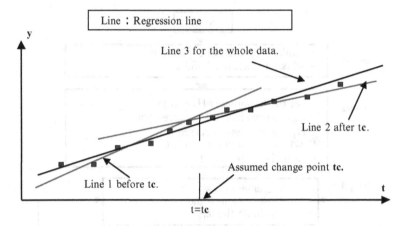

Fig. 13.6 Chow test in the situation where a hypothesis is set up that the structural change has occurred at $t = tc$

$$\lambda_i = \lambda_{i-1} \frac{P(\varepsilon_i|H_1)}{P(\varepsilon_i|H_0)} \quad (13.26)$$

where, if the data y_i goes in the tolerance band, $P(\varepsilon_i|H_0) = \theta_0$ and
$P(\varepsilon_i|H_1) = \theta_1$; otherwise, $P(\varepsilon_i|H_0) = (1-\theta_0)$ and $P(\varepsilon_i|H_1) = (1-\theta_1)$.

Step 6: Execution of testing.

1. If the ratio λ_i is greater than $C_2 (= (1-\beta)/\alpha)$, dismiss the null hypothesis H_0, and adopt the alternative hypothesis H_1, and then end.
2. Otherwise, if the ratio λ_i is less than $C_1 (= \beta/(1-\alpha))$, adopt the null hypothesis H_0 and dismiss the alternative hypothesis H_1, and then set $\lambda_i = 1$ and return to Step 3.
3. Otherwise (in the case where $C_1 \leq \lambda_i \leq C_2$), advance to Step 7.

Step 7: Observe the following data y_i incrementing i.

Evaluate the error $|\varepsilon_i|$ and judge whether the data y_i goes in the tolerance band or not. Then, return to Step 5 (calculation of the ratio λ_i).

13.4.2 Chow Test

The well-known Chow test [9] checks the significant differences among residuals for three regression lines, where regression line 1 is obtained from the data before a change point tc, line 2 from the data after tc, and line 3 from the whole data so far, by setting up hypothesis of change point at each point in the whole data. Figure 13.6 shows the conceptual image of Chow test.

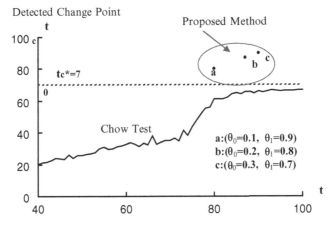

Fig. 13.7 Relation between the observing time t and detected change point tc ($\beta_{11} = 0.2$, $\beta_{21} = 0.4$, $\sigma = 1.0$)

13.5 Experimentation for Change Point Detection

We have experimented with the proposed method for both artificial and real-time series data, in comparison with the well-known Chow test. Those artificial time series data are generated based on aforementioned equations (13.24) and (13.25). In this section, we show the experimental results.

13.5.1 Results for Artificial Data

One of the experimental results is illustrated in Fig. 13.7, where horizontal axis shows observing time t (detection operation has started from t = 41). The vertical axis shows the detected change point tc, whose value is the average of experimentation results for 100 sets of generated time series data where the true change point tc* = 70. Figure 13.7 shows that Chow test outputs the change point at the time when every data is observed after t = 40. This means that Chow test cannot detect the change point properly. And, the time point when Chow test can work well is long late enough after the true change occurs.

On the other hand, the proposed method detects the change points **a, b, c**, where each of them corresponds to a set of parameters θ_0, θ_1 that are used in the SPRT, as shown in Fig. 13.7.

Similarly in the subsequent, we use a terminology "proposed method **a, b, c**" which corresponds to different parameter values of θ_0, θ_1 shown in Fig. 13.7.

Fig. 13.8 Time series of
retail price index in China

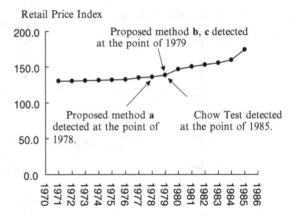

Fig. 13.9 Relation between
the observing time and
detected change point in time
series of retail price index in
China (Fig. 13.5)

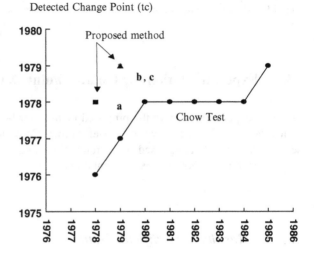

13.5.2   Results for Artificial Data

The results for real-time series data of retail price index in China are shown in
Figs. 13.8 and 13.9. It is regarded that the true change point is 1979. So, important
point in the evaluation of methods is as to whether the method detects true change
point as quickly and correctly as possible. In our proposed method, the number of
data used for making prediction expression is 5 (1971–1975).

As aforementioned, we can see from Fig. 13.9 that, when long enough after the
true change point, Chow test works well. However, until then, it outputs false
detection. On the other hand, our proposed method detects the change point very
well, with 8 or 9 years earlier than Chow test.

Other results for real-time series data of power generation quantity in Japan are
shown in Figs. 13.10 and 13.11. In 1986, "oil shock" happened worldwide and oil

Fig. 13.10 Time series of power generation in Japan

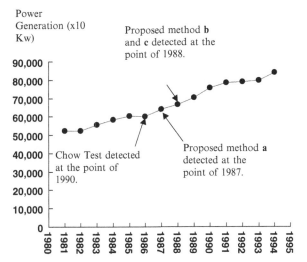

Fig. 13.11 Relation between the observing time and detected change point in the time series data of power generation in Japan (Fig. 13.7)

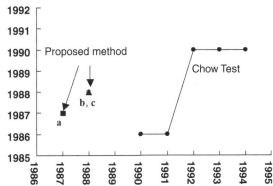

prices suddenly rose. Then, specialists in economics regard that the structural change occurred in the year of 1986.

From Figs. 13.10 and 13.11, we can see that Chow test correctly detects the change point of 1986, at 1990 and 1991. Until then, it detects no change point. And after 1991, it outputs 1990 as change point.

In this case, the number of data used for making prediction expression in our method is 5 (1981–1985). Our method outputs 1986 or 1987 as change point. For this case, we consider that our method works better than Chow test.

Also from this case of power generation in Japan (Figs. 13.10 and 13.11), similarly to the case of retail price index in China (Figs. 13.8 and 13.9), we can see the same kind of characteristics of Chow test that, if time passes enough after the structural change point or if there is drastic change such as abrupt trend change in the time series data around the change point, Chow test can detect the point very well. However, if not, it may miss the point or output false detection. On the contrary, we consider that our method works efficiently.

13.6 Application to Multiple Regression Model

13.6.1 Multiple Regression Model

In our experimentation for time series data based on multiple linear regression model, the data is generated by the following equations.

$$y = a_{11}x_1 + a_{12}x_2 + b + \varepsilon \quad (t \le t_c^*) \tag{13.27}$$

$$y = a_{21}x_1 + a_{22}x_2 + b + \varepsilon \quad (t_c^* \le t) \tag{13.28}$$

where $\varepsilon \sim N(0,\sigma^2)$, that is, the error ε is subject to the normal distribution with the average 0 and the variation σ^2, and tc* means the change point. In addition, we have set tc* = 70.

We have experimented with SPRT and Chow test for the artificial data based on the above (13.27) and (13.28). The concrete values of parameters are shown in Table 13.1. Figure 13.12 shows an example of the graph of generated time series data by the above equations. Figure 13.3 shows the situation of change point detections.

One of the results is illustrated in Fig. 13.15, where horizontal axis shows observing time t (detection operation has started from t = 41). The vertical axis

Table 13.1 Parameters for generating time series data

Equation (13.4) (time t = 1, 2,...,69)	Equation (13.5) (time t = 70, 71,...,100)	σ
$y = 2x_1 + 3x_2 + 10$	$y = 3x_1 + 3x_2 + 10$	5

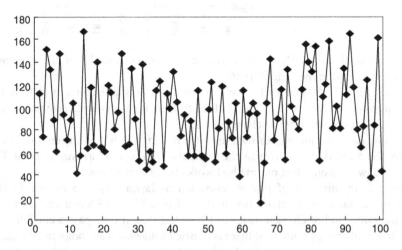

Fig. 13.12 An example of time series data based on multiple linear regression model. Change occurred at tc = 70

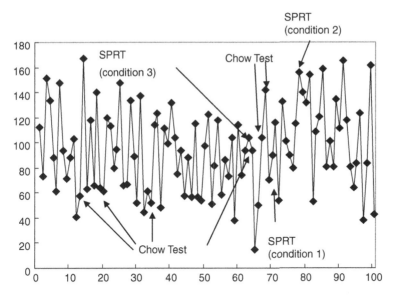

Fig. 13.13 Example of situation of change point detections by SPRT and Chow test, where tc* = 70, and detection operation has started from t = 41

shows the detected change point tc, whose value is the average of experimentation results for 200 sets of generated time series data where the real change point tc* = 70.

From Fig. 13.14, we can see that Chow test outputs the change point at the time when every data is observed after t = 40. This means that Chow test cannot detect the change point properly. And, the time point when Chow test can work well is long late enough after the real change occurs.

On the other hand, the SPRT detects the change points in the case of **a, b, c**, each corresponding to different parameter values of θ_0, θ_1 that are used in the SPRT.

13.6.2 Extended Change Point by SPRT

The SPRT detects a change point at the time when the probabilistic ratio λ_i is greater than C_2 $(=(1-\beta)/\alpha)$. Then, the detected change point equals to the terminated time point and its detection tends to be delayed from true change point. Thus, in this section, we extend the definition of detected change point by SPRT. As such extension, we adopt the number tc − **M** where tc is ordinary aforementioned change point and **M** is the number of times when the observed data continuously goes of tolerance zone until the ratio $\lambda_i > C_2$. The number **M** can be obtained from the (13.29).

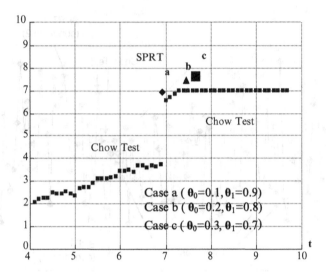

Fig. 13.14 Relation between the observing time t and detected change point tc, where tc* = 70, and detection operation has started from t = 41

Table 13.2 Parameter values in SPRT and M

α	β	θ_0	θ_1	M
0.05	0.05	0.1	0.9	2
		0.2	0.8	3
		0.3	0.7	4

$$\left(\frac{\theta_1}{\theta_0}\right)^M > C_2\left(=\frac{1-\beta}{\alpha}\right) \tag{13.29}$$

Then we have the following equation using Gauss notation. So, the value of M depends on the parameters (see Table 13.2). That is, $M = 2$ (case **a**), $M = 3$ (case **b**), $M = 4$ (case **c**).

$$M = \left[\log_{\frac{\theta_1}{\theta_0}}\frac{1-\beta}{\alpha}\right] \tag{13.30}$$

Applying the extended definition, we obtain the improvement of hitting percentage in the sense that the detected change point justly equals the true change point. It means pinpoint hitting percentage. Table 13.3 shows the resultant percentage when using the old definition of detected change point. On the other hand, Table 13.4 shows the resultant one when using extended definition.

Table 13.3 Frequency of change point detection and percentage of true change point (TCP) detection

Case	Time series point					Percentage of TCP detection (%)
	70	71	72	73	74	
a	7	141	4	12	1	0.35
b	1	7	105	5	12	0.05
c	1	1	5	98	2	0.05

Table 13.4 Detected change point frequency and percentage of true change point (TCP) detection

Case	Time series point					Percentage of TCP detection (%)
	70	71	72	73	74	
a	7	141	4	12	1	74.90
b	1	7	105	5	12	56.50
c	1	1	5	98	2	50.10

Fig. 13.15 Example of images where someone passes by at low speed (time is counted from upper left to lower right)

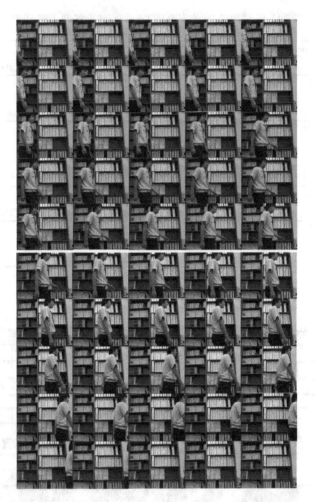

Fig. 13.15 (continued)

From those experimental results, we can expect that, if we adopt the interval
[tc − M, tc] as existing range of true change point, the hitting percentage will
considerably increase.

13.7 Application to Remote Monitoring System

As a simple automated change detection method of the scenes from a monitoring
camera, we apply the SPRT method to the time series data of compressed JPEG file
quantity (Kbyte).

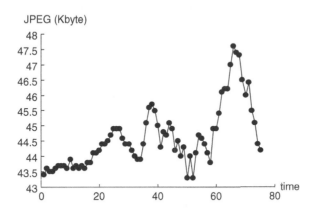

Fig. 13.16 Example of images where someone passes at high speed (time is counted from *upper left* to *lower right*)

JPEG (Kbyte)

Fig. 13.17 Total time series of image data, that is, sequence of JPEG file volumes in Fig. 13.15

Figures 13.15 and 13.16 show two sets of images when a person has moved at low speed and high speed, respectively, in front of a bookshelf. Figures 13.17 and 13.18 show two graphs on time series data of JPEG file volumes, corresponding to Figs. 13.15 and 13.16, respectively.

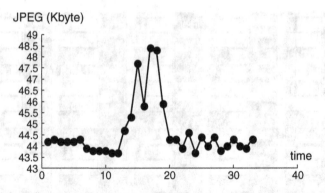

Fig. 13.18 Total time series of image data, that is, sequence of JPEG file volumes in Fig. 13.16

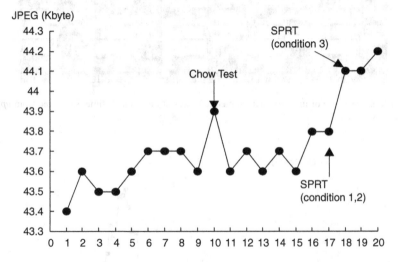

Fig. 13.19 Change point detection (low-speed passing-by movement in Fig. 13.15) using SPRT and Chow test. (condition 1 means ($\theta_0 = 0.9$, $\theta_1 = 0.1$), condition 2 is ($\theta_0 = 0.87$, $\theta_1 = 0.13$), and condition 3 is ($\theta_0 = 0.8$, $\theta_1 = 0.2$))

We assume that change point is the time point when the some change happens, that is, when some person appears in the image data. The SPRT can detect the change point quickly from the sequence of image data. We show experimental results of change detection using two tests (SPRT and Chow test) and discuss those effectiveness.

The results of change detection by the two tests (SPRT and Chow test) are shown in the graphs in Figs. 13.19 and 13.20, respectively, where the SPRT detects change

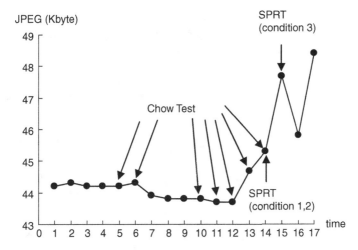

Fig. 13.20 Change point detection (high-speed passing-by movement in Fig. 13.16) using SPRT and Chow test. (condition 1 means ($\theta_0 = 0.9$, $\theta_1 = 0.1$), condition 2 is ($\theta_0 = 0.87$, $\theta_1 = 0.13$), and condition 3 is ($\theta_0 = 0.8$, $\theta_1 = 0.2$))

points in the case of condition 1 ($\theta_0 = 0.9$, $\theta_1 = 0.1$), condition 2 ($\theta_0 = 0.87$, $\theta_1 = 0.13$), and condition 3 ($\theta_0 = 0.8$, $\theta_1 = 0.2$). The number of samples in the stage of learning and analysis, where samples are used for concretely deciding prediction model (regression line), is seven in both cases of low-speed and high-speed passing-by movement and in both tests.

From the results in both cases of low-speed and high-speed passing-by movement, we find that the SPRT can detect the change quickly and correctly after the change happens. Moreover, the SPRT method is simple and takes very low computational cost (i.e., necessary time and memory storage for computation). On the contrary, the Chow test tends to make a mistake in the early stage after the change happens, and to take long time for correct change detection. In addition, the computational cost is considerably high. Then, we consider that the performance of SPRT is very effective in comparison with Chow test, even if the time series data of sequence of JPEG file volumes is fluctuated by lighting and so on.

13.8 Continuous Change Point Detection

In order to continuously detect the structural change of the scene images from a monitoring camera, we apply the ESPRT method to the time series of compressed image data (JPEG file) quantity (Kbyte).

Fig. 13.21 Example of time series images where someone moves in, stops walking, moves again, and moves out at high speed what we call "fast-in fast-out case" (time is counted from the *upper left* to the *lower right*)

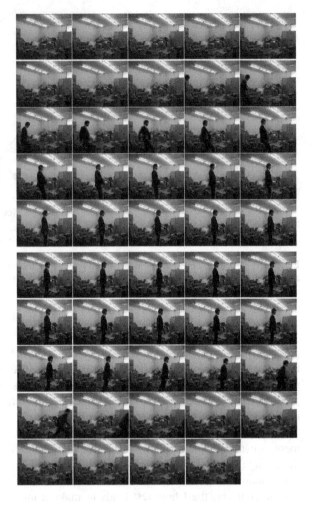

Figures 13.21 and 13.22 show two kinds of images when a person has moved into and out of the scene at high speed and low speed, respectively. Figures 13.23 and 13.24 show two graphs on time series data of JPEG file volumes, corresponding to Figs. 13.21 and 13.22, respectively.

We assume that there are four change points in both of the two kinds of time series images. The first change point is the time when some person appears in the scene image, and the second is when he stops walking, the third when he begins to move again, and the fourth when he moves out of scene.

The results of change detection by SPRT and Chow test are shown in the graphs in Figs. 13.25 and 13.26, respectively, where the SPRT detects change points in the case of condition 1 ($\theta_0 = 0.9$, $\theta_1 = 0.1$). The number of sample points for learning

Fig. 13.22 Example of time series images where someone moves in, stops walking, moves again, and moves out at low speed what we call "slow-in slow-out case" (time is counted from the *upper left* to the *lower right*)

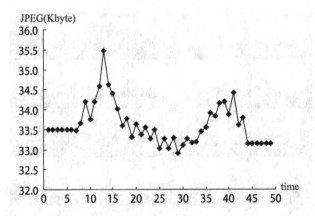

Fig. 13.23 Time series data of JPEG file volumes in Fig. 13.1 (fast-in fast-out case)

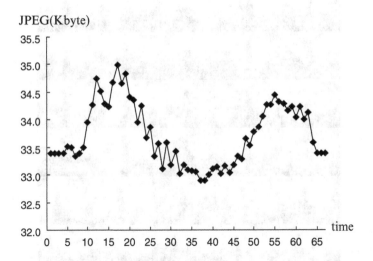

Fig. 13.24 Time series data of JPEG file volumes in Fig. 13.2 (slow-in slow-out case)

and analysis is five, where those samples are used for deciding prediction model (regression line) in both cases.

If SPRT detects the change at tc, the ESPRT estimates the true point as tc − 1 under the condition 1. Then after the first detection, next five points from tc − 1 to tc + 3 will be used as learning samples for reconstructing the next prediction model.

The experimental results show that ESPRT method continuously detects the change point better than Chow test in the two kinds of time series images.

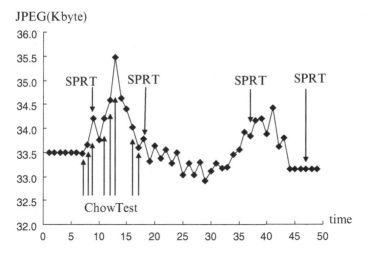

Fig. 13.25 Change detection results by SPRT and Chow test for the time series data in Fig. 13.23 (fast-in fast-out case)

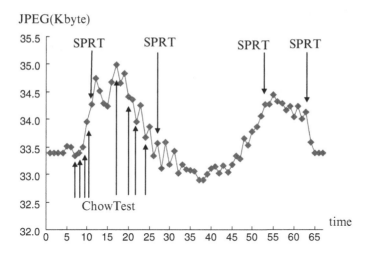

Fig. 13.26 Change detection results by SPRT and Chow test for the time series data in Fig. 13.24 (slow-in slow-out case)

13.9 Conclusion

Although the normal definition of correlation and many statistical methods such as multiple linear regression analysis and principal component analysis is based on the notion of linearity, we have newly proposed a definition of correlation that meets our intuition or Kansei very well using the mutual information in information theory. Moreover, we have presented the equivalent relation between Bayes' updating and SPRT (sequential probability ratio test) using the notion of binary channel. Also we have shown that the SPRT seems more effective than Chow test for structural change detection of time series data, from various experimental results. We consider that the SPRT and Bayes' updating method in binary channel will be a useful tool for decision making in the field of Kansei engineering.

References

1. Gallager RG (1968) Information theory and reliable communication. Wiley, New York
2. Thomas MC, Joy AT (2006) Elements of information theory, 2nd edn. Wiley-Interscience, Hoboken, NJ
3. Emmanuel D (2009) Classical and quantum information theory: an introduction for the telecom scientist. Cambridge University Press, Cambridge
4. Judea P (2001) Causality: models, reasoning, and inference. Cambridge University Press, Cambridge
5. Joachim D, Christopher MB (2002) Information theoretic sensor data selection for active object recognition and state estimation. IEEE Trans Pattern Anal Mach Intell 24(2):145–157
6. Hiromichi K, Tetsuo H, Ken N (2008) Structural change point detection method of time series using sequential probability ratio test-comparison with Chow test in the ability of early detection. IEE J Trans EIS 128(4):583–592
7. Katsunori T, Tetsuo H, Tetsuya I, Hiromichi K (2010) Extended SPRT for structural change detection of time series based on multiple regression model. Int J Artif Life Robot 15(4): 417–420, Springer, ISSN:1433–5298
8. Katsunori T, Tetsuo H, Hiromichi K (2011) Multiple regression model based sequential probability ratio test for structural change detection of time series. Experimental evaluation of effectiveness and extension. IEE J Trans EIS 131(2):442–450 (in Japanese)
9. Chow GC (1960) Tests of equality between sets of coefficients in two linear regressions. Econometrica 28(3):591–605

Chapter 14
Kansei Engineering and Service Engineering

Takashi Uozumi

Abstract What are differences and similarities between Kansei engineering and service engineering? Control theory and measurement technology provide an analogous perspective. However, tools for service engineering are also useful for implementation of Kansei-type agents. For Kansei engineering, an individual sense of value is an important factor. Therefore, relations of a target system are analyzed by the covariance structure analytical method and expressed with ontology to construct a general structure of the system. Then individual relations are examined using a Bayesian network to treat them precisely. We present practical applications as examples.

14.1 Introduction

As computer performance has improved, individual adjustment of them has become feasible. Kansei engineering and service engineering technologies are attractive to accomplish that task. Similarities between technologies do exist, but differences exist also in terms of ideas. While presenting application systems that the author has developed, we discuss technologies that are expected to become necessary in the near future.

14.1.1 *Encountering the Unknown*

Ancillary systems for expanding human exercise capabilities such as inventions from bicycles and automobiles to airplanes are around us. They have become

T. Uozumi (✉)
Department of Computer Science and Systems Engineering, Muroran Institute of Technology,
27-1, Mizumoto-cho, Muroran-shi, Hokkaido 050-8585, Japan
e-mail: uozumi@csse.muroran-it.ac.jp

K. Saeed and T. Nagashima (eds.), *Biometrics and Kansei Engineering*,
DOI 10.1007/978-1-4614-5608-7_14, © Springer Science+Business Media New York 2012

indispensable in our daily life. Our life space is enlarging, and the real experience of sightseeing from the world of movies alone as well as in the business world has become increasingly easy. While physical function is expanding, roles of computers as a part of the expansion of intellectual function is making progress after emergence of the internet, but it is insufficient yet. One reason is that computers used at present are inflexible. It occurs frequently that a huge gap stretches between the intention of a computer software designer and that of users. The author's professional interest is to create a computer that is friendlier to human beings. As tools to attain this, we usually use multiple agents and artificial intelligence technology.

While enjoying such daily life, a spaceship came to land on Earth. I happened to meet with the space aliens who had traveled inside it. They seemed to have learned our languages secretly. Although conversations with them were realized in many situations and subjects, there remained important discrepancies in matters relating to images. Although I did not notice it well at the beginning, I realized that their sensory capabilities were far beyond ours. I noticed that, surprisingly, they can sense visual frequencies and hearing frequencies more than twofold higher than ours. I also learned that their ancillary spectacles and ancillary ears are designed to see and hear millimeter waves, infrared rays, ultraviolet rays, and even radioactive particle emissions. Furthermore, I understood that their hearing sense covers the range from low frequency to the ultrasonic range and that they understand the songs of dolphins and bats.

I asked them to please give some devices for me to use. After using them, another world appeared in front my eyes and my ears felt even a slight pain. That world where I can see what I cannot see usually see and where I can hear what I cannot usually hear was distressing for me before I became accustomed to it. Even smell was detected in the form of a fusion of images and audio. I was quite astonished at how the world which I came to know after using this device differs from the world we usually experience. The device has active functions as well as passive functions and can scan any object by emitting ultrasonic waves. I noticed that with the expanded sensory region, the range of interest is greatly widened as well.

Despite that, as the information amount increased, I felt frustrated with my small brain. Its processing speed and capacity cannot catch up with the greatly increased volume of information. I complained about whether the performance of my brain is competent for this wider and deeper world. Then, he brought a device and told me to use it. He said this device was tuned specially for humans: "I think you can use it." After using it, I said "How do you do it?" He told me that this is a sub-brain that has functions of two kinds. One is a function to assist sorting out of sensory information and is designated as an "image brain", which performs automatic adjustments from gain adjustment and coloring to tone when image processing by my brain is unable to catch up. The other is a "calculation brain", which calculates branching of logical judgment and probabilistic ranking. Both are in the initial state and have a learning function. Therefore, they learn from the conversation with me and enrich their functions one by one. He said I have to be careful because the sub-brain particularly has no previous knowledge about the sensory capabilities of human beings and it therefore needs substantial education. Otherwise, it does not know if it can see and hear human beings and no conversation could be established. I woke up at this point in the dream.

Although such a dream is unrealistic at present, it is highly anticipated that it will be realized in the near future.

14.2 Kansei Engineering and Service Engineering

At the beginning of the 1990s, the economic bubble burst in Japan and the concept of values was reconsidered. In the latter half of the 1980s, Nagamachi [1] proposed Kansei engineering. The Japan Society of Kansei Engineering was established in 1998.

Since 2003, the international conference on "Service-oriented computing theory" has been held every year [2]. In addition, IBM (USA) proposed "service science" in 2005. In 2005, Singh and Huhns published "Service-oriented computing theory" [3], and an international workshop was held in 2007 [4]. Many people explained the definition of the term Kansei within the academic society while definitions of "Service" are also diversified [5, 6]. Meanwhile, according to the strategy for promoting studies and entity developments, it seems that Kansei engineering is performed in a sensory fashion while service engineering is done logically.

Kansei is related to a receiving capability and transmission capability, while other chapters deal with the definition of Kansei. Here, the author will discuss the receiving capability only and consider how computer agents understanding Kansei should be implemented.

A service is either an object service or a related service where the sender provides services to earn profits, and the receiver asks the sender in anticipation of some changes or selects the article presented. After it is provided, the receiver will harbor either satisfaction or disappointment. Conventionally, the service was regarded as the presence of ancillary, decorative, and peripheral objects performed by the provider considering differentiation of competitors. Now, to secure long-term profit as well as short-term profit, people have been aware of the importance of related services.

Conventionally, direct measurement of values and evaluations of the service in the form of "sales amount" was regarded as indirect measurement of the satisfaction level of consumers. However, the satisfaction level of consumers is not simple. The era in which people were satisfied with material civilization is passing away. People now begin to seek new concepts of value in a deluge of information and facing a lack of resources in the future. To cope with these difficulties, I proposed one paradigm from a Kansei engineering viewpoint. However, strategies of Kansei engineering that cover a wide range of Kansei are not definite, while service science engineering produces strategies by narrowing down a target to services. For service and Kansei, the direction of growth such as management and data mining and the direction of narrowing methodology are crossed.

14.3 Measurement and Control in System Engineering

In system engineering, the relation between control and measurement is often discussed. Control can be theorized easily, while theorization of measurement is difficult. Control is a means to maintain the set value in a limited area and is suited for mathematical formalization such as linear control theory and optimum control theory. Meanwhile, measurement requires information collection from manifold environments. To do this, direct tools such as surgical knives or forceps used by medical doctors and wider range of tools such as X-rays and ultrasonic wave electronic measuring devices are used. The important matter here is a structural model and a cause-and-effect relation in the brain of the medical doctor for an in vivo system to be targeted, and meta knowledge about which tools or medicines should be used when and where important. Judgment of the right person for right job principle is necessary. Therefore, theoretical uniformity becomes difficult.

If viewed as described, service engineering is comparable to control and Kansei is comparable to measurement. Therefore, theorization is difficult in one area and easy in another area. However, theory is not required necessarily for implementation on a computer.

To maintain an artificial system in a stable manner, technologies of control and measurement that are inextricably linked are indispensable. At the same time, to maintain a life system and social system with a stable manner, two approaches are necessary. One is a means for grasping the psychological state from the physical condition of a living body from a Kansei viewpoint. The other is a means for maintaining a user's physical condition in a good state from a service viewpoint. What is necessary here is a computer. Specifically, a computer agent that understands protocols of services is necessary. It is necessary for the agent to understand Kansei and to communicate with human beings, and the meaning of Kansei which human being possesses should be understood. As a means for definition of such meanings, ontology has been attracting attention.

14.3.1 Ontology

From birth, human beings acquire enormous amounts of knowledge in family circumstances, social surroundings, and the education environment. They range from knowledge of object to knowledge of relationship. They perform communications with others based on this knowledge. To date, many knowledge representation methods were developed in the artificial intelligence area, and ontology has been used as an effective means including deployment to the web. It is used for representation of background knowledge and implicit knowledge of our group because if ontology specific to an individual is derived from ordinary ontology; its difference could be used as a personal profile. In addition, semantic network and concept of frame can be expressed, and deployment to Bayesian network as probability theory is also possible, which constitute grounds for that reason. Ontology is gained in many ways. Some people gain it while being taught. Others gain it through repeated bodily sensations. How to be interested in and how to develop an interest in ontology and the ability to increase cognition are regarded as being of higher-level Kansei capability. We are performing ontology formation to a greater or lesser degree by learning under unknown circumstances without teachers where people will gain it without being told. However, it is said that autonomous knowledge acquisition is useful for implementation to computers.

Tools used in service-oriented computation theory are agent technology and are represented by ontology, inference technology, etc. For Kansei engineering, sensing technology and modeling technology are also required. Although not applicable necessarily to the transmission capability of Kansei such as design, for implementation of receiving capability of Kansei on computers, many areas are overlapped with service-oriented technique. Moreover, to cause a computer to understand Kansei, multiple translation functions are unavoidable. It might be said that the presence of a translation function equals Kansei.

When patients complain about their physical condition to a medical doctor, they use many personal Kansei terms to convey it accurately somehow. However, for a medical doctor to understand complaints of the patient, multiple translation jobs become necessary. First, the medical doctor forms an early phase of a mental model and a physical model and modifies them based on linguistic expressions of the patient. Furthermore, the physician translates it into physiological and anatomical terms using experiences as a doctor and forms a hypothesis (mental model of medical doctor) for pathogenesis of disease and a disease name from association with the knowledge of physiological mechanism.

Furthermore, a medical inference is promoted on the condition that no one would tell a lie in the medical world. However, lies, jokes, and mistakes account for a significant part of daily life. A translation agent is unavoidable even in this case.

In a social framework, those who make something and those who use it are rarely coupled directly. A number of people and organizations stand between them. If they swell out excessively, harmful effects will be generated, but they have indispensable roles such as consolidation of appropriate opinions, intermediate function, and shipping of products. These intermediate agents are necessary to undertake consistency between domain knowledge and the main system as the translation agent. Particularly, what is required for Kansei will be an agent having domain knowledge.

14.3.2 Spiral Loop

A model is constructed using various tools, catching information (sensing) through one's own sensory organs, and verifying it with an existing knowledge model, if any, from the information, and performing a new conceptualization if the information does not meet with the knowledge model. Input information includes noises and mistakes. Therefore, various results (candidates for hypothesis) will be obtained stochastically as a result of matching with the model. A process for selecting one that is presumed to be the optimum from these candidates for hypothesis depending on the situation is decision-making control. Monetary benefit has priority in some cases, and the scale of pride of life is used for selection in some cases. Furthermore, a feeling of charity will be used for selection in some cases. What should be selected with what feeling is also regarded as Kansei capability. Because a result selected by decision-making is transmitted to the outside environment, modification of the model is performed in a spiral fashion by sensing its reaction. A serial process of sensing, modeling, probabilistic inference, decision-making, and sensing including observation skill of situations of the other party constitutes Kansei capability.

With information collection via the Web, we have no other choice but to presume that the obtained information is nearly correct. It is of course possible to incorporate the same or similar questions cleverly so that respondents might not notice them to check the reliability of replies in a psychological test fashion. However, an increase in the number of question items might result in no response or reduction in the response rate.

Two groups are necessary for measurement of the Kansei of individuals. One is [psychological measurement]. The other is [physiological and physical measurement]. Relative value is obtained from the former. Absolute value is obtained from the latter. Results of brain activity are reflected in both groups. In the engineering field, biased views for the latter are decreasing, while many groups still hesitate to agree to the former.

Measurement of Kansei in the group of individuals and society is further insufficient. Although simulation is made for measurement of group actions and results in social behavioristics and social psychology, forecast is extremely difficult in many cases. Its contribution in the engineering sense is slight.

A difference exists between modeling of individuals and of party or organization to which a plural number of people are concerned. Conservation law is established to a large degree for Kansei of human beings. A person's character is not changed easily, as represented by the proverb: The child is the father of the man. For this reason, it might be said that modeling is comparatively easy. Meanwhile, for a party or an organization involving interests, situations differ between a case led by a leader and a case not led (solidarity is available or not), and in this case, modeling is not so easy. In many cases, the Kansei element is greatly emphasized in economic activity and election forecasts. Here, we consider modeling of individuals. Modeling in keeping with Kansei is indispensable to support medical diagnosis, various consultations, and counseling.

Information made available by sensing is sample-like information. Estimation of the status of internal environments with little information is not possible. What is necessary to attain this is so-called background knowledge, common sense, and implicit knowledge. In other words, because medical doctors have anatomical knowledge as the implicit knowledge in their background, it is possible for them to infer a state in patient's body from superficial diagnosis and medical interview. If this background knowledge is not implemented to the computer, modeling will become insufficient. It takes time.

14.3.3 Probabilistic Inference

After modeling is made to some extent and testimonial information is obtained by sensing, mechanical inference becomes possible. Because information obtained by sensing is not of 100 % information and modeling is made using hidden variables before setting and latent variables and is not conclusive, probabilistic inference is used as a matter of course. Bayesian network (BN) plays a central role, while recently influence diagram has been attracting attention because it is used frequently in IT administrative strategies a short time ago, and balance score card (BSC), SWOT analysis, etc., are approached from service engineering. Priority of probability inference is promoted mechanically in the artificial intelligence field. It depends greatly on situations in a taken-for-granted world. Selection of inference result such as a household has priority or relationship with friends has priority is not simple. Therefore, inference for selection of other party becomes necessary.

14.3.4 Decision-Making Control

Hypothesis candidates are calculated using inference mechanism in the higher probability order. Candidates with higher probability are not necessarily selected. Kansei is used when considering which should be selected. Rather, Kansei-related decision criteria lie in this decision-making step. It is considered that selection criteria exceeding cost function, utility function, and optimality are acting on Kansei. It is considered that decision-making is performed by characters such as [following type], [self-assertiveness type], and [isolation type] used in the psychology and situations. If selected by costs and optimality, a gamble ought not to be available.

To implement such diversified functions in computers, we performed model construction by covariance analysis and analyzed cause-and-effect relations in Bayesian network based on sensing of physical information from living body and psychological information. As a concrete example, the relationship between cosmetics and mood, the relationship between health and foods, psychological counseling system are introduced, and implementation using a multiple agent system is shown. Although the orientation of Kansei engineering and service engineering differs, they use many common techniques in computer implementation aspects. They will move to a big fusion through these techniques.

14.4 Kansei-Type BN Learning Method

As a party who provides services called a product, it is very interesting what impressions users might have of a product. In the cause-and-effect relation of a disease, links based on physiological evidence are set up easily. However, a relationship with psychological factors such as impressions has been studied only scarcely because it is related to uncertainties, such as situation dependence, and individual differences. Here, we performed experiments for cosmetics for which people have clear preferences and aversions; face packing was demonstrated and constructed BN that is learned from physical information such as physiological information. Furthermore, we constructed structural equation model for analysis of psychological information (questionnaire) to check possible relationship between physical information and psychological information (Kansei engineering-related information) [7, 8].

In the experiments, colored and colorless materials in which lavender is blended as a sedation pack are used. The primary ingredients are aloe vera leaf essence and bifidus fermentation essence. Colored and colorless materials in which cranberry and strawberry are blended are used for whitening, and primary ingredients are *alpha-arbutin*, placenta essence, vitamin C, and mulberry bark essence. In all, 24 students and university staff, of 18–52 years old (average 27.4, SD 8.0), participated to this experiment. Objects and methods of the experiment were explained. Written consent was received.

Measurement data were taken intermittently using a micro-camera and an infrared ray camera at face washing before face packing, coating of packing, 10 min after complete rest after coating, and after removal of packing for skin moisture, skin oily substance, melanin pigment composition, and the skin state. At the same time, an electrocardiogram, brain wave, and brain blood flow were measured intermittently at times other than face washing. Participants were requested to respond to the questionnaire before and after the experiment. We attempted model construction based on this psychological and physiological information.

Human beings are pleased when praised and are discouraged or angered when not praised. Although such a cause-and-effect relation shows a general tendency, individual differences of psychological cause-and-effect relation are more significant than a physical cause-and-effect relation, and if averaged for several people, connections of linkages will be weakened. In contrast, if a difference from the general model is detected, then an individual profile will come out. With an algorithm which handles physiological information and psychological information equally (BayoNet 5.02; Mathematical Systems Inc.), an arrow was not drawn between physiological information and psychological information. Then they were separated into BN of physiological information and BN of psychological information. As one reason for this, correlation is weaker between heterogeneous information than between homogeneous information. Then, we used looser criteria for heterogeneous information than for homogeneous information. With some structure learning algorithms, the presence or absence of the arrow is determined according to result of verification of the correlation between variables. Using this sort of algorithm, criteria of correlation applied to variables of homogeneous information were changed from those applied to variables of heterogeneous information.

Detailed procedures are as follows: (1) Continuous variables are discretized. (2) Limiting conditions relating to presence/absence and direction of the arrow are

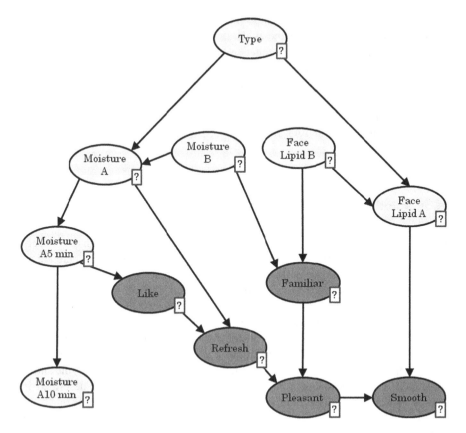

Fig. 14.1 Learned Bayesian network

determined (in child–parent matrix) from prior knowledge. (3) Correlation factor matrix is obtained. (4) Presence/absence of the arrow is determined based on the criteria of 0.35 for variables of homogeneous information and 0.11 for variables of heterogeneous information.

To simplify the structure, the arrow being drawn from the grandparent node to grandchild node was removed. In this case, comparison of network before and after the simplification was made by leave-one-out cross validation (LOOCV) method to check that any variable that increases forecast error by more than 10% did not exist.

Figure 14.1 shows the BN learned from the above. It is understood that a model in which heterogeneous information is mixed is realized. This was compared with BN being output from Greedy-K2 algorithm, and performances which compare favorably with it were obtained. Using this BN, it is possible to perform qualitative analysis: Although psychological information variable Like is influenced by skin moisture 5 min after packing, it is not influenced immediately after packing. Furthermore, quantitative inference to forecast which pack will result in greater effects becomes possible if the skin condition before pack coating and desirable psychological state are input as the evidence.

With this method, the reference of correlation coefficients is simply manipulated. No professional knowledge is used at all. That this method is applicable easily to other area is advantageous. When applied to the medical field and body temperature is used as the physiological information and chilly sensation is used as the psychological information, it is possible to associate psychological symptoms and the psychological condition [8].

14.5   Food and Health-Care System

Interest in foods and health is indispensable for a wealthy life. Although the concept of Chinese cooking using Chinese herbs is known for foods and health, there are no definite rules. Therefore, we performed structuring by ontology. When food knowledge based on Yakuzenn (Chinese cooking in which Chinese herbal medicine is combined with normal food ingredients), which has the same concept derived from ancient China with the same principles underlying a normal diet and medical treatment, is sorted out in advance in the form of ontology, users who are not familiar with the concept can use its knowledge. Using the inference rule based on that concept, we attempted two different methods to acquire an inference rule and to implement it. One is to use a design method of the inference rule described in ontology specified [9]. The other is extraction of rules by data mining [8].

With ontology, the Semantic Web Rule Language (SWRL) language for description of inference rules is originally available. The rule described by SWRL is useful also by the rule engine Jess of Java. JADE, a Java library, is used for the development of multiple agents. Therefore, rules available on Jess can eventually be used by the agent.

According to the theory of that Chinese concept, foods have properties of providing tastes and indicating the extent to which the body should be warmed (or cooled) by them. The latter falls into five categories and is designated as five vital energies (five natures). Five tastes include sweet and [light] taste which means a plain taste. We devised such an inference rule that after a user's physical information, the clinical history and present symptom are set and input altogether; food health care (cuisine, foodstuff) to be recommended to the patient concerned is output. For example, when a user's body is cold, foodstuffs having febrility, of five natures, is recommended. Additionally, we set a rule for diagnosis of hypertension and obesity from a user's physical information. This enabled establishment of a more practical rule that food and health care are determined according to diagnosis results. The inference rule is specified by SWRL. Therefore, inference is possible using a free software ontology editor Protégé (Standard Center for Biomedical Informatics Research) (see Fig. 14.2). Implementation using Jess is a future task.

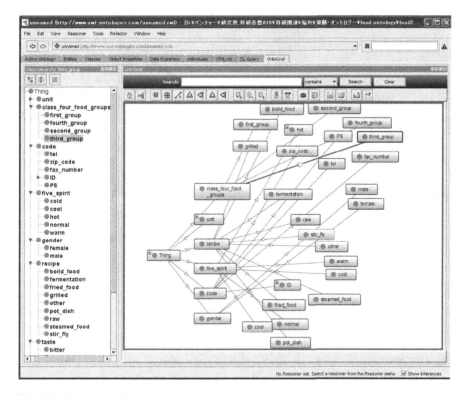

Fig. 14.2   Inference with food ontology (Protégé snapshot)

14.6   Multiple Agent System

If situations in which Kansei engineering service is actually used are considered, measuring equipment and software are not necessarily functioning in synchronized fashion. Therefore, each should preferably function autonomously. The whole system is then constructed using a multiple agent method using this concept. It is possible to develop multiple agent system using Java with a free software framework: Java Agent Development Framework (JADE, Telecom Italia Lab.). To date, we have developed an experiment support system, a data mining support system, and a tongue diagnosis system.

14.6.1   Experiment Support System

The experiment support system is a pilot support system to perform simple experiments to check the physiological reaction when one listens to music using real-time electrocardiographic analysis. Music player and electrocardiographic

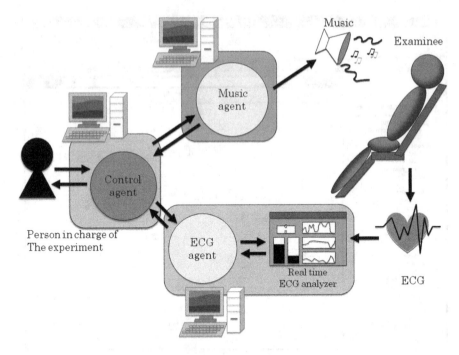

Fig. 14.3 Whole system for Kansei measurement support system

analysis software are operated individually by an exclusive agent. The person in charge of the experiment simply gives instructions to the control agent. This system was developed devoting attention to the fact that, in general, there is difficulty in operating many devices simultaneously (Fig. 14.3).

This system consists of agents of three types. (1) The control agent displays changes in the sympathetic nerve component and the parasympathetic nerve component being transmitted from the electrocardiographic analysis agent in real-time fashion in addition to entry of an experimental protocol, designation of musical composition used, and instruction for experiment start. (2) The music reproduction agent performs regeneration and stop of music file and loudness control according to the request from other agents. (3) An electrocardiographic analysis agent supports the start and completion of electrocardiographic measurements being linked with a real-time electrocardiographic analysis system (which is developed by MATLAB (which executes high-speed processing by compilation) analyzes electrocardiographic data obtained; calculates sympathetic nerve component and parasympathetic nerve component, the R–R interval and P–R interval; and sends them to the control agent.

Many procedures should be observed properly to perform physiological experiments. If a failure occurs on the way, then the experiment should be repeated, which brings psychological stress. For this reason, automation of measurements is useful and allows for a reduction in necessary labor.

14.6.2   Data Mining Support System

This system supports data mining for a database of measurements by household medical measurement equipment and falls into database management one, data mining one (by R), and an inference agent. All that is required for the user is to give instructions to the agent for user interface. This was developed devoting attention to such convenience that renewal of database can be performed independent of other processing.

We developed a system that supports introduction of a rule for consolidating several psychological tests [10]. Specifically, a rule for introducing results of vocational preference inventory (VPI) based on results of the Baum test is extracted using a rough set. We attempted this integration several times based on the idea that using advantages of a projection method that only slightly accepts false replies and advantages of questionnaire test with which results and their interpretation are clear-cut, and disadvantages of both might eventually be compensated by each other. However, the use of exclusive software is recommended depending on the method such as rough set. Therefore, disadvantages of this system are that the software to be used is wide ranging and that jobs are made cumbersome and complicated. With the presently developed system, an exclusive agent is assigned to each step of database and data mining (pretreatment, rough set, rule extraction). Therefore, all that is required for the researcher is a simple information exchange with user agents (Fig. 14.4).

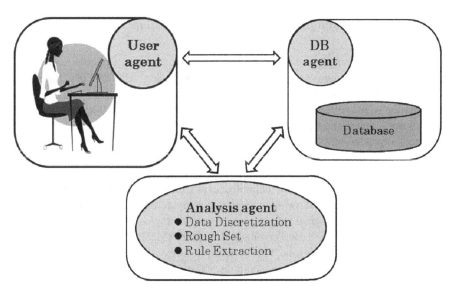

Fig. 14.4 Whole system for data mining

Table 14.1 Tongue color classification

k-average method	Identification accuracy of cherry red and rose pink is 97%, while that of garnet and rose pink is 11%
Discrimination analysis	Identification accuracy of garnet and cherry red is 82%, while that of garnet and rose pink is 69%
SVM	Identification accuracy of garnet and rose pink is 89%, while that of showy pink and rose pink is 51%

14.6.3 Tongue Diagnosis Support System

The tongue color and tongue coating are identified by tongue diagnosis. This diagnosis is considered important in oriental medicine. Meanwhile, with Western medicine, this is used as ancillary information at medical interviews because cause-and-effect relations between this diagnosis and disease are not clear. However, many people who worry about their health condition check the tongue's color and its state of roughness every morning in front of the mirror. To perform this checking quantitatively, image information of the tongue obtained using a camera is compared with a standard color using color templates and mapped on the Munsell color system. Furthermore, the hue, brightness, and chromaticity information are classified, using the k-average method, discrimination analysis, and support vector machine (SVM), and compared (see Table 14.1). If diagnosis rules are regulated by a rule base, presentation to the users is possible. This is also an example of collaboration work system by the image processing agent and diagnosis inference agent [11].

14.6.4 Psychological Medical Interview System

As civilization advances and affluence increases, the number of people who suffer from mental and emotional difficulties has been increasing. Although psychological diagnoses are performed here and there, the contribution from engineering viewpoints is not remarkable. One reason that developments from engineering aspects are not sufficiently advanced yet is regarded as attributable to lesser consistency and reproducibility of cause-and-effect relation of psychological diagnosis than diagnosis of physical disorders. Meanwhile, as Web services are used extensively, many diagnosis systems are provided via the network. If the interface part is seen solely apart from diagnosis rules, technologies of CGI and image analysis are used as the foundation. We have developed several systems to date from the standpoint of fusion study of physiological information and psychological information.

The Minnesota Multiphasic Personality Inventory (MMPI) is a system developed by the University of Minnesota. This system produces 10 clinical scales and 4 adequacy scales based on replies to as many as 500 questions. The diagnosis is already standardized, and results are obtained immediately after one replies on the computer screen. The data are collected by CGI and calculated, and a graphical display is given.

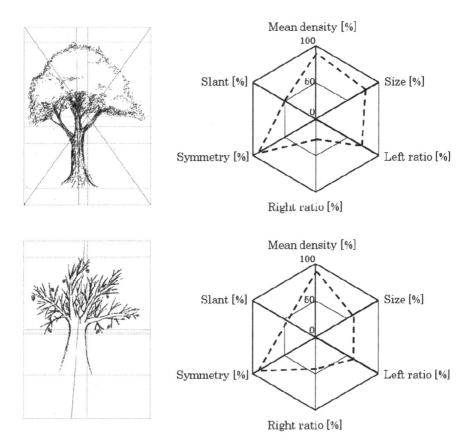

Fig. 14.5 Static analysis of tree test examples

Furthermore, with the Baum test stated previously, one is requested to draw one tree on A4-size white paper. It is said that one's psychological state at that point of time can be known from the drawing. Although the diagnosis rule is not concerned from an engineering standpoint, an analysis method is of image processing. Static information is obtained after the picture is read by a scanner and analyzed, and dynamic information is obtained using a tablet PC. Dynamic information provides information about the pen pressure, stroke order, pencil inclination, continuity, etc. (Fig. 14.5).

Analysis of ego using transactional analysis is used frequently in the psychological field. This analysis is also based on questionnaires, and therefore, acquisition and analysis of the data by CGI and graph display are made possible with ease. We attempted utilization on the Web referring to the system developed by the medical faculty of The University of Tokyo. Data patterns are subjected to automatic classification using a fuzzy set (see Fig. 14.6).

These systems function on the web, but they are not released to the public from viewpoints of security of personal data and are used for research purposes only.

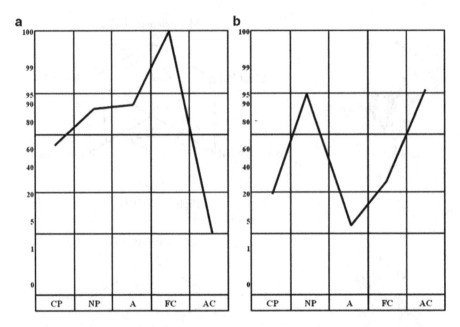

Fig. 14.6 Ego-grams drawn by a Java applet

We are developing a structuring association test (SAT) and its commercialization jointly with Tsukuba University. This method consists of a stress source estimation test and a stress check test for adults, juveniles, and lower grades to allow for self-counseling. With this system, the self-value scale, depression scale, self-compassion/dissociation/negation scale, and the PTSD scale are calculated. Commercialized products of this system are sold in stand-alone fashion instead of network marketing.

Many tests are available for psychological items and Web service technology is useful, while the security problem is the most important issue. We are of the opinion that the test should not be used without security management, similarly to a medical network. Computerization is indispensable for the chronological processing of enormous amounts of test data. Furthermore, a lack of unified diagnosis rules presents a problem. As stated previously, it is considered that narrowing of common rules from several diagnostic tests will be effective in the future.

14.7 Conclusions

In 2011, an artificial intelligence program developed by IBM played against humans on the *Jeopardy* quiz show, and won. Moreover, the computer level for chess has exceeded that of human beings. It is said IBM will proceed with development of medical diagnostic programs in the future. In the 1980s, the medical faculty of Stanford University developed the expert system Pathfinder for lymph node disease and Utrecht University (Netherland) developed a medical diagnosis support system called Promedas, which became the core of a venture business [12]. In that year, Dr. Tanaka of Shimadzu Corp. who received the Nobel Prize developed a system to diagnose diseases from a drop of blood. The style of future medical care might be changed and improved by it. Medical diagnosis can be performed by hospitals in only an instant to check changes in daily physical condition. We consider that a Kansei-type computer should provide relief from individuals' health problems using information about cosmetics, facial state, foods, health, and what is more, daily checking of tongue color. Kansei is related to the concept of psychological analysis of individuals' values and needs. Therefore, psychology should be implemented from the viewpoints of computation theory.

References

1. Nagamachi M (2010) Kansei/Affective Engineering, CRC Press
2. http://icsoc11.icsoc.org/
3. Singh MP, Huhns MN (2005) Service-oriented computing. Wiley, England
4. Service-oriented computing: agents, semantics, and engineering, 2007. In: AAMAS 2007 international workshop, SOCASE 2007, Springer
5. (2011) Special edition: service science led by job site. J Jpn Soc Artif Intell 26(2)
6. (2010) Special edition: service science, digital practice. Inf Process Soc Jpn 1(1)
7. Wakatsuki J et al (2011) Construction of graphical models for temporary application of facial packs. Int J Comput Inf Sys Ind Manage Appl 3:399–406
8. Abrishamian A et al (2012) A discovery of physiological and psychological connection based on Bayesian network. Trans JSKE 11(2):1–7
9. Li L, Uozumi T (2012) Study on food care ontology and inference rule toward health management support systems. In: The 7th spring conference of JSKE 2012, Takamatsu, Japan, pp 122–124
10. Tsubosaki D, Uozumi T (2011) Construction of psychology diagnosis support system with multi-agent system. In: The 13th annual conference of JSKE, P07
11. Ikeda N, Uozumi T (2005) Tongue diagnosis support system. Hokkaido J Med Sci 80(3): 269–277
12. http://www.promedas.nl/